Sociology

Concepts and Uses

Sociology
Concepts and Uses

Jonathan H. Turner
University of California, Riverside

McGraw-Hill, Inc.

New York   St. Louis   San Francisco   Auckland   Bogotá   Caracas   Lisbon
London   Madrid   Mexico City   Milan   Montreal   New Delhi   San Juan
Singapore   Sydney   Tokyo   Toronto

This book was set in Palatino by ComCom, Inc.
The editors were Phillip A. Butcher, Bob Greiner, and Cybele Eidenschenk;
the production supervisor was Louise Karam.
The cover was designed by Wanda Lubelska.
The photo editor was Barbara Salz.
Arcata Graphics/Martinsburg was printer and binder.

Photo Credits

1: *Bettmann;* **4:** *Bettmann;* **6:** *Image Works;* **8:** *Bettmann;* **9:** *Archiv/Photo Researchers;* **11:** *Otto Neumann/Bettmann;* **17:** *Barbara Rios/Photo Researchers;* **33:** *Fujifotos/Image Works;* **47:** *Shmuel Thaler/Jeroboam;* **61:** *Joel Gordon;* **77:** *Richard Frieman/Photo Researchers;* **97:** *Mark Antman/Image Works;* **115:** *Harvey Finkle/Impact Visuals;* **139:** *Barbara Rios/Photo Researchers;* **173:** *Spencer Grant/Photo Researchers;* **189:** *Ron Delany/Jeroboam;* **207:** *Ulrike Welsch/Photo Researchers.*

SOCIOLOGY
Concepts and Uses

This book is printed on acid-free paper.

1 2 3 4 5 6 7 8 9 0 AGM AGM 9 0 9 8 7 6 5 4 3

ISBN 0-07-065596-0

Library of Congress Cataloging-in-Publication Data is available:
LC Card # 93-28039

INTERNATIONAL EDITION

When ordering this title, use ISBN 0-07-113701-7.

About the Author

JOHNATHAN H. TURNER is Professor of Sociology at the University of California, Riverside where he has taught sociology for twenty-five years. He is the author of two dozen books, plus the editor of several more, and he has published articles in most of sociology's major journals. He has been associate editor for most of the major journals in sociology, and he is currently editor of the journal, *Sociological Perspectives*. He has also served on the editorial board of the University of California Press.

Although his primary interest is in developing sociological theory, he has maintained an active research agenda in several more specific areas of specialization, including inequality and stratification, ethnic group relations, bioecology, social change, social institutions, and American society. He is also of the belief that scientific sociology and humanistic social policy are highly compatible enterprises. This short introduction to sociology is designed to communicate both the substance and relevance of sociology—as a science, as a practical vocation, and at times, as an advocation.

To my grandchildren,
Ghislaine Marie Roelant
Katherine Marie Mueller

Contents

Preface

For over twenty-five years I have taught introductory sociology. Indeed, it has always been my favorite course. Yet, I have always been a bit frustrated over the kinds of texts available, including the ones that I have written. Not all instructors, and certainly not all students, want or need a large and lavishly produced text, which, in the end, costs the student a fortune and limits the ability of instructors to assign additional books and materials in their course. They would prefer, perhaps, a "plain wrapper" or "generic brand" text which lacks the gloss, color, and high price of a regular text but which, at the same time, covers the basic subjects of the standard introductory course. It is for these instructors and students that this book was written.

My goal was simple: write a short text that communicates the same amount of basic information of a larger text and, at the same time, deliver it at a cost that is substantially below all large hard-cover texts and smaller paperback texts as well. To do this, I took out the pictures, cartoons, four-color graphics, glossy pages, suggested readings, and "filler" of a large text. And I collapsed related subjects together to reduce the number of total chapters and pages, but without a significant loss of coverage.

My feeling is that it is rather easy to "get lost" in many texts, as one sorts through graphics, pictures, inserts, margin notes, and other features of these books. Indeed, it is often hard to find the running text without searching for it. While these extra materials are, no doubt, interesting, I am not sure that justice is done to our field. It might be better, I think, to simply lay out in a coherent and easy-to-follow way the basic concepts and approaches of sociology as a discipline, without distracting the reader. In fact, I think that this approach can be even more interesting, for two principal reasons: First, students can get through chapters much more quickly and, as a result, more readily absorb and retain material. Second, students can see that there is coherence to what sociologists study because they are not taken off on tangents as they read along. In a sense, I think that we insult students with the presumption that we must constantly entertain them with extra materials. In contrast, I believe that sociology, per se, is interesting without all of the filler and fluff. We do not need to make our texts like MTV.

Acknowledgments

I wish to thank the following reviewers for helping me improve the manuscript: Lee K. Frank, Community College of Allegheny College; Peter Kivisto, Augustana College; Boyd Littrell, University of Nebraska, Omaha; and Peter Turner, Herkimer County Community College.

Jonathan H. Turner

Sociology
Concepts and Uses

CHAPTER 1

The Nature and Origins
of Sociology

When the social world undergoes dramatic changes, as illustrated by the transformation of the landscape with industrialization, people begin to think about the world around them. How could they account for these dramatic and sudden changes, as the old feudal order gave way to a new way of organizing the social world? It is in this context that sociology was born, as scholars increasingly came to see society as something that could be analyzed systematically.

THE RELEVANCE OF SOCIOLOGY

Sociology is the study of human social behavior, interaction, and organization. In a very real sense we are all sociologists because you and I are always analyzing our behaviors and our interpersonal experiences with others in organized situations. The goal of sociology is to make these everyday understandings of the social world more systematic and precise, while extending the depth and breadth of insights beyond our personal experiences. For, we are simply small players in a large and complex world of other people, symbols, and social structures, and only by extending our perspective beyond the here and now can we come to appreciate fully the forces shaping and constraining our lives.

This emphasis on constraint often runs against the personal beliefs of many Americans who like to view themselves as rugged individuals, using their free will and initiative to shape their destiny. To a degree, we can all do so, but we are never totally free of constraints. We must operate in a social environment that profoundly influences how we feel about ourselves and the world around us, how we see and perceive events, how we act and think, and how far and where we can go in life. At times, this constraint is obvious, even oppressive and debilitating; more often it is subtle and even unacknowledged. Yet it is there, constantly shaping our thoughts, feelings, and actions.

Examine the situation of a college student. There are broad cultural values and beliefs emphasizing the importance of education and, thereby, forcing students to perceive and believe that they *must* go to college. For some, there may be parental pressures and expectations, making these pressures to go to school even greater. There are the constraints of school itself—class attendance, reading lists, exams—circumscribing what one can do. There are pressures of class background—how much money one has to spend—determining whether a student must also work while going to school. And, if work is necessary, there are the constraints of the workplace itself, as well as the problems of scheduling and reconciling school and work. There may be one's own family of spouse and children further cramping a busy schedule. There are the constraints of the economy and job market affecting students' decisions about their college major and life goals. There are governmental forces affecting funding for students (tuition, loans, grants, fellowships) and for the college or university as a whole. These governmental and economic constraints are, in turn, tied to the world political economy as balances of geopolitical power and economic trade ebb and flow. The point, I hope, is clear: All of us live in a complex web of forces dictating so much of what we see, feel, and do. None of us is a free agent; true, we can pick and choose our way through daily life, but our options are always limited.

Sociology examines these constraints, and as such, it is a very broad field, for it studies all the cultural symbols that humans create and use to interact and to organize society; it explores all the social structures that order social life; it examines all the processes, such as deviance, crime, dissent, riots, migrations, and social movements, that flow through the social order; and it attempts to understand the transformations that these processes work on culture and social structure.

In changing times, where culture and structure are undergoing dramatic transformations, sociology becomes especially relevant (Nisbet, 1969). As old ways of doing things change, personal lives are disrupted, and as a result, people seek answers as to why the routines and formulas of the past no longer work. The world today is undergoing dramatic transformation—the collapse of the Soviet empire, the rise of volatile ethnic relations, the flight of jobs to countries with lower-priced labor, the shifting fortunes of commerce and trade, the difficulty of financing government services, the changing job market, the spread of a deadly disease (autoimmune deficiency syndrome—AIDS), the increase in famine with overpopulation, the disruption of ecological balances, the redefinition of gender roles for men and women, and many other changes. As long as social life and daily routines hum along, the need for sociological insight is not fully appreciated. But when the basic fabric of the society and culture changes, people seek sociological knowledge. This is true not only today, but it was the very reason that sociology emerged in the first place as a distinct discipline in the early decades of the nineteenth century.

THE EMERGENCE OF SOCIOLOGY

Humans have, no doubt, thought about themselves and the universe throughout history. Yet it was not until the late eighteenth century that a confluence of events in Europe set the stage for the emergence of sociology. As the old feudal estates began to give way to free labor moving into industry in urban areas and as new forms of government began to break the hold of monarchies, the foundations of society—employment and income, living arrangements, community, family, and religion—were being altered forever. As might be expected, people were worried about the new emerging order, and they began to think more systematically about what all the changes meant for the future (Turner, Beeghley, and Powers, 1989).

The resulting intellectual movement is sometimes termed **the Enlightenment** because the hold of religion, tradition, and dogma on intellectual thinking was finally broken. Science could now emerge fully as a way of thinking about the world, and physics and, later, biology were able to overcome persecution by religious elites and establish themselves as a path to knowledge. Along with the growing influence of science came a burst of thinking about the social universe. Much of this thought was speculative, pondering the nature of humans and the first societies unfiltered by the complexity of the modern world. Some of this thought was moralistic, but not in a religious sense. Rather the proper type of society and the fundamental relationship of individuals to one another and to society were reevaluated in ways consistent with the economic and political changes wrought by the spread of commerce and then industrialization. In England, this kind of thinking was termed the *Age of*

Reason; and scholars like Adam Smith (1776), who first articulated the laws of supply and demand in the marketplace, also pondered the effects on society of rapid population growth, of escalating economic specialization, of declining community, and of weakening moral sentiments. In France, a group of thinkers known as **the philosophes** also began to expound a vision of the social world that championed a society where individuals were free from arbitrary political authority and were guided by agreed-upon moral standards and democratic government.

Yet another force behind the emergence of sociology—the French Revolution of 1789—accelerated systematic thinking about the social world. The violence of the revolution was a shock to all of Europe, for if such violence and force could throw out the old regime, what was to replace it? How could society be reconstructed in order to avoid such cataclysmic events? It is at this point, in the decades around the turn of the eighteenth and into the nineteenth centuries, that sociology as a self-conscious discipline was forged.

Auguste Comte (1798–1857) and the Founding of Sociology

The long French legacy of the Enlightenment and the shock waves of the French Revolution led Auguste Comte in his five-volume *Course of Positive Philosophy* (1830–1842) to sound the call for a discipline devoted to the scientific study of

Auguste Comte
(1798–1857)

society. Comte wanted to call this discipline "social physics" to emphasize that it would study the fundamental nature of the social universe, but he was eventually forced to settle on the Latin-Greek hybrid term, *sociology*.

The central problem for sociology was the one that had been articulated by earlier thinkers in the Enlightenment: How is society to be held together as it becomes larger, more complex, more varied, more differentiated, more special-ized, and more partitioned? Comte's answer was that common ideas and be-liefs—a *consensus universalis*, in his terms—needed to be developed to give society a "universal" morality. This answer was never developed, but the con-cern with symbols and culture as a unifying force was to remain the mainstay of French sociological thinking, right up to the present day.

Comte's main contribution to the development of sociology was not so much the substance of his ideas, but his strong advocacy for the acceptance of sociology as a legitimate field of study. Establishing a new discipline is never easy, because there are always some vested interests opposed to new ways of thinking. This was to be a discipline devoted to the study of society, and the old academic disciplines, such as philosophy, ethics, theology, and law, were threatened by this newcomer. Thus it was that Comte spent much of his monumental work justifying the right of sociology to even exist.

One tactic that Comte employed to make sociology seem legitimate was to postulate a **law of the three stages** in which thinking is considered to move along in an evolutionary sequence. The first stage is the *theological,* where thought about the world is dominated by considerations of the supernatural, religion, and god; the second stage is the *metaphysical,* where appeals to the supernatural are replaced by philosophical thought about the essence of phenomena and by the development of mathematics, logic, and other neutral thought systems; and the third stage was to be the *positivistic* where science, or the careful observation of empirical facts and the systematic testing of theories, become the dominant modes for accumulating knowledge. And with the positivistic stage, knowledge *can be used* for practical purposes to better people's lives.

Society as a whole, as well as thinking about each domain of the universe, moves through these three stages, but at different rates: astronomy and physics move first, then chemistry and biology, and finally sociology emerges as the last mode of thinking to enter the positivistic stage. In Comte's eyes, the analysis of society was ready to take a seat at the table of science—a claim which was challenged in Comte's time, as well as today. And as the laws of human organization were developed, Comte (1851–1854) believed that they could be used to better the human condition—again, a theme as controversial today as in Comte's time.

A second legitimating tactic employed by Comte was to postulate a **hierar-chy of the sciences** in which all the sciences were ranked in terms of their complexity and their movement into the positivistic stage. At the bottom of the hierarchy was mathematics, the language of all sciences higher in the hierarchy, and at the top, emerging out of biology, was sociology, which in a moment of overexuberance Comte proclaimed as "the queen science." For, if sociology was the last science to emerge but was also the most advanced in terms of its subject matter, it must be a legitimate mode of inquiry—or so Comte hoped.

The First British Sociologist: Herbert Spencer (1820–1903)

Writing after Comte's major work, Herbert Spencer was the first sociologist of the nineteenth century to carry forward scientific sociology. Like Comte, Spencer (1873) believed that human arrangements could be studied scientifically, and in his monumental three-volume work, *The Principles of Sociology* (1874–1896), he developed a theory of human social organization and presented a wide range of historical and ethnographic data to support this theory. For Spencer, all domains of the universe—physical, biological, and social—evolve in terms of similar principles (Spencer, 1862). And the task of sociology is to apply these principles to what he termed the **superorganic** realm, or the study of the patterns of relations among organisms.

Spencer's basic question was a version of Comte's: What holds society together as it becomes larger, more heterogeneous, more complex, and more differentiated? Spencer's answer, in general terms, was very simple: Large, complex societies develop (1) interdependencies among their specialized components and (2) concentrations of power to control and coordinate activities among interdependent units. For Spencer, then, societal evolution embodies growth and complexity which is managed by interdependence and power. If patterns of interdependence and concentrations of power fail to emerge in a society, or are inadequate to the task, dissolution occurs, and the society falls apart.

In developing this answer to Comte's basic question, Spencer analogized to organismic bodies, arguing that societies, like biological organisms, must perform certain key functions if they are to survive: They must reproduce them-

Herbert Spencer
(1820–1903)

selves; they must produce sufficient goods and commodities to sustain members; they must distribute these products to members of the society; and they must coordinate and regulate the activities of members. As societies grow larger and become more complex, revealing many divisions and patterns of specialization, these key functions become distinguished along three lines: (1) the operative (reproduction and production), (2) the distributive (the movement of materials and information), and (3) the regulatory (the concentration of power to control and coordinate).

Spencer is best remembered for founding an approach in sociology known as **functionalism** (J. Turner, 1985b). This approach emphasizes that analyses of specific cultural and social ways in a society should occur with an eye to what functions they serve for the larger society. Functional sociology thus asks a basic and interesting question: What does a cultural or social phenomenon *do for* the maintenance and integration of a society?

The Later French Tradition: Émile Durkheim (1858–1917)

Much of Spencer's mode of analysis was adopted by the first great French sociologist, Émile Durkheim, but Spencer's ideas were modified to fit the long French lineage (J. Turner, 1984b). Like Spencer, Durkheim (1895) advocated the search for sociological laws, but unlike Spencer, Durkheim took the Comtean position that sociological knowledge could be used to build a better society. Like Spencer, Durkheim (1893) saw the essential question of sociology as revolving around how to explain the integration of society as it becomes larger and more complex, but unlike Spencer, Durkheim (1891) remained true to his French heritage and emphasized the importance of common ideas as an integrating force. Like Spencer, Durkheim (1895) adopted a functional approach, arguing that sociological explanations must seek to discover how an element of the social world fulfills a need of society, but unlike Spencer, Comte emphasized only one need—the need to integrate members of society into a coherent whole.

What marks Durkheim's contribution to sociology is the recognition that systems of cultural symbols—that is, values, beliefs, religious dogmas, ideologies, and the like—are an important basis for the integration of society (J. Turner, 1981). As societies become complex and heterogeneous, the nature of cultural symbols, or what Durkheim (1893) termed the **collective conscience,** changes. In simple societies, all individuals have a common collective conscience that regulates their thoughts and actions, whereas in more complex societies the collective conscience must also change if the society is to remain integrated. It must become, at one level, more "generalized" and "abstract" in order to provide some common symbols among people in specialized and partitioned activities, whereas at another level it also becomes more concrete to ensure that relations between, and within, specialized positions and organizations in complex societies are regulated and coordinated. Social order, therefore, is possible in large, complex societies when there are some common symbols that all individuals share, coupled with specific sets of symbols that guide

Émile Durkheim
(1858–1917)

people in their concrete relations with others (J. Turner, 1990). If this balance between the abstract and specific or the general and concrete aspects of the collective conscience is not realized, then various pathologies become evident (Durkheim, 1893, 1897).

Durkheim (1912) later examined society at a more interpersonal level in an effort to understand how the collective conscience is generated. In his study of reports on the religion among Australian aborigines (Spencer and Gillian, 1899), Durkheim was less interested in religion, per se, than in the interpersonal processes producing a collective conscience. What he discovered was the significance of people's interaction, as this produced a sense that there is a supernatural "force" above and beyond them. In sensing the power of this force arising out of the animation and energy of interaction, the aborigines constructed totems and engaged in rituals to honor the supernatural powers symbolized by the totem. From this observation, he concluded that worship of the gods and the supernatural is, in reality, worship of society and of the bonds generated by people's interaction and contact with one another. Thus, the glue that holds society together is sustained by concrete interactions of individuals. In developing this argument, Durkheim took sociology in a new direction toward the study of more micro, interpersonal activities. For most of the nineteenth century was decidedly macro, emphasizing the big picture—evolution, the state and its stability, the economy, the church, the class system, and other structures where the actions of real people were underemphasized. Durkheim was one who began to look beneath the surface at what people actually did in creating and sustaining these "big structures."

The German Who Sought Refuge in England: Karl Marx (1818–1883)

Karl Marx wrote his major works between Auguste Comte and Herbert Spencer, and well before Émile Durkheim. Unlike these other figures, however, Marx was suspicious of any pretensions that sociology could uncover timeless laws like those in the natural sciences. Instead he felt that each historical epoch was built around a particular type of economic production, organization of labor, and control of property, with the result that historical epochs reveal their own unique dynamics. Hence, feudalism operates in terms of one dynamic, and Marx's (1867) main focus, capitalism, proceeds in terms of yet another set of dynamic *processes*.

What are these processes? For Marx, the organization of a society at a particular point in time is determined by the **means of production,** or the nature of production and the organization of work. Thus, the organization of the economy is the material base, or in his terms, the **substructure,** that circumscribes and directs the **superstructure,** consisting of culture, politics, and other aspects of society. The operation of human society is thus to be explained by the economic base (Marx and Engels, 1846).

For Marx (1867), there is always what he referred to as "contradictions" inherent in the organization of this economic base. For example, in capitalism he saw that the collective organization of production (in factories) stood in contradiction to the private ownership of property and the extraction of profit by some from the cooperative labor of others. Whatever the merits of this argument,

Karl Marx
(1818–1883)

Marx's approach emphasized a basic source of tension in human societies between those who control resources and those who do not. In arguing this way, Marx became the inspiration for a sociological approach known as **conflict theory** or **conflict sociology**. In this approach, all patterns of social organization reveal conflict-producing inequalities, where those who own or control resources can consolidate power and develop legitimating ideologies to maintain their privilege and where those without resources eventually become oriented to conflict with the more privileged (Marx and Engels, 1848). At the very least, there is always a smoldering tension between super- and subordinates in social systems, and this **conflict of interest,** as Marx phrased the matter, periodically erupts into overt conflict and social change.

Sociological analysis must, therefore, concentrate on the pattern of inequality and the tensions between those with power, privilege, and material well-being, on the one side, and the less powerful, privileged and materially well off, on the other side. For Marx and subsequent generations of conflict theorists, this is where "the action is" in human social organization.

There is yet another important facet to Marx's work: the activist role of the sociologist. The goal of the analyst is to expose inequality and exploitation in social situations and, in so doing, to play an active role in eliminating these conditions. Sociologists are not to just stand on the sidelines; they are to work to change the social world in ways that reduce inequalities and domination of one segment of society by another. Marx, of course, wanted to help bring down capitalism and usher in a new era of collectivism, but the general thrust of his program—to find inequalities, expose them, and work for their elimination—is still a source of inspiration for many sociologists today who wish to intervene in the social world as activists.

The Founding Father of German Sociology: Max Weber (1864–1920)

Max Weber is said to have had a "silent dialogue" with Marx in which he sought to correct for the excesses in Marx's thinking about inequality, power, and social change (Bendix, 1968). Like Marx, Weber (1904) was suspicious of any claims that sociology could be like the natural sciences and formulate universal and timeless "laws" of human social organization. Unlike Marx, however, Weber (1904) argued that sociological analysis should be **value-free,** or objective, and neutral on moral matters. The goal of sociology is to describe and understand how and why social patterns come into existence and how they operate rather than to intervene and change these patterns.

Sociology must, Weber (1922) argued, always seek to understand phenomena "at the level meaning" of the actors. That is, what do the participants see and feel in the course of their involvement in social situations? Yet, these insights alone are not enough; it is also necessary to examine the larger cultural and structural picture created when many participants are involved in complex arrays of relationships. Sociological analysis must, therefore, move back and

Max Weber
(1864–1920)

forth between the experiences of the actors and the larger cultural and social patterns in which actors are involved.

As we will see at many places in the next chapters, the substance of Weber's sociology still influences the focus of present-day sociology. In his silent dialogue with Karl Marx, for example, Weber felt that control of the means of economic production was only one of several bases for inequality; status, honor, and prestige constitute another basis, as do power and politics (Weber, 1922). Thus, inequality is not a simple matter of "haves and have-nots" with respect to who controls the means of production; it is a more multidimensional process with inequalities and rankings of people along several dimensions—as a part of a particular class (economic), a status group (prestige, honor), and a party (power). For Marx status and power simply follow from class; for Weber, such was not always true.

Another silent debate with Marx concerned conflict and change. For Marx, inequality inevitably produces conflict between super- and subordinates and, hence, social change; for Weber, inequality increases the probability of conflict, but the specific conditions of a situation can facilitate or impede the emergence of "charismatic leaders" who can mobilize subordinates to pursue conflict (Weber, 1922). Thus, conflict is not inevitable and inexorable; it is a more probabilistic chance event which depends upon the specifics of a situation.

A third silent debate that Weber had with Marx was over the impact of "ideas," or systems of symbols, in producing social change. For Marx, cultural ideas—values, beliefs, religious dogmas, political doctrines, and the like—are a *superstructure* that followed from a material *substructure* revolving around the means of production. For Marx, it is this *sub*structure, or the means of production, that drives social change; for Weber, ideas can also cause social change and alter the means of production. For example, in Weber's (1904–1905) famous *The Protestant Ethic and the Spirit of Capitalism*, he argued that the content of beliefs among early Protestant religious sects, advocating thrift, frugality, savings, and hard work, was more responsible for the emergence of industrial capitalism in Europe than more material forces in the economy itself, as Marx had argued.

Weber continues to influence sociology because of his interest in isolating and understanding the basic forces of modern societies—the emergence and operation of capitalism, the domination of social life by bureaucracies, the growing power of the state, the multidimensional bases of stratification, the significance of law in modern social relations, the urbanization of populations into cities, the effects of cultural ideas. In these and many other specific concerns, Weber sought to sort out the historical causes of a modern situation (or at least modern in his time), to develop objective ways of describing the essence of this modern condition, and to understand what it means to the individuals involved. His insights, as well as the nature of his approach to gathering these insights, still inspire many contemporary sociologists (J. Turner, 1993b).

The Early American Tradition

Sociology was established as an academic discipline in the United States before Durkheim in France and Weber in Germany achieved this goal, and yet, early American sociology was highly derivative. It first tended to emphasize Comte and Spencer, later Durkheim and Weber, and eventually Marx. There were, of course, some notable accomplishments, primarily the systematic use of statistics to analyze data—an emphasis that still typifies American sociology (Turner and Turner, 1990) as well as some adaptations of Spencerian and Comtean ideas to the analysis of communities and later organizations (as we will explore in later chapters).

The most significant approach to emerge in the early decades of this century in American sociology was the concern of several philosophers, and a few sociologists, with the process of face-to-face interaction among individuals. The leading figure was the philosopher, George Herbert Mead (1863–1931), who served as the source of inspiration for an approach that came to be known as **interactionism** (Blumer, 1969). This approach emphasizes that society is ultimately created and sustained by the mutually signaling and interpreting of gestures among individuals who confront each other in face-to-face situations and who seek to confirm their images of themselves and to meet their basic needs by negotiating and constructing agreements about how they are to behave and respond. Since we will explore this school of thought in the next chapter, and examine G. H. Mead's (1934, 1938) thinking in detail in Chapter 5, we need only recognize the shift in emphasis from sociology's European founders. Though most early American sociologists sustained the macro emphasis of the founders, American scholars began to address in far more detail than Durkheim's late micro-level analysis the process of interaction and its significance in understanding social reality.

THE STUDY OF SOCIOLOGY TODAY

As we move into the body of the text, the influence of these early thinkers can still be seen, although the many intervening decades have produced a rich body of research and many new approaches to the study of human behavior, interaction, and organization. Let me outline, very briefly, what is to come.

In the next chapter on theory and methods, the nature of research methods, scientific theory, and various theoretical approaches inspired by the founders of the discipline will be examined. Here we will confront the basic question that the founders debated: Is sociology to be a science, and if so, what kind of science is it to be? Are sociologists to take an active role in social intervention, or are they to remain neutral?

In Chapter 3 on symbols and culture, we return to the questions posed by Comte, Durkheim, Weber, and Mead: How are human behavior, interaction, and organization mediated by symbols and systems of ideas? How do symbols enable humans to construct large and complex social patterns, and at the same time, fine-tune their daily interactions?

Chapter 4 turns to how humans create and sustain social structures, or patterns of relationships. All the founders of sociology recognized that human relationships are ordered, revealing a structure, and that the study of society always involves an examination of these structures. Our goal in this chapter is to review the concepts and approaches that sociologists use to understand structures—from the smallest group to the society as a whole—giving order to our daily lives.

Chapter 5 returns to the basic processes underlying the production of culture and social structures: interaction among people in face-to-face contact. Here we will return to the work of George Herbert Mead and those who followed his lead in trying to understand how you and I interact and, in so doing, how we use symbols to create social structures.

Chapter 6 examines a very special kind of interaction: the process of socialization. By virtue of our interactions with others, from infancy to death, we continue to acquire those capacities which make us human and which enable us to use culture and participate in social structures. For without socialization, society could not exist.

Chapter 7 explores two of the basic structures that humans create and use to organize themselves: (1) groups of people in face-to-face contact and (2) more complex organizations of groupings into hierarchies and formal systems of authority. For much of our daily lives is spent in groups and formal organizations, the basic units of organization in modern societies.

Chapter 8 returns to the issues of inequality so prominent in early sociological thought. As societies are built and culture elaborated, inequalities become ever more evident. These inequalities can be traced along class lines, as emphasized by Marx, and along other lines as well, including gender and ethnicity. In all cases, we shall see that these inequalities produce tension and conflict in human societies.

Chapter 9 explores basic institutions, which all the early sociological masters saw as a basic organizing principle of human society. Each institution—economy, family, government, education, religion, medicine, and science—has been created to meet biological needs and socially constructed needs; and it is within these institutional domains that groups and organizations operate and the inequalities play themselves out.

Chapter 10 examines the relationship of a population's size and characteristics to the structure of society, its geographical distribution, and its effects on the environment. Early sociologists clearly recognized that the size and diversity of a population have enormous effects on urban living, the use of space, the development of culture, and the creation of social structures. More recently, we have all become aware of how ecological balances are influenced by cultural beliefs, living space, and social structures.

Chapter 11 pulls together a topic given forceful expression by Marx, but also by Spencer, Durkheim, and Weber. For all these founders, the social order was tenuous, ever in a state of potential dissolution by widespread deviance and dissent. Which forces produce such deviance and dissent, and which promote conformity, order, and integration? Ultimately, this is the fundamental question of sociology.

Chapter 12 examines the force that initially prompted the emergence of sociology—social change. What processes generate change in cultures, social structures, behaviors, and interactions? How can these be understood? We thus end where we began this review of sociology, for sociology emerged in the early decades of the last century and persists today in the remaining years of this century because we seek to understand the dynamic and change-producing forces affecting all our lives.

SUMMARY

1. Sociology is the study of human behavior, interaction, and social organization.
2. Sociology is relevant to each of our daily lives because it provides a vehicle for understanding the sources of constraint in our thoughts, perceptions, and actions.
3. Sociology emerged under conditions of change associated with (a) the decline of feudalism and the emergence of commerce, industry, and urbanization; (b) the intellectual movement known as the Enlightenment in which science and secular thought about the physical, biological, and social worlds could flourish; and (c) the traumatic shock over the violence and sudden change associated with the French Revolution of 1789.
4. The name, *sociology*, was proposed by the French thinker, Auguste Comte, who believed that a science of society could emulate the natural sciences. Comte also felt that discovery of the laws of human social organization could be used to reconstruct society in a more humane way.
5. Herbert Spencer in England similarly argued that laws of human organization could be developed. These laws would focus on the growing size and complexity of society as these forces created pressures for (a) increased interdependence and exchange among people and organizations of a society and (b) increased use of power to regulate, control, and coordinate activities of these members and organizational units.

Spencer founded a sociological approach known as functionalism, where the effects of a social pattern on the maintenance of society are emphasized.

6. Émile Durkheim borrowed from Spencer, but continued the Comtean and French tradition of emphasizing the importance of cultural ideas for the integration of society. Like Spencer, he was a functionalist and believed that laws of human organization could be discovered, but he added to Spencer's approach the importance of discovering the causes and functions of cultural symbols for integrating society.

7. Karl Marx, a German who was expelled from his homeland and eventually settled in England, emphasized the conflictual nature of society, founding an approach known as conflict theory or conflict sociology. In Marx's view, inequalities in the distribution of resources set the stage for the transformation of society as those without resources organize to engage in conflict with those who control production, who possess power, and who manipulate cultural symbols to legitimate their privilege. Unlike Comte, Spencer, and Durkheim, Marx did not believe that general laws of human organization, transcending historical epochs, could be developed.

8. Max Weber, the other major German founder of sociology, engaged in a lifelong but silent dialogue with Marx, emphasizing that inequality is multidimensional and not solely based upon the economy, that conflict is contingent on historical conditions and is not the inevitable and inexorable outcome of inequality, and that change could be caused by ideas as well as the material and economic base of a society. He also stressed that sociology must look at both the larger-scale structure of society and the meanings that individuals give to these larger-scale forces. Like Marx, he doubted that there were general laws of human organization, but unlike Marx, he felt that it is necessary to be value-free, or objective, in the description and analysis of social phenomena.

9. Early American sociology adopted European ideas to specific problems associated with urbanization and industrialization, but it did initiate two important trends: (a) the widespread use of quantitative, statistical techniques and (b) the theoretical approach which was to become known as interactionism, where concern is with the processes by which society is sustained and changed by the behaviors of individuals in micro face-to-face encounters.

10. Sociology is now a large and diverse field analyzing all facets of human culture, social structure, behavior and interaction, and social change.

KEY TERMS

collective conscience   Émile Durkheim's term for systems of cultural symbols that people in a society share and use to regulate their affairs.

conflict of interest   Karl Marx's term for the basic tension and incompatibility of goals between those who control resources and those who do not.

conflict sociology/conflict theory   The view that the main dynamic of human social relations and patterns of social organization is tension and conflict over the unequal distribution of resources.

Enlightenment, the   A broad intellectual movement in the eighteenth century in which nonreligious thinking about the universe was encouraged.

functionalism   An approach to the analysis of phenomena in terms of their consequences for the needs or requisite of the larger social whole in which they are located. This approach was first used in sociology by Herbert Spencer.

hierarchy of the sciences   Auguste Comte's view that the sciences could be arranged in a hierarchy based on when they emerged and how complex their subject matter is. Sociology, not surprisingly, was at the top of the hierarchy, just above biology.

interactionism   An approach to the analysis of social phenomena, inspired by early American philosophers and sociologists, that stresses the importance of understanding the dynamics of face-to-face contact and interaction among individuals.

law of the three stages   Auguste Comte's view that ideas, and society as a whole, pass through three stages: (1) the theological, where religious ideas dominate; (2) the metaphysical, where systematic thought is stressed, and (3) the positivistic, where science comes to dominate.

means of production   Karl Marx's term for the nature and organization of the economy in a society.

philosophes, the   A lineage of eighteenth-century social thinkers in France who championed the idea of individual freedom from arbitrary political authority. It was from this lineage that Auguste Comte, the founder of sociology, was to draw many of his ideas.

sociology   The systematic study of human social behavior, interaction, and organization.

substructure   Karl Marx's label for the material, economic base which influences other aspects of a society.

superorganic   Herbert Spencer's view of sociology's subject matter: the organization of living organisms.

superstructure   Karl Marx's term for those structures and cultural systems determined by the economic base of a society.

value-free   Max Weber's term emphasizing that sociology should seek to eliminate bias and moral considerations in an effort to produce objective analyses of social phenomena.

CHAPTER 2

Theoretical and Methodological Approaches in Sociology

Social reality involves the ebb and flow of people who act, interact, and organize. If we just walk outside and look around us, the world is a buzz of activity, as people move about in their daily routines. How are we to get a handle on this booming and buzzing reality? How are we to understand what is going on? The answer to these kinds of questions is through the dual activities of theory and research. Theory is our vehicle for explaining how the social world operates; methodology is our way of conducting careful research that can help us create or test theories.

17

In the contemporary world, science has become the dominant way to understand the universe. Science is not the only way because religion, ideologies, philosophies, and personal intuition are also used to make sense of the world. Thus, science has competitors; and this competition is more intense in some arenas than in others. Few nonscientists question the claims of physicists about how the physical universe works; the same is true of chemists, biochemists, and biologists, although deeply held religious beliefs about "creationism" often stand in a hostile stare down with biologists' commitment to Darwinian evolution. In the social arena, however, science hardly reigns supreme. Humans and their creations—society and culture—are often not seen as amenable to scientific study. And, over 150 years since Auguste Comte's (1830–1842) confident presumption that sociology could be a natural science, sociologists themselves are still divided on the question of whether scientific sociology can, or should, be so endowed. For just as Karl Marx and Max Weber questioned the possibilities of scientific sociology, so do many contemporary sociologists (Halfpenny, 1982; Denzin, 1970). Still, for the moment, let us assume that this controversy over the scientific status of sociology did not exist and examine how scientific sociology proceeds.

THE NATURE OF SCIENCE

The goal of **science** is to enable us to understand and accumulate knowledge about the universe. The vehicle for such understandings is **theory**, which seeks to tell us why phenomena exist and how they operate (J. Turner, 1991). Scientific theories have some special characteristics which set them apart from other types of explanations like those in religion, political dogma, and personal opinions (J. Turner, 1985a).

One distinctive characteristic of scientific theories is their *abstractness*. They are stated in very general terms because the goal is to explain phenomena in all times and places. For example, Albert Einstein's famous formula, $E = mc^2$, says nothing about a particular emission of energy (E), or body of matter (m), or the speed of light (c) at a specific moment in time; what it says is that energy, matter, and the speed of light are fundamentally related in all times, in all places, and in all manifestations of energy. In a word, this revolutionary equation is abstract because it rises above the particulars and states what is true in all times and places in our universe. Sociological theories can also display this quality. For example, as I noted in the last chapter, Herbert Spencer (1874–1896) proposed that as a population grows in size, its members become differentiated into ever more specialties and partitions which then are integrated by interdependencies and concentrations of power. This theory is also abstract because it does not address a particular population at a specific point in time, but *all* populations in *all* times and places.

A second unique characteristic of scientific theories is that they are subject to **tests**. Some have even proclaimed that scientific theories are designed to be proved wrong (Popper, 1959, 1969), because the goal is to subject theories to tests and retests until we have some confidence that the theory is not easily proved wrong and is, therefore, plausible. For if a theory stands intact after repeated assaults from empirical data, then it is considered for the time being as the best explanation of the way things are. When theories stand the test of time—that is, repeated efforts to disprove them—then they become provisionally accepted as truth, as the way things are (Popper, 1969).

This is the way all science works. It is not an efficient process, but it is the way we keep our theories tied to real events. We hold theories skeptically and constantly check them against the facts. Compare this approach to alternative ways of trying to understand the world. In religious interpretations, the powers of gods and supernatural forces are seen to control the flow of events, and there is a presumption that things should and ought to occur; and if this view does not correspond to the way actual events unfold, beliefs in the power of the gods or the correctness of one's presumptions are not rejected, as they would be for a scientific theory. Rather, a new interpretation is offered that sustains beliefs. Similarly, personal biases are often retained when the facts contradict them; indeed, we cling to our prejudices and perceptions because they give us comfort and because we are used to them. Political ideologies have this same quality; people hold on to their political beliefs even when programs enacted in the name of these beliefs fail. In contrast, scientific theories are ultimately rejected or changed when they do not correspond to the empirical facts.

Theories are not casually tested, although we often begin with only an intuitive sense that the data correspond to the theory. Eventually the theory must be assessed in a systematic way, in terms of some general procedures, often termed the **scientific method**. The general idea behind the methods of science is to develop unbiased procedures for collecting data and then to specify clearly

---

BOX 2-1   *What Makes Science Unique?*

1. Science does not seek to evaluate what *should*, or should not, exist or occur.
2. Science seeks only to understand why phenomena exist and how they operate.
3. Science generates such understanding by developing abstract and nonevaluative theories that explain the how and why of phenomena.
4. Science then subjects these theories to empirical assessment, rejecting or modifying theories if the facts do not support them.
5. Science uses methods of data collection that can be replicated by others to make sure that the data used to test theories are not biased.
6. Science accumulates knowledge when theories find consistent support in empirical tests and when those that do not receive such support are rejected or modified.

the steps that we have taken. In this way, others can come along and check up on us and verify that we were honest and did not make any dumb mistakes or impose biases. Without data that we can trust, or have confidence in, we do not know if we have accurate records of events nor do we know if the data really do bear on the theory that we are testing.

Thus, science impinges on sociology to the degree that we use theories to explain the social world and, at the same time, to test these theories against what really occurs. As theories are developed and tested, knowledge accumulates and we know more about the social world around us.

THEORY IN SOCIOLOGY

It would be nice at this point to report on the great accomplishments of sociological theory to explain human behavior, interaction, and organization. But at present, there is little agreement about which theories are the best, nor has there been a stampede by researchers to test each of our many theories and to see which one looks best. Indeed, sociology reveals an unfortunate tendency for theorists to create theories that are not very amenable to tests and for researchers to collect and analyze data without paying much attention to theory (Turner and Turner, 1990). Thus, it is sad but true that theorists and researchers tend to go their own separate ways. On the theory side of the schism the result is for sociology to evidence a series of theoretical approaches, mostly untested but interesting nonetheless, that provide eyeglasses for looking at and for interpreting events in the social world (Ritzer, 1975, 1988; J. Turner, 1991). Let me outline in broad contours some of the most prominent of these perspectives, saving for later chapters specific theories that have been developed within these broad perspectives. We have already encountered some of these perspectives in our review of the emergence of sociology in the last chapter. Here, we will be more explicit on the underlying elements of these broad approaches (J. Turner, 1991).

Functional Theorizing

Functional theory was created by Herbert Spencer and carried forward by Émile Durkheim into the twentieth century. At one time in the 1950s, this kind of theory dominated sociology; now, it represents just one of several approaches. All **functional theories** examine the social universe as a system of intercon-nected parts (Turner and Maryanski, 1979). The parts are then analyzed in terms of their consequences, or functions, for the larger system. For example, the family might be seen as a basic social institution that helps sustain the larger society by regulating sex and mating among adults and by socializing the young so that they can become competent members of a society. Moreover, one can examine any structure—say, your current college or university—in func-tional terms. All that is necessary is for you to ask one question: How does some aspect of your school—the student body, fraternities and sororities, student government, faculty, staff, administrators, etc.—contribute to the operation of the overall system?

Most functional theories posit "needs" or "requisites" of the system. When this is done, a part is examined with respect to how it meets a need or requisite. For example, many social systems have needs for making decisions, coordinating people, and allocating resources; and so, if these constituted a basic requisite, one would ask: What parts of the system meet these related needs? And then, we would explain how a particular part—for example, government if our focal system is a society—operates to meet this basic need.

There are many problems with functional theories. One of the most important is that they often see society as too well integrated and organized (Dahrendorf, 1958, 1959). For if every system part has a function or meets a need, societies would seem to be smooth-running and well-oiled machines. We all know, of course, that such is not the case; conflict and other dysfunctional processes also exist. Yet, functional approaches still have an appeal because they force us to look at the social universe, or any part of it, as a systemic whole whose constituent elements operate in ways that have consequences for this whole.

Conflict Theories

Karl Marx and Max Weber were the intellectual fountainheads of conflict theories, although other early sociologists also saw the social world in conflictual terms. Unlike functional theories, which emphasize the contribution of parts to a larger whole, **conflict theories** see social wholes as rife with tension and conflict among their subparts (Collins, 1975). Though there are many diverse conflict theories, they all share this point of emphasis in common: Inequality is the driving force behind conflict; and conflict is the central dynamic of human relations. Indeed, it would be hard not to notice the tensions and conflicts that emanate from inequality. For example, in your sociology class there is an inherent tension between you and your instructor over a basic resource: your grade. The instructor controls the grade, and this means that he or she has power over you. You are, then, in a situation of great inequality, and the tension is just beneath the surface. If you do not get the grade that you wanted, you may get angry, and if you could, you would do something about it. The same basic force operates in all social relations between such diverse actors as individuals, ethnic groups, offices and personnel in an office, societywide strata, or nations.

If we look around our own society, we see the tension-producing effects of inequality everywhere. Workers and managers in companies often exist in an uneasy standoff; poor people have aggression for affluent people; women have resentments for the extra income and power that men can command in the society; ethnic minorities intensely resent their second-class status; and so it goes. All these sources of tension which erupt into many diverse forms of conflict—violent crime, riots, protests, demonstrations, strikes, and social movements—stem from the unequal distribution of valued resources like money, power, prestige, housing, health care, and job opportunities. Conflict is, therefore, a basic contingency of social life; we feel its potential everywhere, from interpersonal relations between men and women, through the often strained interaction with different ethnics, to the resentments against the power of parents, teachers, and employers.

Interactionist Theories

It is fine to talk about "parts," "wholes," "functions," "inequalities," and "conflicts," but what about actual people who must face and deal with one another? **Interactionist theories** try to answer this question, as we will see in detail in Chapter 5 when we return to the work of George Herbert Mead (1934, 1938) and all those who built upon his insights. For the present, let me outline the basic position of interactionist theories.

Humans interact by emitting symbols—words, facial expressions, body position, or any sign that "means" something to others and ourselves (Goffman, 1959, 1961, 1967; J. Turner, 1988). By signaling with symbolic gestures, we mark our mood, intentions, and course of action; and conversely, by reading the gestures of others, we get a sense of what they think and how they will behave. We can even do this when other persons are not physically present—for example, when you think about asking for more money from a parent, protesting a grade given by a teacher, or dazzling someone of the relevant sex. Here there is an exchange of gestures in your head as you mentally interact with this person. Thus, the world as we experience it is mediated by symbols and gestures; and we use these gestures to adjust to each other, to build up images of ourselves and situations, and to construct a definition of what will, or should, occur in situations.

For interactionists, then, the explanation of social reality is to come by carefully examining the micro world of individual people who mutually interpret gestures, build up images of themselves, and define situations in certain terms (Blumer, 1969; Stryker, 1980). The macro, or big, structures of society—the state, economy, stratification, and the like—are constructed and sustained by micro interactions (Collins, 1981, 1986); and for interactionists it would be impossible to understand the social world without examining these micro-level encounters. Imagine yourself, for example, in a classroom; all that occurs in this setting is an emission of gestures—for example, by you as you move to your seat past others who may have to accept your apologies as you squeeze by them, by you and others with whom you talk before (and often during) lecture, or by your instructor as he or she seeks to penetrate your mind. So, a "structured" classroom is teeming with gesturing, interpreting and reinterpreting, and defining situations. From an interactionist perspective, you are not a "worker bee" who dutifully follows the script of classroom demeanor (though this is certainly relevant); for you are constantly signaling and interpreting in order to adjust and, at times, create new scripts for interaction. Interactionism thus provides a corrective to any tendency to view "structure" and "culture" as somehow outside of us or as imposing itself on passive interpersonal robots.

Utilitarian Theories

A final group of theories borrows a simple set of assumptions about humans from modern economics which, in turn, adopted the core ideas of Scottish philosophers such as Adam Smith (1776) during the Age of Reason (Camic, 1979). In the eyes of **utilitarian theorists,** humans are rational at least to the extent that they have goals and purposes; they calculate the costs of various alternatives to realizing these goals and choose the alternative which maximizes their benefits (or what economists call *utilities*) and minimizes their costs. We are thus beings who try to derive some benefit in a situation, while reducing our costs (Hechter, 1987; Coleman, 1991). For example, you may calculate how much work you are willing to put out (your "cost") in order to receive a particular grade (your "benefit") in this course or, if I may be idealistic for a moment, a body of knowledge that you can use over a lifetime (in the long run, a much more rewarding benefit). Thus, all situations involve an "exchange" of resources: You give up some resources (your cost) in order to receive something that you perceive to be more valuable (your utility).

For utilitarian theorists, then, all social relations are ultimately exchanges among actors who incur costs in order to get benefits from one another and who calculate the cost-benefit ratio. Your instructor incurs a cost (energy and time in preparing lectures, talking to students, reading exams, etc.) in order to receive a salary (from the university) and, perhaps, your undying loyalty and admiration. Similarly, you come to class, read, think, and humble yourself on exam days (your costs) to receive grades, knowledge, and perhaps a monthly stipend from someone like your parents (your benefits or utilities). We do not have to be consciously aware of these calculations; more often than not, we make them implicitly. It is only when we are not sure of what to do in a situation that we become aware of hard-nosed cost-benefit calculations. But ultimately, utilitarian theorists argue, you exchange time, energy, and money in school settings for grades, credentials, and knowledge which you calculate to be even more valuable than alternative avenues for spending your time, energy, and money.

For rational choice and exchange theorists, interaction, society, and culture are ultimately created and sustained because they offer payoffs for rational individuals. These payoffs are rarely monetary, although they certainly can be, but more typically they are less tangible "goods"—self-feelings, affection, pride, esteem, power, control, and other "soft" currencies that cement society together. You can see this by simply looking at a situation where you got angry or perhaps had your feelings hurt; in such a situation, an anticipated reward (usually nonmonetary) was not received proportionate to your cost and investment, a fact which indicates that beneath the surface of your feelings are implicit calculations about costs and rewards.

The State of Theory in Sociology

There are many specific variants of these broad theoretical perspectives. We will encounter some of them as we move into the subject matter of sociology. From the point of view of science, it would be nice to have more focused and precise theories which have been systematically tested and which would now organize this introduction to sociology. But such is not the case. Moreover, many sociologists do not believe that such can, or should be, the case (Seidman and Wagner, 1992). Instead, current sociological theories can only help us interpret particular facets of the social world, and so, for the present our theories are not like those in the "hard" sciences (Giddens, 1971, 1976, 1984).

Sociology has many pieces of theory, typically inspired by the early founders, but most have not been systematically tested or accepted as the best explanation of the social world. For some, the goals of science in sociology are illusionary, and Comte's dream for a science of society is just that, a dream. For many others, sociology has not yet become a mature science, but the potential is there in the theoretical ideas that have developed within these four approaches: functional, conflict, interactionist, and utilitarian theories. Moreover, there are many less "grand" theories, only loosely connected to these four and other general approaches, that help us understand many social processes, as we will come to see.

METHODS IN SOCIOLOGY

In science, **data** on the actual world need to be systematically and carefully collected so that procedures can be replicated by someone else. For if we simply describe some data without telling others *how* and *why* these data were collected, no one can check up on us to see if our "facts" are really true. Thus, in science a general procedural approach—*the scientific method*—guides research, or the collection and analysis of information about the world.

This scientific method is often viewed as having stages or steps, but we should not get too carried away here and view science as a kind of lockstep march to truth and knowledge. Rather, the practice of science, or carefully crafted research, simply depends upon attention to several matters (Babbie, 1992).

One is a statement of a **research problem**, or what it is that one is trying to discover. This may sound obvious, but it is fundamental because one needs to narrow the focus of inquiry. Otherwise, we will run around like data-collecting magpies. In science, research problems are often dictated by a theory and a desire to see if the theory is plausible. In sociology as well as in the more advanced sciences, research is often conducted for reasons other than explicit theory testing. One reason for conducting research is that we are simply curious about some aspect of the world. Another is that a client—a governmental agency, a business, a charity—desires information on a topic. Yet another is that previous research reveals gaps in our knowledge, or stimulates new questions. Thus, while the idealized view of science would see all research as guided by theory, the reality is quite different. There are many other reasons for conducting research, and the scientific method can be easily accommodated to them.

Another important matter in the conduct of research is the question of what a researcher expects to find. It is often useful to formulate a **hypothesis,** which may be taken from a theory, but not necessarily, about the expected results. In this way, researchers have a criterion or yardstick against which to measure their findings. Without a hypothesis to guide the collection and analysis of data, or at least a loose expectation about what is likely to be found, it is once again difficult to focus one's efforts; indeed, we might gather unneeded, or even irrelevant, information that does not bear on the research problem.

Eventually, after stating a problem and what your expectations are, a **research design** is constructed. This design is a game plan and set of procedures for gathering information as it relates to one's research problem and hypotheses. There are many basic types of designs, but they all try to state clearly *how* information is to be collected. The choice of a design depends upon many factors—the nature of the problem, the amount of money one has to spend, and the preferences of the researcher. In sociology, there are four basic types of designs employed in research: (1) experiments, (2) surveys, (3) observations, and (4) histories. Each of these is briefly summarized below.

Experiments

The idea behind an **experiment** is to test the effect of a particular phenomenon on some aspect of the social world, typically people's responses to a particular stimulus or situation. The key ingredient of an experiment is the control of extraneous influences that might contaminate the researchers' ability to assess the effects of focal stimulus in a situation. In the classical **experimental design,** this is achieved with two matched groups of subjects: (1) the **experimental group,** which receives the stimulus or is exposed to the situation of interest, and (2) the **control group,** which does not receive the stimulus or is not exposed to the situation. The differences between the two groups allow the investigator to determine how much, if any, the stimulus or situation affected individuals. This classical design is rarely used in sociology, but the goal of controlling extraneous influences still guides the research. A more typical experimental design in sociology isolates individuals from the outside world and then observes their responses to a stimulus or to a particular situation of interest to the investigators. By temporarily isolating individuals, some control over outside influences is achieved and it becomes possible to record people's responses to a stimulus or situation. For example, let us say that we wished to examine the effects of placing individuals in a situation of power. We might isolate a group of individuals in a laboratory, construct a task for them to perform, and create a situation where one individual has power. By observing and recording responses, we could examine the effects of having power. Such is the general nature of experiments in sociology.

Surveys

The most common research design in sociology is the **survey,** where people are asked questions about a topic of interest to the investigator (Rossi et al., 1985). These questions can be asked by an interviewer who sits down with the respondent or, more typically, by a questionnaire that the respondent simply fills out. The most ideal survey is one that has the following characteristics: First, the respondents are the entire population of interest or, more typically, a representative sample from this population. Second, all respondents agree to answer the questions. Third, the respondents answer precisely the same questions. These three features are often hard to achieve in practice, however. It may be impossible to ask all of the population; there may be too many, or they may be hard to reach. It may be difficult to get them to respond, because they are busy, unconcerned, forgetful, or even hostile to intrusions in their lives. It may be that items on a questionnaire are interpreted differently by varying respondents, or if actual interviews are conducted, the interviewers ask the questions in a different tone or the synergy of the interaction between the interviewer and respondent produces different responses. If samples are large enough, many of these problems are obviated, or cancel each other out. Yet, the extensive use of surveys reveals other problems (Cicourel, 1964): They reveal only what people *say*, not what they may actually think and do; they structure respondents' answers rather than let respondents communicate in their own way; they are easily subject to lies and misrepresentations; they do not easily examine phenomena that cannot be collapsed into questions. Sociologists use them, however, because they are quickly administered and amenable to the application of statistics (Collins, 1984; Lieberson, 1985, 1992). Moreover, sociologists are often interested in what people think, perceive, and believe; and a survey is a relatively easy way to get at surface cognitions, perceptions, feelings, and emotions.

Observations

Sometimes it is best to leave the confines of the experimental lab, to throw away the questionnaire, and to go out among people in real-life situations and observe what they are actually doing. **Observational research designs** do just this (Whyte and Whyte, 1984; Whyte, 1989): They place the investigator in a more naturalistic situation, and they have the investigators observe and write down what they see. In this way, nuances, context, interactions, histories, and flows of events can be discovered. One type of observational study is **participant observation** where the investigator actually becomes a member of the group, organization, or community being studied. As such, the observer can not only be more intimately involved, but he or she can actually experience the world in a manner similar to those being observed. Another type of observational study is the **unobtrusive observation** where the investigator does not actually participate as a member, but stands aside, out of the way and records what is occurring. This type of study loses some of the intimacy and insight possible with participant observation, but it does mitigate against the pitfall of having the researcher's actions influence the flow of events and, hence, the research findings. Oftentimes, observational studies are a preliminary step in survey research, because they enable those designing questions to select and phrase them in ways that will make sense to the respondents. The great advantage of observational studies is that one is examining the real world, not the artificial constructions of experimental designs and lists of survey questions (Whyte, 1989). The great disadvantage, however, is that different investigators may see different things in terms of their personal biases. Moreover, observational studies are hard to replicate—to see if indeed what the investigator says occurs actually does—because the group may not exist any longer or because various investigators simply observe different things or excite different responses.

Histories

At times we want to know what happened in the past. One can, of course, ask people in interviews about their past, but often we want to look further back at long reaches of history. It is at this point that history and sociology converge. All the early founders of sociology—Spencer, Marx, and Weber, in particular— used history to develop or illustrate their ideas; and in recent decades there has been a dramatic revival of **historical research** to test or illustrate theories, or to describe the ebb and flow of events in past societies. At times, historical research draws upon the previous research of historians who have gone to the archives and dusty records or upon the data of archeologists who have dug up the past; and at other times, sociological researchers go themselves to the records or to the archeological dig. The major difference between history and historical sociology is that, more typically but not always, the sociological research is interested in using history to test or illustrate a more general theory, whereas the historian seeks only to describe the events of a particular time in the past. Although this is a blurred distinction, it does capture a sense of the differences between history and sociology. The great problem with using historical records is that they are always incomplete and subject to different interpretations (which, of course, keeps historians in business); and as a result, history can rarely provide a definitive and conclusive "test" of a theoretical idea.

Once the data are collected by one of these research designs, they are subjected to **analysis**. The type of analysis depends on the research design and the nature of the data, but the goal is to be careful, systematic, and unbiased. From the analysis will come our conclusions about what we found; and so, we had better be careful because others will check up on us.

And a final step in the scientific method is to assess the plausibility of the hypothesis or, if hypotheses were not offered, to indicate what the data tell us about the phenomena studied.

These steps may seem like common sense, but they are much more: They

FIGURE 2-1. Elements of the scientific method.

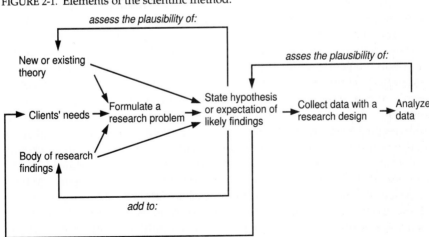

force us to be systematic, to remain unbiased (or at least to reduce our biases), and to let others know *what* we discovered and *how* we discovered it. Without the guidelines of the scientific method, we could not trust one another's findings, and we would not know how to check them and reassess them. The result would be that knowledge would be haphazard and often inaccurate; and we would not accumulate trustworthy knowledge about the world.

DOES SCIENCE TAKE AWAY HUMANISM?

My fellow sociologists often proclaim that sociology is "an art form." The general idea is that sociologists should stop handing out impersonal questionnaires and, instead, get in touch with the actual workings of people. Moreover, we should use our intuition as much as our intellect to extract information about the world. Sociology should still involve the use of general conceptual ideas, it is held, but only as these ideas are influenced by our active participation with people in real-life settings. By knowing firsthand about the concerns, dilemmas, problems, and frustrations of individuals in society, we can use our conceptual knowledge to help them and make their lives better and more satisfying. Sociologists of this persuasion see their mission as diagnosing those sources of strain among individuals that stem from patterns of social organization and then suggesting possible solutions.

Many professional sociologists first dedicated themselves to sociology for humanitarian reasons. They felt that certain social conditions were wrong—ethnic and sexual discrimination, privilege in the face of abject poverty, unhappiness and alienation, and other social ills—and they wanted to do something about these ills. Indeed, this was certainly the motivation of Karl Marx and many other sociologists. They wanted to help people and make a better world. Scratch the surface of even the most hard-nosed methodologist or climb into the armchair of a good theorist, and one can find humanistic motivations in the most professional of our professionals. Of course, this fact means that there is always an implicit ideology lurking in the thinking of a sociologist. Sometimes this ideology is explicitly advocated, but whether implicit or explicit, most sociologists do hold views about "what's wrong with society" and a general plan for "what should be done to solve these problems." True, at the same time we are realists and recognize that it is impossible to mold society to our will and fervor. Moreover, we recognize the bias in our thinking, and we try to suspend it when "doing science." Indeed, something often happens to sociologists as they move through school, especially on the road to a Ph.D. Somehow the humanistic motivations and ideological fervor recede and get buried under a veneer of technical skills and academic professionalism. One consequence of this is that those scholars who remain openly humanistic and ideological tend to view experiments, statistics, impersonal scientific methods, and abstract theory as the "enemy" to their more practical concerns. They tend to see theory and methods as negating both their intuitions into sociological situations and their desire to help people.

This apparently unbridgeable gap between intuition on the one hand and research on the other is unnecessary. Our reasoned hunches, feelings, and intuitions are marvelous sources of sociological data. Although we often empha-size the methodological problems of such data—personal bias and unverifiabil-ity, for example—we should also recognize the great advantage they give us over natural scientists. Since we are humans who study humans and their patterns of social organization, we can use our intuition to gather information. We often have intimate familiarity with our subject matter in a way that a geologist or a physicist can never have. In short, our intuition and feeling can give us a real leg up on what is occurring. Yet, we should not go overboard on this issue, as many sociologists do.

Our intuition can be wrong, biased, or only partly right. And if we try to base a corrective program on faulty information or on ideological grounds (that is, on what we think *should* occur), we can potentially do more harm than good. Indeed, we can hurt people and create even more difficult social settings for those we are trying to help. Thus, we need to qualify our enthusiasm for intuition and for data gathered and interpreted in light of our actual experiences in a social setting. We should not throw this intuitive advantage away or suppress it, any more than we should repress our humanistic concerns and desires to help people and to make a better world. But we need to supplement these. This supplementation comes by recognizing what science is and what it can do in mobilizing and channeling intuition and ideological biases for constructive purposes.

If we want to realize our humanism—and this motive is what gets most of us started in sociology—we need to be skilled at gathering and interpreting information about situations we want to change and people we want to help. We also need to understand *why* and *how* the situations operate. And we need to be able to anticipate the consequences of any changes we initiate and to collect accurate information on these changes. We cannot rely on intuition and our personal ideologies in these matters. We need theory that has withstood efforts to disprove it to tell us how and why things operate, and we need to use this theory in ascertaining what needs to be done to improve a situation. We will also need to collect accurate information and analyze it carefully to know just what exists in a situation and just what the consequences of our theoretically informed actions are.

If we have no theory, we have no framework for understanding and inter-preting the social world. Hence, we do not know what we have done or what to expect. If we do not have methods, we cannot have confidence in our theories, since they have not been tested, and we cannot know exactly what in a situation needs to be changed. We can use our familiarity with a situation and our creative intuition to bring to bear relevant theories and to develop systematic ways of gathering information. But our intuition cannot substitute for theory, carefully constructed methods, and detailed analysis. This is why science is an important tool for approaching social issues and problems of interest to humanists.

SCIENTIFIC SOCIOLOGY AND SOCIAL ENGINEERING

As I mentioned in Chapter 1, the titular founder of sociology, Auguste Comte, believed that a science of society could be used to make a better society. He realized that if sociology could develop and test theoretical laws like those in the physical and biological sciences, it would be possible to achieve a level of understanding about human organization that would facilitate the construction of new social forms. Thus Comte saw that science and humanism are not antithetical: Once there is understanding of how and why the social world operates, this knowledge can be used to construct a better world. In entirely different guises, Karl Marx and Émile Durkheim felt the same way. They desired *to use* their conceptual understandings of how the world works *to construct a better society.*

Words like "construct" smack of social engineering, of social control, of an Orwellian world of Big Brother, of a dull and lifeless society of technocrats. Engineering is fine, many would argue, as long as we use it to build bridges and roads. But unfettered engineering of theoretical knowledge creates things like nuclear bombs and other potentially harmful devices. These fears about engineering are, of course, well-founded. But it could be argued that harmful uses of engineering are the result of organization into societal forms that encourage and sustain harmful uses of engineering. If we knew more about the social universe, we might be better able to limit the misapplication of knowledge. On the other side of the issue, however, we might misuse knowledge of social organization to create even more monstrous things.

This issue in some ways is moot. The development of theory and the use of research methods are going to produce more knowledge about how the social world operates. This knowledge—even in its current crude state—is going to be used for social engineering (Hunt, 1985). We call social engineering by other names in sociology—sometimes sociological **practice,** at other times **clinical sociology** and **applied sociology**—since the label "social engineering" has such unsavory connotations. But we should know what these more benign labels mean: They are efforts to construct certain types of social relations using theoretical ideas and research findings. As with all engineering, it can be used for both good and bad purposes—what is good and bad, of course, being relative and variously defined. Thus, we should not view scientific sociology as an arcane activity, for in point of fact, it is being used to change our daily lives; and it is likely to be used even more in the future.

SUMMARY

1. Science is the systematic effort to understand the universe in terms of theoretical ideas that have received consistent support in carefully conducted research.
2. Theory is, ultimately, the vehicle for understanding the universe, and it reveals two distinct characteristics: (a) abstractness and generality; and (b) testability. Knowledge accumulates when abstract theories are tested and retested.
3. Theory in sociology is not as well developed as in the natural sciences. Currently, four general theoretical approaches guide theory in sociology: (a) functional theorizing where concern is with understanding how social phenomena operate to meet the needs of the larger social whole in which they are implicated; (b) conflict theorizing where

emphasis is on the conflict-producing effects of inequalities; (c) interactionist theorizing where attention is drawn to the use of gestures in face-to-face communication and adjustments of individuals to one another; and (d) utilitarian theorizing where emphasis is on the calculation of costs and benefits in the pursuit of goals.

4. Data on the empirical world are collected systematically in accordance with the tenets of the scientific method. These tenets include (a) stating a research problem; (b) formulating a hypothesis; (c) collecting data which in sociology is done with either experiments, surveys, observations, or history; (d) analyzing the data; and (e) drawing conclusions with respect to the plausibility of theory, previous research, or needs of a client.

5. While there are biases when humans study humans, this fact also gives social science an advantage: We have an intuitive familiarity with our subject matter.

6. Sociological knowledge will, as it accumulates, be used to construct and reconstruct social relations. Such efforts do not need to be antihumanistic; indeed, they can be done in the name of humanism. Hence, science and humanism need not stand in contradiction.

KEY TERMS

analysis A stage in the scientific method in which the data collected are systematically assessed and in order to determine what has been discovered.

applied sociology The effort to use sociological knowledge in dealing with problems and events.

clinical sociology A term used to describe the activities of sociologists who use sociological knowledge to assess a situation for a client and to develop solutions for this client.

conflict theories Explanations that seek to understand phenomena in terms of the tensions inherent in the unequal distribution of resources.

control group Those subjects in an experimental design who are not exposed to a stimulus of interest and who are used as a basis of comparison with those exposed to the stimulus.

data Information about the empirical world.

experimental group Those subjects in an experimental research design who are exposed to a stimulus of interest to the investigator.

experiment/experimental design A research design in which extraneous influences are controlled in an effort to isolate the effect of some specific stimulus.

functional theories Explanations that seek to understand phenomena in terms of their consequences for a larger social whole.

histories/historical research A type of research design in which information about the past is gathered systematically.

hypothesis A statement of what one expects to be found in a research project. Hypotheses are often derived from theories and represent the predictions that a general theory makes for a specific empirical case(s).

interactionist theories Explanations that seek to understand phenomena in terms of the mutual, face-to-face gesturing activities of individuals who attempt to confirm self and to construct joint lines of conduct.

observations A type of research design in which the activities of individuals in their natural setting are recorded.

participant observation   A type of observational research design in which the researcher becomes actively involved with those being studied.

practice   A term often used to describe sociological work that is used for practical purposes and for changing a situation.

research design   The explicit procedures that are used in collecting empirical data.

research problem   The first step in the scientific method devoted to establishing what kind of information is to be gathered in a research project.

science   The process in which theoretical explanations about the operation of phenomena in the universe are systematically tested with empirical data.

scientific method   The procedures employed in the collection of data. These procedures are designed to test theories or, at the very least, to collect data in ways that are objective and replicable by other researchers.

survey   A type of research design in which a sample of respondents is asked an established set or schedule of questions.

tests   The careful gathering of empirical data in order to assess the plausibility of a theory, or hypothesis derived from a theory.

theory   Abstract statements that explain how and why phenomena in the universe operate. Theory is the vehicle in science for understanding.

unobtrusive observation   A type of observational research design in which the investigator seeks to remain uninvolved with those being studied.

utilitarian theories   Explanations that seek to understand phenomena in terms of the rational calculations of actors of their costs and benefits.

CHAPTER 3

Symbols and Culture

Social life is regulated by systems of symbols that give us instructions for acting, interacting, and organizing ourselves. For many animals, these instructions sit on the genes of their cells and provide biologically based blueprints for living. To a limited degree, this may also be true of humans, but these biological instructions are supplemented, and indeed usually supplanted, by cultural codes that provide us with the necessary guidance to move about in space, talk to others, form relationships, and construct the large-scale structures of modern societies. Humans without symbols, or culture, would be lost, and the world as we know it would collapse. While the symbols and instructions they contain may seem like a burden, especially in a modern world where the information revolution is generating ever new systems of symbols and where one cannot escape a world saturated with signs and symbols (as is the case in the picture above), we would not know how to act, how to form relationships, and how to build and live in the structures of modern life without such systems of symbols.

A WORLD OF SYMBOLS

Humans, and to a limited degree a number of nonhuman animals as well, can do an amazing thing: They can represent facets of the world, their experiences, and virtually anything with arbitrary signs. We call these signs symbols when people come to agree on what a sign stands for and what it represents. The words that you are now reading are signs (black marks on a page) whose meaning we agree on; and hence, each word is a symbol. These words are organized into sentences, paragraphs, and chapters. They are part of an organized *system* of symbols.

What is true of language is true of almost anything we can think up. Flags, crosses, clenched fists, facial frowns, books, bibles, and computer programs are all signs that carry agreed-on meanings. And typically, they belong to systems of symbols, for they invoke other related symbols and meanings. It is through such systems of symbols that we remember the past, take cognizance of the present, and anticipate the future. Without this amazing capacity, our world would consist of mere sense impressions. We would be enslaved in the here and now. We would have no music, art, mathematics, joking, swearing, reading, worshiping, or any of the other things we as humans take for granted. Our life would be dull and routine, but we would not "know" this since we would be incapable of representing it with symbols.

We can get a sense for the significance of symbol systems by observing ants and other social insects, like termites and bees. We call them "social" because they are organized, but they are organized by information much different than our systems of symbols. The information guiding these insects and their conduct is coded on the genes within their chromosomes so that their place and role in insect society are largely predetermined and genetically orchestrated (although all organisms make unique adjustments to the particulars of their environment).

Human systems of symbols are not genetically programed. They are imaginatively created, used, and changed as we confront one another and the conditions of our environment. But they are the functional equivalent of the genetic codes of social insects in that they shape our actions and, most important, our patterns of social organization. And the sum total of these systems of symbols among a population of humans is what sociologists generally call **culture** (Kroeber and Kluckhohn, 1973; Parsons, 1951). In everyday talk, we often use the term *culture* differently to refer to fine wine, good scotch, tasteful dress, or premium beer. But these are not culture, per se, but the material products of activities guided by culture. They are physical things created by using symbols to organize people to produce things. Yet, they can also be cultural symbols in themselves if they "say something" about us to others. Thus, serving a premium beer as opposed to an "el cheapo" discount brand is a statement and it affects the nature, in however slight a way, of your relation to others, as does driving a Mercedes Benz, a Lexus, or a BMW. Thus, cultural products (which result from cultural symbols as they organize manufacturing) can become symbols themselves and influence the behavior, interaction, and organization among people.

I should add a note of caution and qualification here: This emphasis on culture as systems of symbols is not universally accepted. There are many diverse definitions of culture (Kroeber and Kluckhohn, 1973), and some want to see culture as the sum total of all human creations (Singer, 1968): symbols, material artifacts, and ways of organization. When this more global definition is used, then a distinction between **material culture** (physical artifacts) and *nonmaterial culture* (systems of symbols and social ways) is sometimes drawn. I will, however, employ a more restricted usage, but it is important to be aware that there is no agreed upon definition of culture in the social sciences (Gilmore, 1992).

Thus, the point of view emphasized here stresses the fact that our world is constructed from and mediated by symbols. Virtually everything we experience, do, desire, and see is tied to symbols. Understanding ourselves and the broader social world thus requires a greater knowledge of culture. We need to recognize that symbols structure our world for us, although not to the extent they do for genetically preprogramed ants, bees, or termites. In short, we should not underestimate the power of cultural symbols to dictate our perceptions, our feelings, and our behaviors, but neither should we overestimate their power. Humans create them and can re-create them as they change their relations with one another, as they reorganize their social worlds, or as they deal with new environmental conditions.

SYMBOLS AND SOCIETY

At one level, culture and the products of culture are simple resources that enable us to get things done. Without language, our communication is limited. Without technology (information about how to manipulate the environment), we could not eat and house ourselves. Symbols, then, are the medium of our adjustment to the environment, of our interaction with others, of our interpretation of experiences, and of our organizing ourselves into groups.

Symbols are more than a convenient medium, however. They also tell us what to do, think, and perceive. To paraphrase Marshall McCluhan, our symbolic media also carry a message, or a set of instructions. As we have seen, they do not shackle us in the same way as does the genetic information on the genes of ants, bees, and termites, but they do limit our options. Even a seemingly neutral symbolic resource like language carries a hidden message (Hall, 1959). For example, the language of Hopi Native Americans is different from English in the way it treats the notion of time (Carroll, 1956). In English, "time" is a noun, which means that it can be modified—cut, saved, spent, lost, wasted. (For example, you may be having a "bad time" reading my words, or you may consider this all to be "a waste of time.") But for the Hopi, "time" is a verb and as such cannot be modified or manipulated like a noun; time simply flows and humans bend to its way. (A Hopi will probably complain less about this book.) Thus, the respective views of the person using Hopi or English will vary, as will their behaviors and patterns of social organization. Culture, then, is rarely just a neutral resource. Culture is a constraint, and it is this constraining aspect of culture that most interests sociologists.

Sociologists study culture by examining how symbolic systems constrain human interaction and organization, and in turn, how patterns of social organization operate to create, sustain, or change culture (Kroeber and Parsons, 1958). We are not interested in every symbolic system, only in those important to the concerns of sociology. We are most interested in those symbols which influence how we see things, act in the world, interact with others, and coordinate our actions and behaviors with people.

SYSTEMS OF SYMBOLS

Symbols are organized into systems which enable them to get quite complex. Although there is enormous diversity in systems of symbols among human populations, these systems are of several basic kinds.

Language Systems

One is the system of **language** codes which can range from spoken words and the words on this page to complex mathematical representations and computer algorithms. The basic kinds of language codes which a population possesses will greatly influence how it will become organized. For example, if a population has only a spoken language, its patterns of social organization will be limited, whereas if this population can develop a written language, it can store information more effectively and, as a result, elaborate its patterns of social organization. And if new languages—mathematics, logic, computer algorithms, and other symbolic codes—can be developed, the range of responses of this population to its environment can increase; and the nature of its members' social relations and their patterns of social organization will be dramatically altered. Think, for example, of what computer language has done to the speed, scale, and scope of relations in the modern world, and you can see the power of language to transform society.

Technology Systems

Another basic cultural system is **technology,** or the organization of information and knowledge about how to control and manipulate the environment. If gathering plants and hunting animals is the basic store of information among a population—as it was for 30,000 of our 40,000 years as a species—social organization and adaptation to the environment will be limited (though it should be emphasized that hunters-gatherers may have been far more relaxed and content with their lives than "modern" individuals). As technology expands, so does the scale of society: We can produce more, get bigger, and become more complex. Thus, technology is one of the driving forces of human organization, and once it reaches certain levels and becomes intertwined with science and engineering, it becomes a cultural juggernaut, transforming how we live, relate to one another, and organize ourselves (Lenski, 1966; Lenski, Lenski, and Nolan, 1991). Indeed, just about every aspect of your daily life—your dress, your transportation, your living arrangements, your perceptions, your aspirations, your modes of communication—is circumscribed by the products that come from new kinds of knowledge or technology. Indeed, we cannot even imagine life without telephone, television, car, apartment, easy-iron clothes, computer networks, information-age talk, compact disks, and so the list goes. If personal relations get lost in this technological shuffle, it should not surprise us.

Value Systems

Humans always hold ideas about what is good or bad, appropriate or inappropriate, and essential or unessential. These are **values**; and when these are organized into a system of standards or criteria for assessing the moral worth and appropriateness of conduct, they constitute a *value system* (Williams, 1970; Rokeach, 1973, 1979).

Values possess a special feature: They are abstract in that they are so general as to be applicable to many diverse situations (Kluckhohn, 1951). Without this abstract quality, which allows us to tailor values to specific situations, people would have a hard time communicating and getting along, because they would have no common moral yardstick to assess others', as well as their own, actions. Imagine a conversation between two individuals holding very different sets of values. They would not agree on what should occur, what would be fair, and what would be appropriate behavior. What is remarkable about most human populations is how they reveal at least some consensus over values. This consensus is rarely perfect, I must caution, for one of the most interesting and volatile dynamics of a society is conflict over values. But a society without some degree of value consensus would be characterized by considerable conflict and tension. It is striking that in a society as large as that of the United States, spread across such a huge geographical area, there is some agreement on what is good, bad, appropriate, and inappropriate. In large part, this general consensus over values is what makes us uniquely "American," and it is what enables us as individuals to move into and out of new situations without great stress. When we share basic values, we can interact, even though we may disagree on many things.

What are some general values (Williams, 1970)? In America, we agree on such values as achievement (doing well, trying to do well), activism (trying to master and control situations), freedom (being unrestrained for pursuit of our fancy), progress (improving ourselves and the world around us), materialism (acquiring material objects, tastefully, of course), and efficiency (doing things in a rational and practical manner). These ideas, and others as well, we share, and they serve us as moral yardsticks for evaluating ourselves and others in most concrete situations. We do not agree on all of these values; indeed, some people reject them all. But there is an amazing degree of consensus over them among most people. While you and I might, for example, assign these values different priorities, we probably agree about them in general terms. And our interaction proceeds with less effort as a result.

Equally important, our whole society and its many components—its economy, political process, educational system, community patterns, and so on—are influenced by these values. In this way, there is some "glue" to hold society together and to give it some degree of coherence.

Values work, of course, on individuals as they make decisions to behave in certain ways. For example, a student reading this book is guided by these core American values: Activism (I'll master this book), achievement (I've got to take a test on it), progress and materialism (I've got to get a degree that certifies me as eligible for a good job), and efficiency (I'm not going to waste time rereading). All these values guide your conduct in an educational system *organized around* these moral premises. Furthermore, entrance into school marked an implicit acceptance of these values by students and willingness to perpetuate the educational system organized around activism, achievement, individualism, and materialism. And what is true for school is also the case for almost all situations: Some profile of values from a value system is guiding the perceptions and conduct of individuals in society.

A functional perspective stresses these consequences of values for guiding people's actions and motivating them to participate in society. If we think back to Émile Durkheim's analysis of the collective conscience and its integrative functions for society, we can see that consensus over values is crucial to a society. There is a great deal of merit in analyzing these functions of values, as Durkheim did long ago and as I have done here, but we must not forget that values can be a source of disintegration in a society. When segments of a population hold varying values, or as I will discuss shortly, different beliefs, the stage is set for conflict. People will clash over their moral standards, and because they hold these dearly, they cannot back down. A conflict perspective would emphasize this aspect of social life, but it would do more: It would stress that values are often tools for the more privileged who have the power to define which values people should hold. I will return to this point later, but it is important to bear in mind.

Belief Systems

Yet another type of symbol system revolves around **beliefs** which are people's cognitions and ideas in *particular types* of situations—education, work, family, friendships, politics, religion, neighborhood, sports, recreation, and all basic kinds of social situations in a society (Turner and Starnes, 1976). Some beliefs represent the application of basic values to particular situations. In a college or university, for example, one should get good grades (achievement), try hard (activism, efficiency), move through the system and know more (progress). Almost all situations—work, play, parties, friendships, sports, and the like—involve beliefs that stem from the application of these and other general values. Even in a personal relationship in America, we wonder how "well we are doing" (achievement), if we are "going somewhere" in the relationship (progress), and what we need "to do to improve it" (activism). Depending on the type of relationship—lovers, parents, casual friends, close friends—somewhat different beliefs apply, but they all invoke the same value premises. In so doing, they give us guidance and make us confident that we are doing the right thing.

Other beliefs are, on the surface, more factual. They are ideas we hold about "what is" and "what exists" in a situation. By "knowing what exists" we feel confident about approaching and acting in a situation. We also hold beliefs about situations that we have not experienced, have yet to experience, or will never experience—work, marriage, old age, poverty, and other distant situations. Members of a population can be seen as "plugged into" one another's social worlds in this way. By holding beliefs about other social arenas and contexts, we vicariously "know about" and can potentially "act in" these arenas. For this reason, new situations are not so totally unfamiliar. We have general values and some beliefs to guide us as we initially fumble about.

Our factual beliefs are not always accurate, however. They are greatly influenced by values and other beliefs about what *should* occur or exist in a particular situation. But because we are convinced that we do indeed know about other worlds, we feel a vicarious comradeship with others and a sense that we could function in these other worlds. For example, most Americans believe that there are job opportunities for anyone who really wants to work and that many welfare recipients are lazy and misrepresent their need (Kluegel and Smith, 1986; Smith, 1985). This belief represents an invocation of such values as activism, achievement, progress, and efficiency to the world of work and welfare. It also contains some supposedly neutral facts: There are lots of jobs out there and lots of people are too lazy to take them. And it carries a presumption: If I were poor and out of work, I would take any job and preserve my dignity. Thus, we feel knowledgeable about a world which, realistically, we are not likely to experience. But the "facts" in these beliefs may be wrong: Most people on welfare cannot work—they are too old, too disabled, and too sick and about half of them work full time or were laid off (J. Turner, 1993b); thus, the more accurate "facts" are that the economy does not have enough jobs to employ all of its citizenry and that wages for many jobs are not high enough to keep people out of poverty (Beeghley, 1983; Ropers, 1991). So our beliefs about what actually exists and occurs can be biased by values and evaluative beliefs. This is not bad; it is inevitable in human affairs.

Indeed, in modern society an entire industry has emerged to poll the public on its attitudes and opinions—which are, in essence, expressions of beliefs. The public opinion industry extends far beyond election polls and general surveys, such as the Gallup and Harris polls; it is also the basic method behind market research and public relations inquiries. The recognition that people's behavior— from voting for president to buying a product—is influenced by their attitudes which, in turn, are shaped by their general values and beliefs has greatly changed the way politicians run for election and the way that corporations do business.

Normative Systems

Values and beliefs are too general to regulate and guide behavior precisely; they give us a common view and perspective and they also get us mobilized to behave in certain general ways (Blake and Davis, 1964). But they do not tell us precisely what to do. **Norms** make up for this deficiency in other symbol systems by telling us what is expected and appropriate in a particular situation. Imagine yourself coming to class not knowing the "rules" of, and expectations for, student behavior. You are mobilized to achieve, to be active, and to progress mentally, but you do not know what to do—where to sit, how to act, what to do with your hands, legs, mouth, and mind. This may be hard to imagine since you do know the general rules of school behavior so well. Yet, if you have never been in a big lecture hall, if you have never owned your own books, and if you have never attended a college lecture, then you may have some early feelings of discomfort. Indeed, you may find yourself watching how to sit in lectures and how to take notes. Thus, one may know the general norms pertaining to basic types of situations—what some sociologists call **institutional norms**—but each person must learn additional norms to fine tune behavior in a special setting.

From an interactionist viewpoint, this process of discovery is very complex and subtle. If we do not know the relevant aspects of culture that apply to a situation, we become intensely attuned to the actions and gestures of others. We read their gestures, seeking to plug ourselves into their mental states in an effort to learn how to behave. We often carry the relevant values, beliefs, and norms already, but lack complete knowledge of *which* ones are most salient, and we may even be ignorant of relevant norms and beliefs. Our mistakes give us away, and we experience the sanctions and disapproval of others, with the result that we become attuned to others' gestures. Or, we may know of our ignorance before we make a mistake, and as a consequence we act tentatively as we pay attention to the movements, words, and gestures of others. Once we acquire a sense for the relevant cultural symbols, interaction processes sustain these symbols in a mutually reinforcing way. Each of us behaves in the appropriate way; such behaviors reinforce values, beliefs, and norms; and as these are reinforced, they gain power to constrain behavior. Acts of deviance do occur and break this cycle of reinforcement, but we usually try to bring the deviant back into line and sustain the cycle. Such is how culture is sustained by the micro interpersonal actions of individuals.

Norms vary in their generality—from broad institutional ones, which are general instructions about how to behave in basic social spheres (work, school, friendships, home, etc.) to more specific ones, which tell us precisely how to function in a concrete setting. We all carry with us the knowledge of crucial institutional norms, and as a result we can enter new situations with at least some guidance. Once there, we can learn the additional norms, through reading the gestures of others. We also must learn how to create new norms in some situations as we interact with others, and this process can become very difficult, especially if people hold somewhat different beliefs and invoke variations of norms that are at odds. When people marry, for example, they often need to negotiate new agreements about how they are going to behave because beliefs about the role of men and women are in rapid flux and because norms about wife and husband activities can differ greatly. In light of this fact, it is not surprising that the divorce rate in the United States is highest in the first year of marriage (Collins and Coltrane, 1991). Most couples have only some highly romanticized beliefs, knowledge of general institutional norms about marriage, and perceptions of their parents' and friends' marriages to guide their relations. There is often just too much to work out, normatively, and as a result, the marriage fails.

Some situations in modern societies, then, require us to improvise and develop normative agreements as we go. Others, such as an assembly line job, are highly constrained, but even here people develop normative agreements about how they are to work on the job. Much of our social life consists of our learning, fine-tuning, creating, and renegotiating norms. This is particularly so in modern societies, where constant social change forces us to move about into ever-new situations.

Stocks of Knowledge

Aside from language, technology, values, beliefs, and normative systems, people carry with them more loosely and implicitly held stores of information. The German sociologist, Alfred Schutz (1932), coined the phrase "stocks of knowledge at hand" to describe the catalogues of relevant information that individuals can draw upon in adjusting to situations. For example, a student entering college possesses stocks of useful knowledge about schools, classrooms, rank differences, occasions for formality versus informality, lectures and speeches, and appropriate sitting and talking demeanor. These **stocks of knowledge** are used to guide a student's orientation to those first classes and encounters, while the more fine-tuned norms of each new situation are learned.

Thus, each of us has a stock of knowledge, forged out of experiences. And we use these stocks to orient ourselves to situations; and when people share similar stocks of information, they can construct a common view of a situation. Even when we do not speak the same language, this is possible, as anyone who has traveled in a foreign country can testify. By gestures we can usually get foreigners to draw from their stocks of knowledge information close to our own, especially with respect to the common situations. This ability to use these implicit systems of symbols gives humans enormous flexibility in their adjustment to new situations.

Part of culture, then, is a quiet "knowledgeability" which is drawn upon constantly, as we adapt to each other, to norms, and to other features of situations. If we could only catalogue values, beliefs, and norms, we would be stiff, robotlike; and if something new came along outside our "programing," we would not know what to do. But we can adjust to nuances because we all carry vast storehouses or stocks of knowledge which can be drawn upon.

To sum up thus far, the organization of human society is greatly facilitated by cultural symbols. Conversely, cultural symbols are created, sustained, or changed by interaction among people. Indeed, as functional theorists argue (Parsons, 1951, Alexander, 1985), the integration of society cannot occur without common systems of symbols. Culture thus meets a basic need of society. And as interactionists emphasize, these systems of symbols are sustained by the fine-grained reading of one another's gestures. The most crucial symbols for under-standing our actions and patterns of organization are systems of language, technology, values, beliefs, norms, and stocks of knowledge. These are the functional equivalents of genetic codes in social insects, but with a big difference: They can be changed and used to create new social forms. If we all did not participate in a common culture, we would be bumping into one another, insulting our friends, and otherwise doing the wrong thing. Yet, we are not insects, and since our guidance system is not genetically coded, there is lots of room for misinformation, inadequate information, conflicting information, and ever-changing information. Thus, society is not like the well-ordered beehive or ant hill because we organize ourselves with cultural, as opposed to genetic, codes. And in cultural symbols there is a great potential for ambiguity, dissen-sion, and conflict.

CULTURAL VARIATIONS

Humans create systems of cultural symbols because we need them. They are developed to facilitate interaction and organization, as functional theorists ar-gue. And because people live and operate in diverse environments, culture naturally will also vary. And as a conflict theorist would emphasize, cultural variations are a source of constant conflict and tension in a society. Just as languages differ, so do other cultural systems, such as technology, values, beliefs,

FIGURE 3-1. The interrelations among interaction, social structure, and culture. Symbols regulate interaction and social structure, but the reverse is true: People change and create culture in their daily interactions; and patterns of social relations in structures (such as economy, politics, inequality, family, etc.) can generate pressures for new systems of symbols. Without this mutually reinforcing cycle, human society would not be possible, and we would have a great deal of difficulty knowing how to behave and how to interact with on another.

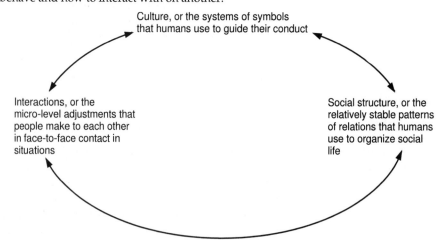

Culture, or the systems of symbols that humans use to guide their conduct

Interactions, or the micro-level adjustments that people make to each other in face-to-face contact in situations

Social structure, or the relatively stable patterns of relations that humans use to organize social life norms, and stocks of knowledge. This fact has enormous implications. Let me review some of them.

Cultural Conflict

Cultural systems like values and beliefs are a set of eyeglasses or a colored prism through which we see the world. Our perceptions are biased by culture so that we see some things and are unaware of others. This is why science has been created as a conscious effort to reduce the biases inherent in the fact that we must have culture to organize our daily lives. Science is a type of belief system, and like other aspects of culture, it emerged to deal with human problems. In the case of science, the desire to gather accurate information and to check ideas against the facts led to the development of beliefs that knowledge is generated by theories that are constantly checked against carefully and systematically collected data. Initially, beliefs about science, and later the development of norms about how scientists should behave, encountered great resistance from other types of belief systems—religion, philosophy, and ideology, to name the most important. And some of these still view science with great antipathy. Such antipathy can create **cultural conflicts** for individuals who simultaneously hold a number of different beliefs, as well as larger conflicts between groups of individuals adhering to different beliefs. Religious fundamentalists question science when its conclusions violate the tenets of religious dogma. And ideologues, whether Marxists, right-wing politicians, or something in between, often refuse to accept scientifically based knowledge. Even in the United States, where science is a dominant cultural belief, this conflict surfaces over such emotionally charged issues as the teaching of Darwinian evolution instead of creationism.

When differences in cultural beliefs become the basis for political organization and action, cultural conflicts become more intense. For example, the current conflict over abortion involves not just disagreement over beliefs about motherhood, life, and conception but actual combat among organized groupings (Luker, 1984). Such conflicts are difficult to resolve because the combatants' beliefs are so different and so strongly held. Similar conflicts have occurred again and again in the United States and in all complex societies where complete consensus over symbols is simply impossible.

Subcultures

Different subpopulations within a larger society like the United States often hold somewhat different beliefs and at times even different values. These different cultural worlds are built up and sustained by face-to-face interaction, as interactionist theorists would stress; for those in frequent interaction develop common symbol systems to give meaning to their affairs. And so, through interaction, people in different subcultures develop somewhat different normative expectations, speech patterns, and ways of expressing themselves in bodily movements. For example, blue-collar workers exist in a somewhat different cultural world than white-collar workers, as do blacks and whites, Hispanics and Anglos, rich and poor, executives and clerks, professors and students. These subpopulations can be termed **subcultures** because their members see the world through somewhat different symbolic glasses and behave somewhat differently; and often, these differences cause conflict, especially when they are accompanied by differences in power, income, wealth, and other valued resources in a society. Yet, we all get along, to a degree, because we share some of the same culture. But our relations are often strained because we recognize our differences and try to tiptoe around them by stylized and ritualized interactions. And, of course, at times these differences in beliefs and norms erupt into overt conflict—and then no amount of effort can save us from confronting our differences.

As the theories of Karl Marx and most other conflict approaches stress, some subcultures possess more power and material resources than others. The wealthy, the holders of political power, and the owners of large corporations, for example, are better able to impose their beliefs on, and to define the norms for, those subcultures without wealth, political power, or economic power (Mills, 1959). Just *how far* they can go is a subject of great debate (Alford and Friedland, 1985), but there can be little doubt that basic values, key beliefs in important arenas, and broad institutional norms have been greatly influenced by those with wealth and power, and more so than those without wealth and power (Bourdieu, 1984). At times, this disproportionate influence is resented by the less influential, and conflict emerges. For example, women, black Americans, gays and lesbians, and other subcultures in America have pushed for redefinition of beliefs and norms about, respectively, gender roles, white Anglo-Saxon culture, and sexuality. Indeed, much of the presidential campaign of 1992 revolved around a defense of the older cultural traditions by those satisfied with the status quo and the introduction of new systems of symbols by those tired of being culturally dominated. Such conflicts are inevitable in a society with many diverse subcultures.

Cultural Contradictions

Not only can subpopulations hold different cultural beliefs and other symbols, but cultural components can themselves be somewhat inconsistent and contradictory. We often hold inconsistent values, beliefs, and norms; and as a consequence, we experience **cultural contradictions**. Fortunately, humans have large brains which allow them to partition or reconcile in an uneasy armistice much of this inconsistency. Thus, biologists who can adhere to Darwinian evolution when they do biology can believe creationism in their personal everyday lives; whites can believe in equality and freedom while holding discriminatory stereotypes about blacks; students can believe in learning and still cheat on exams; and professors can believe in a dispassionate search for truth and hate those whose research conflicts with their own. But there are limits to these mental gymnastics. Too much inconsistency can create a problem for the individual; and if too many people in a society are confronted with cultural contradictions, widespread personal pathologies can result. Or, cultural contradictions can lead people to change society, as was the case in pre-Civil War days when abolitionists reacted against the beliefs of people who asserted both that "all men are created equal" (women too, let us hope) and that slavery was acceptable. Thus, major contradictions in values, beliefs, and norms usually create both personal and social turmoil. They are the stuff of change and reorganization in a society.

Ethnocentrism

Finally, all cultural systems make people in a society ethnocentric—that is, individuals tend to view their system of values, beliefs, and norms as better than those of others. This **ethnocentrism** leads to intolerance, and intolerance leads in turn to conflict and tensions. Thus America's belief in its moral superiority can lead it to interfere in the affairs of other nations whose ways are, from an ethnocentric view, inferior. Many other societies have done this, and so we should not be too hard on ourselves. Ethnocentrism also operates within a society: Members of certain subcultures can view those in other subcultures as inferior, and this, too, can lead to conflict.

By looking around virtually any college campus in America, ethnocentrism is immediately evident. The effort to increase the cultural, class, and ethnic mix of students has brought individuals with somewhat different beliefs and normative expectations about demeanor and behavior. Each subculture—African American, Hispanic American, Anglo and Angloized white American, Asian American, middle class, working class, and so on—views the other suspiciously and applies the standards of its subculture in evaluating the others. This ethnocentrism is, of course, aggravated by the dominance of white, middle-class, and Anglo-Saxon values, beliefs, and norms in most American colleges; for, members of other subcultures must constantly confront the domination of many cultural symbols different from their own.

SUMMARY

1. The information guiding much human activity is symbolic rather than genetic. Unlike social insects, humans create the codes guiding their behaviors, interactions, and patterns of social organization.
2. Culture is the system of symbols that a population creates and uses to organize itself, to facilitate interaction, and to regulate behavior.
3. There are many systems of symbols among a population, but among the most important are (a) language systems that people use in communication, (b) technology systems that embody knowledge about how to manipulate the environment, (c) value systems that carry the principles of good and bad, right and wrong, (d) belief systems that organize people's cognitions about what should and does exist in particular situations and domains, (e) normative systems that provide the general and specific expectations about how people are to behave in situations, and (f) stocks of knowledge that provide the stores of implicit information that people unconsciously use to make sense out of situations.
4. Culture varies within and between societies, and this situation often leads to conflict

between those holding different values, beliefs, or norms. Some conflict remains at the symbolic level, but conflict often erupts into open combat between parties with different beliefs.

5. Subcultures emerge and persist in complex societies, each revealing some distinctive systems of symbols. At times conflict is evident among subcultures, especially when some subcultures have been able to impose their symbols on others.

6. Systems of symbols often reveal contradictions and inconsistencies, a situation that can put individuals in personal turmoil and, at times, groupings into conflict.

7. Ethnocentrism is an inevitable by-product of cultural variations, with individuals viewing as inferior those cultural symbols unlike the ones that they hold. Such ethnocentrism produces prejudices that often erupt into conflict.

KEY TERMS

beliefs   Systems of symbols organized into cognitions about what should exist or occur, as well as what does exist and occur, in specific types of social situations.

cultural conflict   Differences in cultural values and beliefs that place people at odds with one another, and hence, in potential conflict.

cultural contradictions   Inconsistencies in the various systems of symbols making up the culture of a society.

culture   Those systems of symbols that humans create and use to guide behavior, interaction, and patterns of social organization.

ethnocentrism   The tendency to view one's own culture or subculture as superior to the culture of other people or societies.

institutional norms   Systems of symbols organized into very general expectations about behavior in basic types and classes of situations in a society.

language   Systems of symbols used in communication.

material culture   The term used by some analysts to denote the artifacts and objects created by humans.

norms   Systems of symbols informing individuals about how they are expected to behave and interact in a situation.

stocks of knowledge   Implicit stores of information that individuals use to guide their behavior and interaction.

subculture   A subpopulation of individuals in a society that possesses at least some symbols that are unique to this subpopulation and, at times, at odds with the broader culture of a society.

technology   Systems of symbols organized into knowledge about how to manipulate the environment.

values   Systems of symbols organized into abstract moral ideas about good-bad, appropriate-inappropriate, and right-wrong. Values cut across diverse situations because they are general and abstract.

CHAPTER 4

Social Structure

Social reality reveals a pattern, or structure, that gives us each a sense for where we belong, what we are supposed to do, and how we are to think and perceive. While social reality is not like a well-ordered beehive, it nonetheless is ordered, as the picture above illustrates. If it were not, we would not know how to behave, and we would be constantly unsure of how others were likely to respond. Without structure, the social world is chaos. Of course, with too much structure it is restrictive, boring, and oppressive. Since humans left hunting and gathering as a mode of existence, they have never achieved the same balance between freedom and autonomy, on the one side, and order and stability on the other. Social life is a constant tug-of-war between our desire to be free and our need to be part of social structure.

Most activities in our daily lives are carried out within social structures. In fact, try to think of situations where you are away from other people and outside of expectations and constraints. Even when we are alone, we are often part of a larger structure whose presence is felt. For example, you may be reading these words in your private room or at a table in the library or cafeteria, but you are not alone; you are part of a structure—home, dorm, apartment, or library—in which others and their expectations are not far away. Moreover, the very act of reading this page is done because you are part of a college or university which imposes expectations and constraints. And even if you think about doing something more interesting, your thoughts probably revolve around choices among alternative social structures.

Social life is thus organized within structures; and because of this obvious fact, we need a vocabulary for talking about structure. Let us begin with the basic elements of all structures; then we can see how they are combined to produce ever larger and more encompassing structures that constrain all of our lives.

THE BASIC BUILDING BLOCKS OF SOCIAL STRUCTURE

Positions

Social structures are ultimately composed of **status positions** which are the place we occupy in a system of interconnected positions (Nadel, 1957; Parsons, 1951). For example, you currently occupy the status position of "student," and this fact locates you within a larger system of positions—fellow students, teaching assistants, professors, staff, administrators or counselors, and all those other positions in a college or university.

By knowing our position, we know where we stand and what is expected of us. Thus, positions make sense only in relationship to other status positions, a topic which we discuss shortly, but for the present, I want to emphasize a simple point: positions carry with them cultural content. For each position, there are usually expectations or norms about how we should behave (Linton, 1936); and these normative expectations are impregnated with values, beliefs, stocks of knowledge, language, and even technology. The position of student carries certain clear norms—come to class, study, take exams, be respectful to teachers, be quiet in class, ask questions, and other expectations that can be listed on a piece of paper. But these norms embody aspects of other cultural systems: A profile of values is being invoked; particular beliefs are being applied; stocks of knowledge are being used; and certain technologies are being employed. Thus, there is an enormous amount of cultural coding for a particular position. In one sense, this can seem like a burden, but in another sense the existence of so much information gives a person options about exactly which codes will be used and how they will be used. There is, then, a dynamic quality to a status position and the cultural systems impinging upon this position. This is so because an active, thinking, and potentially creative human being ultimately occupies a position and must decide how and in what way cultural forces are to guide behavior in a particular position. We are not, as I should emphasize again, worker bees or ants; rather, humans have the capacity for agency in their behaviors (Giddens, 1984).

Roles

When we behave in a position, we take account of norms and other systems of symbols; and then we fashion this behavior in ways that fit our needs and personality as well as the particulars of a situation. This behavioral activity associated with incumbency in a status position is termed **role**. It is the dynamic aspect of a status position, and it reveals how cultural systems are being invoked (Linton, 1936; Heiss, 1981; Biddle, 1992). To occupy the status of student, for instance, involves paying attention to behaviors dictated in cultural scripts while at the same time, reconciling these expected behaviors with (a) personal needs and (b) the expectations of others occupying the same or different positions in a situation (R. Turner, 1978). Roles are thus complex activities because they involve interplay among many forces—culture, personality, other people, and other positions. Let me explore this complexity by introducing some additional concepts.

Status Sets

All of us occupy many different status positions, lodged in various structures. For example, we have positions in families (child, father, or mother), in churches (worshiper), in organizations (student, worker, fraternity or sorority member), in groups (friendship, study, lunch time), in communities (resident), in political parties (voter), in society (citizen), and so on. The complex of positions that each of us occupies is often termed **status set** (Merton, 1957).

A status set marks the structures in which we belong and the systems of culture into which we are plugged. By knowing people's status sets, we can learn a great deal about them because we can get a sense for the cultural systems and attendant expectations that orient and guide their behavior. For example, it is easy to spot different types of students—let us say, "party animal," "married with children," "part time," "full time with job," "commuter," "dormy," "Greek," "geek," and so on; the differences in these students reflect varying webs of affiliation with social structures. For each position in a particular configuration, somewhat different cultural systems are invoked and used to orient perceptions and guide behavior. By listing all the positions that each of us occupies and, then, assessing the structures and culture in which these positions are lodged, it becomes possible to get a rough picture of "who we are" sociologically.

Role Sets

For any particular status position, there is always a cluster of behaviors to be emitted. The total of these behaviors constitutes a **role set** (Merton, 1957). For example, the role set of a student (the status position) might include going to

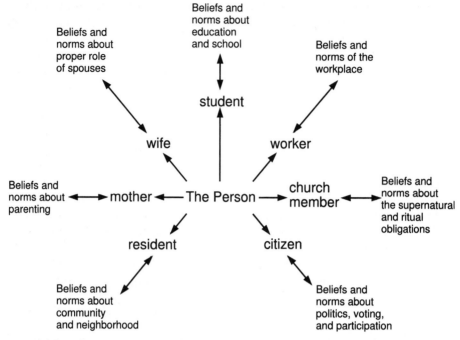

FIGURE 4-1. A hypothetical status set. Each position in this person's status set plugs her into somewhat different cultural scripts composed of beliefs and norms which, in turn, reflect values and other cultural systems such as technology. By constructing a similar diagram for each of us, we can learn a great deal about ourselves and about the symbolic codes that guide our perceptions, orientations, and actions.

class, being with friends, using the library or computer room, studying, taking exams, participating in fraternity or sorority activities, holding a part-time job, and playing a sport. By virtue of occupying one master status—student—a variety of role behaviors can become relevant. Some of these place individuals into new status positions—say, "jock" on a particular team or "worker" in a part-time job—but our focus here is on the configuration of behaviors associated with a particular position. Some status positions are robust and require many different behaviors, whereas others are simple and do not demand too many different behaviors. Compare the difference between "mother" or "student" positions, on the one hand, and "shopper" or "customer" in a store on the other; there are great differences in the amount and variety of behaviors associated with these behaviors, and so the role sets are very different.

Role Strain and Role Conflict

Participation in social structures is rife with strain. One source of strain is that the behaviors associated with a position are too robust and demanding, requiring too many different or even incompatible behaviors. If such is the case, **role strain** is likely (Goode, 1960). A full-time student who is active socially will often suffer role strain by trying to engage in too many activities. First year college students are the most likely to suffer role strain as they jump into far too many things, leading them to suffer fatigue, physical illness, or even emotional distress. Thus, depending on the number, variety, and intensity of behaviors associated with a position, the level of role strain will vary.

Role conflict comes when we occupy different status positions that come into conflict or are incompatible. A mother of three children (one status position) who goes to school (another status) is likely to experience considerable role conflict, trying to juggle and balance very different demands. For example, the hypothetical woman whose status set is delineated in Figure 4-1 is a very likely candidate for role conflict, and certainly for role strain. Similarly, a student who has a part-time or, worse, a full-time job will also experience role conflict. Role conflict is inevitable in complex societies where we all occupy different positions in varying structures with their own demands. Usually, role conflict can be mitigated by separating occupancy in different positions in time and space. If a student mother could do all her work at school and then go home to assume her mother status, the conflict would be reduced. But in this instance, such is usually not the case, for student mothers must also study at home, and here is where the conflict becomes more intense.

Thus, built into status sets and role sets are sources of tension, strain, and conflict. These problems are the price we pay for living in complex societies; and each of us must learn to manage these sources of strain and conflict or suffer the consequences.

Networks of Positions

So far, I have not really said anything about structure per se: I have merely touched on some of the *elements* of structure. Let us now tackle this matter head on: Social structures are composed of (1) **networks of interrelated status positions** as well as (2) the cultural systems and roles associated with the positions in this network. Structure is thus evident when positions are *connected* to one another, such that our roles in one position are affected by, and conversely have an effect on, roles in other positions. For example, a family is a structure composed of three basic positions—father, mother, children—and it is the relationships, or network connections, among these positions that make the family a social structure. What each family member does has an effect upon, while being constrained by, the role behaviors of other family members.

This may seem so obvious that it is a waste of time to talk about it, but when social structures get big and complex, we need some way of looking at them and talking about them. By visualizing social structures as networks of status positions, we have the elementary tools to analyze large-scale structures (Wellman and Berkowitz, 1988; Burt, 1980; Marsden and Lin, 1980). But we need to introduce some simple ideas if we are to use the notion of networks to examine social structures (Maryanski and Turner, 1991, pp. 540–557).

Dimensions of Structure

What are some of these simple ideas? One is very obvious: the number of different types of positions in a network. Structures with two or three positions are very different from those with many positions, as a simple comparison of your family and your college will immediately reveal. Another dimension is also straightforward: the number of people in positions of a given type. A network with a thousand incumbents in a particular position—say, the student position—and comparatively few in other types of positions (faculty, for example) will be very different from one where the distribution of people in various positions is more equal (for instance, a friendship network like a lunch group or, more formally, a sorority).

Yet another useful consideration is the nature of the connection among positions. Is the connection loose, as is the case among casual friends? Is it temporary as will be the case with students in a class? As utilitarian exchange theorists (Coleman, 1991) would emphasize, are there important resources—for example, money, love, honor, grades—flowing among the positions, and if so, which ones? As conflict theorists (Collins, 1975) might stress, are there differences in the power of positions, and if so, how much? And, to what degree is every position in a network connected to every other position (this is often termed *density* of the network)?

By considering these various dimensions of networks among positions, we can describe very different kinds of structures. An American family is a simple structure; it is composed of a few positions; these positions are densely connected to one another (that is, its members are all directly connected to one another); there are only a few people in each position; the connections are usually close; they are rarely temporary; the resources flowing among the positions are highly valued (love, affection, support and, of course, money); and the power differences (parent-child and perhaps mother-father) deeply affect how roles are played. Compare this kind of structure with a classroom, sorority or fraternity, athletic team, or workplace: The nature and types of positions, the number of people in positions, the density of connections, the permanence of connections, the resources being used, and the power relations are different from those of the family and, as a result, the underlying structures are different.

TYPES OF SOCIAL STRUCTURES

Stripped to their basic forms, there are relatively few basic types of social structures. Of course, once cultural content is added, the range of substantive diversity for each type increases, but the basic nature of the type remains. For example, a group is a small, face-to-face cluster of positions and, as such, constitutes a basic structural form; but the substance of a group—family, work, play, recreation, etc.—can vary enormously in terms of the cultural symbols guiding its operation.

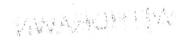

BOX 4-1 Comparing Social Structures

1. Social structures are composed of networks connecting status positions, cultural symbols associated with these positions, and roles dictated by cultural scripts, personal needs, and expectations of others.
2. These networks of positions can be described by some basic dimensions:
   a. The number of different types of positions
   b. The number of people in each type of position
   c. The nature of connections among positions, including:

   (1) Looseness of ties
   (2) Duration of ties
   (3) Resources exchanged in ties
   (4) Variations in power among positions
   (5) Density of ties

3. By examining any structure—from our family through our workplace to the entire economy—in terms of these dimensions, it is possible to compare and contrast social structures. Use (2) above as a checklist in describing the social structures in which you participate.

What, then, are some of the basic forms of social structure? An answer to this question frames much of the subject matter of sociology, as will be evident in later chapters. For the present, let me briefly discuss basic forms of structure, leaving for later chapters a more detailed explanation.

Group Structures

As noted earlier, **groups** are comparatively small social structures composed of one or a few types of status positions, small numbers of incumbents in these positions, dense ties among some of the positions, and clear cultural expectations about what people are supposed to do. Groups vary in their permanence—from a temporary gathering of friends over lunch to permanent ties among members of a close-knit family. Another important consideration is that groups vary in size, and this, in turn, influences important dimensions of their structure. Sometimes this difference is described in terms of a distinction between *primary* and *secondary* groups. Primary groups are small, close-knit, and intimate, whereas secondary groups are larger and more impersonal (Cooley, 1909). The difference between a small seminar class where ties develop among members and a large lecture class whose size precludes personal ties among all its members (that is, lower density) captures the essential differences between primary and secondary groups.

Much of our participation in social structure begins with a position in a group which, in turn, is lodged in a larger structure like an organization. For instance, your classes, friendships on campus, and other group activities at

school are embedded in the more inclusive organizational structure of the college or university, and hence, it is through your membership in a series of groups that you are related to the larger college structure. Groups plug us into larger structures, and as a result, they are critical for understanding not only ourselves but the larger society as well. Groups are also the arena where symbolic interactions occur, as interactionist theories emphasize; for in occupying positions and playing roles in a group, we interact with one another, building up, sustaining, or even changing the cultural symbols that guide our conduct and that serve as standards for our self-evaluations. We will examine group processes in Chapter 7.

Organizational Structures

Organizations are larger and more formal structures composed of a diversity of status positions, revealing differences in authority and, at the lower levels, evidencing larger numbers of incumbents in each position (Weber, 1922). Organizations are assembled to get something done—making money, educating students, winning a war, producing a good or service, and so on—and they tend to develop distinctive cultural systems revolving around their goals and structure. We usually think of organizations as *bureaucratic* structures, although it is best to conceptualize them more generally as *complex organizations* because of the unsavory connotations of the term *bureaucrat* and because organizations evidence considerable diversity in their structure. Complex organizations are, as we will come to see in Chapter 7, the principal integrative structure of modern complex societies; and as such they connect people in groups to the broader forces in society.

Community Structures

People reside and move about in physical place; and when there is organization to this place—roads, schools, churches, government, workplace, and other structures—it can be termed a **community**. Communities are thus social structures organizing people's residence as well as their activities in physical or geographical space (Hawley, 1981). As is perhaps obvious, but nonetheless fundamental, communities can vary in size, from the small rural town to the giant megalopolis. And hence, our goal in Chapter 10 will be to understand how the size of communities has changed how we all live.

Institutional Structures

Groups and, at times, organizations are structured to meet basic contingencies of biological and social life. For example, to survive biologically, humans must eat and reproduce, and so there will be social structures—the economy and kinship systems, respectively—designed to ensure that this is so. Or, to remain effectively organized, especially as the size of a population grows, it will be necessary to develop ways—political structures—to regulate and control the larger population. Those structures that are created to solve basic human and organizational problems are termed **institutions** (J. Turner, 1972); and as the problems of organization for a population increase, so do basic institutional structures. For example, in very simple societies, only a few basic institutions are evident—family, economy, and religion—but as the scale of society increases, additional institutions—government, law, education, science, and medicine—become elaborated to deal with new human needs and organizational problems, as we will see in Chapter 9.

Categorical Structures

Humans classify one another in terms of distinguishable characteristics and, then, respond to one another differently. The only universal categories are sex and age, which means that all human populations categorize people on the basis of their sex and age and, as a result of these distinctions, respond to them differently. By virtue of being treated differently, those in a category take on similar characteristics, thereby reinforcing their distinctiveness and making them members of a categorical unit. For example, we respond differently to males and females as well as to babies, young people, old people, and middle-age persons, and on the basis of this differential treatment, these people come to form a categorical unit. **Categorical structures,** therefore, are created and sustained by virtue of differential treatment of those who reveal identifiable characteristics (Hawley, 1986).

As populations of humans grow and as societies become more complex, many additional kinds of categorical structures are created: ethnic categories, social class distinctions, religious categories, occupational categories, regional distinctions, and educational differences. Among the most important of these additional categories are ethnicity and class because members of such categories usually receive varying shares of valued resources—for instance, money, power, prestige, health, opportunities—as a result of differential treatment; and as conflict theories would emphasize, categories often become a source of intense conflict in society. Because these categorical structures are so important to understanding society, especially its tensions and conflicts, they are sometimes viewed as a distinctive kind of structure, a *stratification system*.

Stratification Structures

When the valued resources of a society are distributed unequally and when, as a result, people can be categorized by virtue of their shares of resources and come to define themselves as distinctive, a **stratification system** exists in a society (J. Turner, 1984a). There are many bases for stratifying categories of people: sex, age, income, ethnicity, and religion. All that is essential for stratification is that members of a category get a distinctive share of some valued resource. For example, if black skin color is used as a basis for economic, political, and educational discrimination, then the low shares of money, power, and prestige among those who have black skin will become codified into a system of ethnic stratification. Or, if sex is used for differential treatment of men and women with the result that men have better jobs, more income, more prestige, and more power than women, then a system of sexual stratification exists. Or, to illustrate further, if people's incomes, education, and jobs are correlated and if the people are distinguished by virtue of this fact, then class stratification exists (say, among the poor, the working class, the middle class, the upper-middle class, and the rich). As we will see in Chapter 8, stratification structures are among the most volatile in any society because they are created and sustained to give some people more of what is valued than others. Rarely do those on the short end take their plight lying down.

Societal Structures

When a population with distinctive systems of cultural symbols is organized within a clear territory by political institutions, we can call it a *societal structure*, or a **society**. Such societal structures can be very simple and small, consisting of only a handful of people; yet, as larger societies have gobbled up, destroyed, or displaced smaller ones, societal structures increasingly embrace larger populations, although larger societies can disintegrate into a series of smaller ones (as was the case recently with the Soviet Union).

In the course of human history there have been just a few basic types of societies (Lenski, 1966; Lenski, Lenski, and Nolan, 1991; J. Turner, 1972; Maryanski and Turner, 1992). *Hunting and gathering societies* dominated for two-thirds of humans' 40,000 years as a distinct species. These societies were composed of small, wandering bands of thirty to eighty people, organized by their families and making only basic distinctions between sex and age categories. There was little inequality; men hunted but in reality sat around a great deal; women gathered indigenous plants and prepared food, and no one worked very hard, perhaps fifteen hours a week. Conflict was rare, and if a dispute could not be resolved, the band split up and moved on. As a biological species, our natural tendency is not to work very hard, or to be locked into highly constraining structures (Maryanski and Turner, 1992); and so, we can see how far our current lives are from the societal form in which our biological propensities were forged. Then, about 15,000 to 18,000 years ago, people began to settle down; and a new form of existence for humans emerged. *Horticulturalists* were the second type of society to emerge. Here, people lived in small villages composed of groups that included numerous kin related by blood and marriage and linked together by political ties and authority. These kin groups, under the direction of a headman, cultivated gardens with women performing much of the dull work. Men helped at times, but they became involved in a new pastime: war. For, horticulturalists were often in conflict with their neighbors, and a new chapter in human history was born. *Agrarian societies* were the third basic type, and they were built by the use of nonhuman power—animals, wind, and water—to cultivate much larger tracts of land which, in turn, created enough supplies to build roads and cities, while sustaining great inequalities between the nobility and peasants. With agrarianism the scale of society shifted; societies became bigger, more complex, more oriented to distant conquest, more unequal, more urban, and more politi-cally centralized. Then, a few hundred years ago a new type of society emerged, *the industrial*, based upon inanimate sources of energy. New social constructions developed—factories, huge bureaucracies, large urban centers, open markets, political democracy, complex infrastructures for transportation and communi-cation, mass education, and all the basic structures with which you are familiar. We are now in the middle of the transition to yet another societal type—*the postindustrial*—where most people work in nonmanual jobs for the first time in history and where new modes of transportation and communication reduce physical distances among people in even the largest society and, for that matter, in all the world (see Chapter 9 for more summaries on these basic societal types).

Yet, no matter how grand societies become, each is ultimately a society composed of all those positions ordered into all those types of social structures discussed above and all those types of cultural systems examined in Chapter 3. Most sociological analysis examines culture and structure within a particular society, but increasingly there is concern with intersocietal structures for the simple reason that contact and communication among societies have increased dramatically.

Intersocietal Systems

Trade, migration, political and economic coalitions, and warfare have typified relations of societies in the past, and today. For as politically organized popula-tions have bumped into one another, it has become necessary to form some kind of relation. War has been a most typical response; trade and exchange have been another; political and economic alliances in the face of a threat have been yet another kind of response; and migration from one society to another has fre-quently forced societies to form some kind of relation—that is, some kind of **intersocietal system**.

If we ponder some of the big issues today for Americans—the aftermath of the collapse of the Soviet empire, the increasing formation of a common Euro-pean community, the patterns of trade with the Japanese and other societies, the prospects of war, and the immigration of foreigners (legally and illegally)—the importance of unraveling the complex web of intersocietal connections becomes clear. For what goes on *within* a society is greatly influenced by what transpires between societies. Indeed, we now operate in a world system, composed of trade and political networks which influence most aspects of our daily lives (Waller-stein, 1974).

THE POWER OF SOCIAL STRUCTURE

Each of us is but a cog in a vast web of structural forms. True, we have big brains and can be creative, but our daily lives are highly circumscribed by structure, as well as the cultural symbols associated with structures.

Social structure and culture thus have power over us; they force us to do what they want. For example, right now, you are reading these words because you are part of a class in a college or university system that, to be blunt, has you doing what it wants. I am sure that most of you would prefer to be elsewhere, but you persist, because there is a power beyond your control, a system of relations dictating your actions. So it is in social life, from the day each of us was born until the moment of our death. Our life is a constant and incessant movement in social structures—family, friends, schools, work organizations, communities, and other social aggregations. What we are as individuals is the product of these structural affiliations. Indeed, all social life is a web of interconnected social structures in which we are at times merely cogs or pawns.

True, we can choose to move in or out of many structures. We can often choose which ones are to be our oppressors, or our taskmasters. But unless we can find a vacant mountaintop for social contemplation and tolerate the loneliness of it all, we must be involved in social structures. These have their own dynamics, which vary somewhat depending on the nature of the structure. It is the goal of sociology to understand these dynamics.

To some extent, the field of sociology is organized around basic types of social structures. Individual sociologists tend to concentrate on a particular type of structure, although our theoretical goal is always to find some common processes that occur in all structures. In light of this fact, we can view the social world, as well as a good deal of sociology as a discipline, to be organized around groups, organizations, communities, social categories (social classes as well as sexual, age, ethnic, and racial categories), various social institutions (economic,

---

BOX 4-2   *What Is the Difference between Sociology and Psychology?*

We often prefer to think about our world in psychological terms—feelings, moods, motivations, and the like. From a sociological perspective these psychological states reflect our experiences in social structures. This point of emphasis is what distinguishes sociology from psychology. Psychology is primarily concerned with personality, cognition, behavior, and other dimensions of the person per se, whereas sociology is devoted to the study of culture and social structures as these influence interaction, behavior, and personality. The two fields meet, and indeed often clash, in the area of *social psychology*, but even here where the subject matter overlaps, large differ-ences are evident. A psychologist will emphasize the effects of social situations on the operation of basic psychological processes—perceptions, cognitions, emotions, and the like—whereas a sociologist will stress how culture and social structure constrain behavior and interaction of individuals in social contexts and, then, how these constrained behaviors and interactions sustain or change culture and social structure. Thus, psychology will tend to focus on the properties and dynamics of the person; sociology will concentrate on the properties and dynamics of the person, behavior, interaction, social structure, and culture as these mutually influence one another.

political, kinship, educational, and religious), societal and intersocietal systems. For all of us, most of our waking hours are spent embedded within these basic social structures; and because of this fact, social structure has great power to influence our thoughts, perceptions, emotions, actions, and interactions.

SUMMARY

1. Virtually every aspect of our being—thoughts, perceptions, feelings, and behavior—is influenced by participation in social structures.
2. Social structures are constructed of status positions, roles, and networks of positions. Each person reveals a status set, perhaps a master status and, for each status position occupied, a role set. Role strain and role conflict often ensue because of too many role obligations in a single position or because of conflict between obligations in different positions.
3. The networks of positions that comprise social structures vary in terms of basic dimensions: number of positions, number of people in each position, nature of connections among positions. These connections can be loose or dense, involve power or hierarchy, transmit varying resources, and exist for varying lengths of time.
4. Basic social structures organizing human populations include (a) groups composed of relatively small networks of people in face-to-face contact, (b) organizations pulling together larger numbers of individuals and groups in hierarchies of authority, (c) communities ordering individuals, groups, and organizations in geographical space, (d) institutional structures composed of complexes of groups and organizations devoted to resolving basic contingencies of human existence and social organization, (e) categorical structures in which identifiable characteristics of people become the basis for differential treatment, (f) stratification structures in which categories of people receive different shares of valued resources, (g) societal systems organizing (a) through (f) above in space and territory, and (h) intersocietal structures connecting societal systems together.
5. Because each person is embedded in a matrix of social structures—from groups to intersocietal systems—human thoughts, perceptions, feelings, actions, and interactions are highly constrained.

KEY TERMS

categorical structures   Structures created when cohorts and types of individuals are defined and treated differently on the basis of their perceived attributes and characteristics.

community   A social structure that organizes the residence and activities of people in physical space.

groups   Small social structures composed of only a few different status positions, small numbers of incumbents, relatively dense ties among positions, and clear cultural expectations about role behaviors.

institutions   Societywide structures that organize groups, organizations, and the community with respect to basic human and organizational needs.

intersocietal systems   Processes that create relations among societies, including trade, war, migrations, and political or economic coalitions.

networks (of interrelated status positions)   The ties and connections that link status positions together, thereby forming a social structure.

organizations   Goal directed social structures revealing hierarchies of positions, linked together by authority and clear norms, with increasing numbers of incumbents at the lower levels of the hierarchy.

role   The behavior of individuals in status positions, as they take account of one another and size up norms and other cultural symbols.

role conflict   A situation where the roles associated with different status positions are incompatible, placing the individual trying to play the roles of these different positions in a situation of conflict.

role set   The expected array of behaviors for a given status position.

role strain   A situation where there are either too many or contradictory expectations in the role set of a status position, thereby creating tension and strain for individuals trying to meet all expectations.

society   A structure which encompasses all other structures (groups, organizations, institutions, categories, and stratification) and which organizes a population and provides political regulation for these structures in geographical space and in relation to other societies.

status position   The location of an individual within a network of positions. A basic unit of social structure.

status set   The complex or array of positions that an individual person occupies.

stratification systems   Structures revolving around (1) the unequal distribution of valued resources to the members of a society and (2) the distinctive categories thereby created by virtue of the shares of resources held by different subpopulations in a society.

CHAPTER 5

Social Interaction

Humans use cultural symbols—language being the most obvious but body position, facial expressions, and almost anything that has meaning to others—to coordinate their actions. For we are constantly sending and receiving messages. Without such interaction, we could not connect ourselves to other people; we could not develop culture; and we could not erect and sustain the social structures so essential to human life. Interaction is, therefore, the most basic social process sustaining society, culture, and our personal well-being.

ACTORS AND INTERACTION

Shakespeare once wrote, "All the world's a stage, And all men and women merely players: They have their exits and their entrances; and one man in his time plays many parts." Much of human life is indeed performed on a stage, but in contrast to theatrical life, our stage is set by cultural symbols and social structure. In a real sense, we are all actors on a stage and play in front of an audience of those who are immediately present and those whom we can imagine. At the same time we try to offer an interpretation of the cultural script and a performance on a stage built by social structure. Social life involves each of us as actors who perform and, in performing, interact with others. No process is more fundamental to social life and to understanding ourselves and those around us.

THE SYMBOLIC NATURE OF HUMAN INTERACTION

At the beginning of this century social scientists did not understand how human interaction occurs. All could agree that interaction among people is the fundamental process underlying the social world, but how and why did it operate? What were the specific mechanisms and processes involved? A University of Chicago philosopher, George Herbert Mead (1934), unlocked the mystery of this process, as I noted in Chapter 1. Mead did not have a blazing insight, but rather, he took bits and pieces from the works of others and combined them in ways that made sense.

The essence of interaction, Mead argued, is the emission of signs and gestures. Any organism must act within its environment, and as it does so, it emits signs or gestures that mark its course of action. **Interaction** occurs, Mead felt, when (1) one organism emits signs as it moves through its environment, (2) another organism sees these signs and alters its course of action in response to them, thereby emitting signs of its own, and (3) the original organism becomes aware of the signs of this responding organism and alters its course of action in light of these signs. Let us imagine a cat and dog. The dog is looking for a post to relieve itself (emitting the appropriate signs); a lounging cat observes the dog moving toward it and panics, running away (its gestures); the dog sees the cat and readjusts its course of action, forgetting about its bladder and instead giving chase.

When these three stages have passed, then interaction has occurred. Note that signs or gestures are the critical vehicle of interaction and note also that these signs do not need to be symbolic in the cultural sense. That is, the cat may not be able to read or interpret the dog's gestures, nor does the dog necessarily understand the panic of the cat. But "their conversation of gestures," as Mead put it, is nonetheless interaction.

Mead also thought that humans interact in a unique and special way, however. The signs that humans send, read, receive, and respond to are symbolic in that they mean the same thing to the sending and to the receiving organism.

In a word, they are cultural. The signs on this page mean more or less the same thing to both of us; and as a result, interaction is special because it is mediated by signs that are given cultural definition. Indeed, with our large brains, we can attach common, agreed-upon meanings to virtually all our movements—talk, facial gestures, bodily stance, spacing relative to others, clothing, hair style, or almost any sign or gesture that we make. This is why we feel "on stage" when in front of others, for we implicitly know that others are reading our gestures and interpreting our performance. And while some animals can also interact symbolically, they cannot do so to the degree that humans can (Seboek, 1968; Aitchison, 1978; Maryanski and Turner, 1992).

Mead observed that the ability to read symbolic gestures allows humans to **role-take,** or *take the role of the other.* What he meant is that by reading the gestures of others, we can imagine ourselves in their place; we can take their perspective and sense what they are likely to do. Thus, if someone comes up to you glaring, fists clenched, and calling you obscene names, you can imagine yourself in his or her position and adjust your responses accordingly. All of us role-take in every situation, but we are usually not that conscious of this process until we find ourselves in an awkward situation where we literally hang on every word and gesture emitted by others. Imagine having a first date with someone, or going to a party where you do not know anyone, or entering a school or dorm for the first time, or being in any number of new situations where you only have broad institutional norms to guide you. You cope—which is to say, you learn the more situationally specific norms—by role taking or seeing others' perspectives and using what you see to guide your responses. This is symbolic interaction, and it is the means by which we plug ourselves into culture and its values, beliefs, and norms. Conversely, by being aware of cultural symbols, we can role-take and thus get along with others in various positions of specific social structures. As a functional theorist might argue, the function of role taking is to connect people to one another and the broader culture, thereby facilitating their cooperation and, ultimately, the integration of society. And so, if we were unable to use cultural symbols and role-take, interaction would be very awkward indeed, and society would collapse.

Mead also emphasized other processes involved in human interaction. One is the process that he termed **mind.** For Mead, mind was not a thing or entity, but a series of processes. For Mead, mind is the covert and behind-the-scenes process of first anticipating the consequences of various possible courses of action and then, on the basis of this assessment, choosing or selecting a particular action. Mead characterized mind as the process of "imaginative rehearsal" in that, like any good actor who must go on stage, we rehearse our act in different ways and assess our audience's reaction to these alternatives. Such mind processes are an intimate part of human interaction, for as we role-take with others, we assume their perspective, and as we become aware of relevant beliefs and norms, these become a part of our mental deliberations. We then imagine how others will respond to us, and we deliberate whether we are doing the proper thing in terms of cultural codes. A rational choice theorist would add something to Mead's portrayal: We would calculate our costs and benefits as we imagina-tively rehearsed alternatives, trying to choose that option which would give us the greatest payoff.

Because we are so facile at this process, we are often unaware of its operation. But think again about a situation where you felt awkward or unsure. Remember how you rehearsed your lines and anticipated what the reaction of others would be. Naturally, one cannot be this attuned all the time; that would be too exhaust-ing. But all of us are always involved in reading gestures, role taking, and covertly (in our minds, as it were) imagining outcomes of alternative responses. For if people could not engage in these processes, interaction would not be flexible and it could not involve more than just a couple of people.

Yet another crucial process involved in interaction is what Mead labeled **self**. According to Mead, each of us sees *ourself* as an object in each situation we are in, just as we see other objects—people, cars, chairs, houses, etc. When we communicate with someone, we read gestures and, by doing so, get an image of ourselves as an object. Thus, the gestures of others become a kind of "looking glass" (Cooley, 1909) or mirror in which we see ourselves reflected. We are all, in a sense, implicitly saying "Mirror, mirror on the wall," except that our mirror is not on the wall but in the gestures of others. In each situation we get an image of ourselves, but we also bring to a situation a more stable and enduring conception of ourselves as a certain type of object or person. Each of us has a **self-conception,** seeking to interpret the gestures of others so that they are consistent with this conception and adjusting our behaviors so as not to violate this conception. Thus, our actions in most situations reveal a consistency as we seek to sustain our conception of ourselves as a certain kind of person. We come to behave in predictable ways, and because of our consistency, others are able to coordinate their responses to us. In the same way, we adjust our responses to others with a typical interpersonal style.

When you say things like "Sorry, I'm not acting myself today," you are acknowledging that others will not see you in the usual way because you acted contrary to your self-conception. Or, when you say "I can't figure out where he's coming from," you are really saying two things: your role taking has been ineffective, and you cannot see consistency, as dictated by his self-conception, in his responses. Hence, you are uncertain as to how to respond.

Thus, George Herbert Mead viewed interaction as a process of sending and receiving gestures, and in the case of humans, sending culturally defined sym-bols that carry common meanings. These gestures are used to role-take and to help you become aware of others' expectations and their possible lines of conduct. With the cognitive abilities provided by "mind," we can rehearse alternatives, imagine their impact, inhibit inappropriate responses, and select a mode of conduct that will facilitate interaction (or, from a rational choice per-spective, that will maximize utilities or rewards). Furthermore, we can see ourselves as objects in situations and bring to them a stable self-conception that gives us a compass for guiding our responses in typical and consistent ways. Such is the nature of "symbolic interaction" as viewed by Mead, and his views on this most fundamental process represent the starting point for further inquiry.

THE DRAMATIC PRESENTATION OF SELF

Since we are all actors on a stage, we are performers who orchestrate our emissions of gestures to present ourselves in a certain light, as a certain kind of person, and as an individual who deserves certain responses from others. Some of us are, of course, better actors than others. But all of us are performers who manipulate the emission of gestures. This view of interaction is known as *dramaturgy*, a term made popular by the late sociologist Erving Goffman (1959, 1967).

Goffman utilized our analogy of the theater and the stage by distinguishing between frontstage and backstage regions of interaction (Goffman, 1959). On the formal **frontstage,** people consciously manipulate and orchestrate gestures in ways to elicit desired responses from others—responses that uphold their self-conception and that conform to the normative demands of the situation. In the **backstage** area, people relax a bit and lower their respective fronts. Backstage allows some privacy with companions who share their knowledge of the rigors of going onstage. For Goffman, much interaction involves moving back and forth between backstage and frontstage areas. If you doubt that such is the case, examine your own daily routines. You are backstage when you are getting ready to go to school, with showers, toothbrushes, hair dryers, curlers, makeup, deodorants, and hair sprays. You are frontstage when you are sitting in class, lounging in the student union, or flirting at a dance.

Without the backstage, life would be unduly stressful. And yet, without the frontstage, social order would be problematic. As a functionalist would argue, society requires that things get done and actions be coordinated; this fact, in turn, demands that humans perform and conform. We go by the rules; we say the right thing; and we carry ourselves in the appropriate way. If people refused to do so, social reality would be cluttered and chaotic.

Dramaturgy also points an important aspect of all interaction: the use of **physical props** during an interaction. One such prop is our bodies, and their arrangement during interaction. A group of people forming a closed circle while they interact is saying something to those outside this circle; two people who walk close together, touching as they move are in a very different interaction than another couple who keeps some distance from each other; or a class with chairs in a circle will have a different feel as opposed to one with rows of theater-style seating. Thus, how we position our bodies is a gesture which "says something" about the flow of the interaction, and we use "body language"—position, looks, touches, and other cues—to create meanings about what is occurring.

Another prop is objects in space—tables, chairs, walls, doors, partitions, benches, and anything that is a physical object which communicates something about an interaction. When a person sits on a table or turns a chair around and rests his arms on its back, this gesture communicates informality. A lecturer who sits on a table interacts very differently than one who stands erect behind a podium. Or, in more personal interaction, we often put up or take down physical barriers to communicate distance or closeness.

Yet, another physical prop is clothing which tells others a great deal and, as a consequence, structures the flow of interaction. We react and respond very differently to a professor in a coat and tie than to one in informal attire. Types of clothing—sorority emblems, athletic badges, sayings on tee shirts, etc.—all influence in subtle ways the flow of the interaction.

Another aspect of dramaturgy is what Erving Goffman (1959) termed **impression management,** where we orchestrate gestures, staging props, and body position to present a **front**. We do so in order to present a particular self to our audience and to receive certain kinds of responses. And so, as we move to frontstage, we manage our gestures and other available equipment. Such management gives each person's behavior a consistency and facilitates the alignment of behaviors. Of course, as Goffman emphasized, fronts can be both deceptive and manipulative, as when a "con man" presents a front that masks his true intentions to steal. All of us do so at times, hopefully to a lesser degree, but we still find ourselves presenting a front that is not quite genuine.

THE IMPLICIT USE OF FOLK METHODS

Dividing the world into stages and following cultural scripts are not enough to sustain a sense of order during interaction. We have all met someone who seemingly does everything in just the right way, and yet, we feel uneasy. Something is missing—we are not quite sure what it is—but something is wrong in how this person talks, gestures, and acts. One possible reason for this sense of uneasiness is the failure or inability of this individual to utilize certain tacit and yet crucial techniques of interaction. When these techniques are not used, our sense of continuity and orderliness in interaction is disrupted (Mehan and Wood, 1975; Handel, 1982). Thus, interaction depends on some additional processes that the sociologist Harold Garfinkel (1967) labeled **ethnomethods,** or simply "folk methods." As we interact with others, we use a variety of interpersonal methods or techniques to create and sustain a sense of orderliness and to provide continuity in interaction. These folk methods are so unconsciously employed that we become aware of them only when someone does not use them, or uses them incorrectly.

Using one of Garfinkel's (1967) examples, try to imagine your response if you were the subject of this interaction:

SUBJECT: I had a flat tire.
EXPERIMENTER: What do you mean, you had a flat tire?
SUBJECT: What do you mean "what do you mean"? A flat tire is a flat tire. That is what I meant. Nothing special. What a crazy question!

Obviously, this interaction is losing its continuity and sense of order, but why? The reason is that the experimenter has violated an implicit and agreed-upon technique in all interactions: the tacit rule that we don't question the obvious and the presumption (not to be challenged) that we share certain life experiences. Ethnomethodologists (those who study such folk methods) have termed this particular method the *et cetera principle* because we communicate with our gestures the implicit command not to question certain things. Let me now reconstruct for you a conversation that I had with a student (again, imagine yourself in this interaction).

STUDENT: I'm having trouble with this material, you know.
ME: No, I don't know.
STUDENT: The material is so, so abstract, you know?
ME: No, I don't know.
STUDENT: Well, I . . . I'll come back some other time.

People frequently use the phrase "you know" in conversations. When that little phrase is used, the et cetera principle, or technique, is being invoked. The speaker is, in essence, asserting that we are to accept his or her pronouncement, even if we "don't know" what is meant. By nodding or by saying "Yeah, I know," we create a sense that you two share the same world and that the world is orderly.

INTERACTION IN ROLES

A role is simply a configuration of behaviors (gestures) that people emit and that others accept as signifying a particular kind and course of action. As we saw in the last chapter, many roles are dictated by norms and by our position in a social structure (Parsons, 1951). For example, as you play the role of student (dressing a certain way, talking in a particular manner, taking notes, attending lectures, and so on), your configuration of behaviors reveals a consistency and style which

---

BOX 5-1 *Conducting a Breaching Experiment*

One way to discover the subtle universe of folk methods is to conduct your own breaching experiment. These are very easy to execute, because each and every face-to-face interaction involves the use of "folk methods." Here are a few suggestions: The next time someone uses the phrase "you know" tell them that you don't know, or take the most obvious statement a person makes ("I'm late for class") and ask them what they mean ("What do you mean, late?"), or best of all stand impassively as someone talks to you and do not utter a sound and try not to gesture with your face or body. If you follow any of these suggestions, an interaction will probably crumble before your eyes.

Another good experiment would be to act like a guest in your parents' house: Ask if you can use the bathroom, seek permission to grab something to eat, ask if it is o.k. for you to go to bed, and so on as if you were a guest. Your parents will wonder "what's wrong" and attempt to reconstruct a common sense of order.

almost everyone can recognize as "just a student." This distinctive role is, in large part, dictated by cultural norms and location in a college or university structure.

Yet, cultural codes and one's position in a social structure are at best only general frameworks (R. Turner, 1962). There is always a lot of room in which to maneuver; it is always possible to present oneself in a particular way (as student jock, student beauty queen, student sorority member, student fraternity member, student intellectual, student crazy, student party goer, etc.). This is what Goffman termed impression-management. Part of this impression-management involves orchestrating gestures to assert *what* role we are going to play. Indeed, others are waiting to read our gestures to discover this role. As part of our stocks of knowledge (Schutz, 1932) all of us carry within ourselves generalized conceptions of various roles—that of student, mother, father, lover, worker, beauty queen, stud, jock, grind, comic, flirt, teacher, jerk, nerd, friend, acquaintance, and so on. For each role we probably have many conceptions about the behaviors appropriate to the role. Interaction is greatly facilitated by the ability to store roles in our memory because once we have established someone's role in accordance with these conceptions, we can anticipate, at least to a degree, how that person will respond to us. Life is much less stressful when we are able to place someone into a role, for we can then take up the reciprocal role and, in a sense, go on "automatic pilot." It is when we do not know the role of an individual that we have to work at the interaction. We have to read gestures more actively, role-take more cautiously, gaze into the "looking-glass self" more carefully, remain more mentally alert, and do a host of rather tiring mental exercises. Life is so much easier when others orchestrate their gestures to tell you what role they are playing.

These interaction processes are given their most articulate expression by the sociologist Ralph H. Turner (1962, 1968, 1980). Turner has argued that not only do we role-take with others (to see what their role is) but we also **role-make**. As part of our dramaturgical presentation, we consciously and unconsciously manipulate gestures—words, posture, voice inflection, dress, facial expressions—to tell others what role we are playing, since others are looking for these gestures as a sign of our role. Moreover, they assume that our gestures will be consistent and that our respective roles are coherent wholes; and so, once they have read some gestures and placed a person in a role, they expect other gestures to be consistent with that role. And people are constantly verifying and reverifying one another's roles just to make sure that they have got them right.

Thus, all interactions involve the processes of presenting gestures to assert a role, seeking to discover others' roles, and rechecking and reverifying roles. However, once we get placed into a role by others, it is often difficult to escape, because others continue to respond to us as belonging in that role. People are rather reluctant to let us out of a role, because they do not want to readjust their behaviors unless forced to. Only through persistent effort can people remake their roles in a situation.

Try now to recall some personal situations where these role dynamics operated. You have encountered situations where you were "misunderstood" and placed in the wrong role; or you have dealt with people whom "you could not figure out" because their behaviors did not reveal a role that you knew; or you have found yourself or have seen others trying to make a role for themselves which they simply could not play and in which they could not be taken seriously. If these situations typified all of social life, interaction would be awkward and difficult. Fortunately, in most interactions we role-take, role-make, and role-verify rather effortlessly. As a result, our interactions proceed smoothly.

INTERACTIVE TYPIFICATIONS

Often others play roles that are so well known and stereotypical that we interact with them as typifications, as nonpersons, or as categories. One does not have to be coldhearted and mean to respond to people as nonpersons; it is just that in a busy life all of us find it easier to do things when we can interact with people as stereotypes. If we had to interact personally with every clerk, passerby, fellow student, teacher, janitor, administrator, or food vendor, treating each as a unique and fascinating human being deserving of our most sensitive and accurate role taking, we would exhaust ourselves, and we would never get anything done. Thus, in a complex society where we must move in and out of many situations, interaction in terms of typifications is essential, a point emphasized by the pioneering German sociologist Alfred Schutz (1932). And for these brief but functionally essential encounters, people mutually *typify*, or construct **typifications**. That is, they immediately place each other in highly stereotyped roles and rather effortlessly do their business. When a person buys groceries at a store, she and the clerk mutually typify each other, interact in very predictable ways, and yet hardly notice each other. Of course, if she becomes a "regular customer" (another type of typification), then both parties work a little harder and try to be a little more personal.

Interactions obviously vary in their degree of mutual typification. Moreover, when they are sustained, they tend to move over time from highly stereotyped to ever more intimate. However, this process must happen over time. If someone "comes on too strong," "pushes himself or herself on you," or "violates your space," you sense a too rapid movement from a typified interaction to one that is more personal and intimate. A first date who confesses his or her most intimate feelings is violating a "new acquaintance" role and typification as a "first date." In this situation you feel awkward, if not embarrassed. A doctor who asks you very personal questions and reveals his or her personal feelings is probably "making a move on you" (your new designation of his or her role) and, as a consequence, is violating your typification of this person as a physician.

To a degree, norms tell us *how* personal or typified situations are to be. But also, we all carry implicit understandings about these matters. We rarely give voice to them unless they are violated, forcing us to do more interpersonal work than we want.

INTERACTION FRAMES

Without the ability to reduce the scope of interaction, we would have to devote enormous amounts of energy negotiating the substance of an interaction. Fortunately, humans take an important shortcut: they use their gestures and props on the stage to **frame** the interaction. Once again, Erving Goffman (1974) provides us with an important insight; and he used the metaphor of a picture frame in which a frame encloses and highlights certain materials (the picture) and excludes all else outside the frame. Humans create symbolic frames with their gestures, indicating what is relevant and irrelevant to the interaction. For example, when someone says "May I talk with you in private," this set of gestures frames the interaction in a particular way. Or, when someone says "I don't want to talk about that," potential topics of interaction are being placed outside the frame.

Framing is so fundamental to interaction that it is often used in deception. Take a "con artist" again; a con artist creates two frames, one that his or her "mark" thinks is the basis for interaction and a more secret one among those who do the conning. Or, think about anyone who appears to be manipulating another: The person doing the manipulating is often creating one frame for appearances and another for private purposes which others are not supposed to see.

Frames are created in many ways. Talk is, of course, the most obvious: "Let's get down to business here," "I'm in the mood for love," "I've got a headache," "We need to talk," "Let's cut the B.S.," and so on. But besides spoken words, we use other gestures and props as well (J. Turner, 1988). For example, the number of people and their positioning frame a situation, as is the case for a lecture where bodies are lined up in rows and this alignment frames the situation in terms of what can, and cannot, occur. Or, the physical distance between the parties to an interaction frames the situation, as becomes evident when someone moves inside our "personal zone." Aside from body positioning, our demeanor—body countenance, for instance—does much of the framing work, as the difference between leaning back against a wall as opposed to standing erect and pushing forward would signal. Physical structures also frame interactions, as students will immediately notice when they pass from the hallway where they were talking with fellow students into a professor's office.

Frames can be changed, or rekeyed in Goffman's (1974) terms. When someone says "Let's not talk about this anymore," she is changing the frame. In fact, any interaction that endures may experience several shifts in frames—for instance, general gossip to work related talk to personal confidences, back to general gossip, and so on. Because we understand the cues for shifting frames, it becomes possible to move smoothly through the ever-changing substance of interaction. Moreover, we can layer interactions in multiple frames, as when people in a work setting (one frame) talk informally as friends (another frame inside the other), with some becoming good friends or buddies (another frame inside the last one) and others lovers (yet another frame). Thus, interaction is layered and laminated in frames, and we can move from one to the other rather easily—as such a simple phrase as "Well, back to work I guess" denotes.

Without framing, interaction would be a lot more work. In our "stocks of knowledge" we acquire understandings about what gestures mean with respect to frames, and rekeying frames. Because we have this facility, we can easily determine what is relevant and appropriate to a situation, and then move on without too many preliminaries. If our facility at framing is weak, however, we will seem lost and "out of it," uttering statements and behaving in ways that seem odd to others.

INTERACTION RITUALS

We have all probably walked by someone familiar, said "Hello," and received no reply in return. It is a very bothersome experience, even if we do not know the person well. The reason for this dismay, perhaps even anger and annoyance, is that an interaction **ritual** has been violated. A great deal of human interaction is mediated by **interpersonal rituals**; that is, each individual engages in highly stereotypical behavior (Goffman, 1967). And interactions among people who are mutually typifying each other are almost all ritualized. For example, "How are you today?" "Just fine," "Nice weather," "Yes," "Have a nice day," "Bye now," and "See you later" are all interactional rituals. The same is true with framing where rituals are often used to initially frame and then reframe a situation. We engage in these interaction rituals because they give us a sense of being woven into the social fabric.

Interaction is most likely to be ritualized under certain conditions (Collins, 1975): between strangers and between people of vastly different rank. People who do not know each other well talk in stereotypes, feeling each other out and making contact without commitment. Those of unequal power, prestige, and wealth interact in ritualized patterns to hide the potential tension between unequals. Those in subordinate positions wish to avoid the costs of supplication, whereas high-ranking people usually wish acknowledgement of their lofty position without arousing resentments and without having to monitor the respect given to them by low-ranking individuals. Recall, for example, a conversation you may have had with a professor: for all of its feigned informality, it is highly ritualized because the interaction is between people of very different rank. Thus, a conflict approach emphasizes an important aspect of interaction: Interactants are often unequal and, as a consequence, are in a state of tension. This tension can be smoothed over by ritual and by maintaining distance, but it is always there, ready to erupt into more antagonistic interaction.

Thus, rituals allow us to keep our masks and to maintain our dignity and at the same time reinforce our sense of belonging to a larger social whole. The most critical rituals are these day-to-day ones, which we perform routinely and uneventfully *unless* someone does not participate. Then, we see how important they are, because our sense of social continuity is disrupted.

Indeed, day-to-day ordinary interactions are structured by rituals (J. Turner, 1986a, 1988, 1989; Turner and Collins, 1989): There are opening rituals ("Hi, how are you") and closing rituals ("See you later"); and in between this opening and closing, there are rituals to repair breaches ("Oh, I'm sorry, I didn't know"), to frame and reframe ("Enough of this, what about . . ."), to sequence talk ("That's really interesting, but did you think of . . .") and otherwise organize the flow of interaction. Those who cannot use these kinds of interpersonal rituals, or who use them in the wrong way, seem awkward and difficult; the interaction becomes jerky, and it lacks continuity and flow.

Thus, rituals are essential to interaction. If you doubt this, violate just one ritual, such as not giving an opening or closing where it is called for or violating any of the many rituals you implicitly understand. If you do this, the interaction will suddenly become strained, indicating how significant rituals are to the social fabric.

INTERACTION WITH REFERENCE GROUPS AND REMOTE OTHERS

Henry David Thoreau implicitly captured an important dynamic of human interaction when he wrote, "If a man does not keep pace with his companions perhaps it is because he hears a different drummer. Let him step to the music he hears, however measured or far away." In all interactions, we deal not only with those immediately present, but with many "distant drummers." We can simultaneously interact with immediate others and with others not present. This process is sometimes obvious with young children who, as they play together, invoke their parents ("Well, my dad says . . ." or "What's your mother gonna think about that?"). All of us also interact with important others who are not present—a spouse, a lover, a parent, a philosopher, or anyone we deem significant to us. Often, the perceived or imputed reaction of these remote others is far more important than the reactions of those right in front of us. We all like to think of ourselves, especially in America, as rugged individualists, and so we disguise or refuse to be conscious of the extent to which vicarious role taking with remote others guides our conduct.

Often these remote others personify cultural values and beliefs, and role taking with them plugs us into the general culture or a particular subculture (Kelley, 1958). And equally often, we assume the perspective of a large group of individuals, without singling out, or even knowing, a particular individual who personifies this perspective (Shibutani, 1955). Rather, we have a general sense for what these **reference groups** expect, and we thereby adjust our conduct. George Herbert Mead referred to this process as role taking with the "generalized other."

The fact that interaction often involves role taking with remote others and reference groups can potentially create tensions with those who do not know about these distant drummers. What they may see is someone who misses cues or who violates the norms of the present situation. Normally, we are quite good at reconciling our behaviors with those both close and afar. But at times, we have difficulty, and as a result, we say and do stupid things, at least from the perspective of those in front of us. At other times, we recognize that we march to different drummers and ritualize our interactions. For example, jocks and intellectuals, blacks and whites, Hispanics and Anglos, old and young, rich and poor, educated and uneducated all ritualize their initial encounters to avoid the tensions and awkwardness created by our role taking with unfamiliar remote others and reference groups (Merton and Rossi, 1968).

INTERACTION AND THE SOCIAL ORDER

Ultimately, society is held together by people in face-to-face contact. Of course, individuals create a universe of cultural symbols and large-scale structures that constrain what they can do when facing each other and when mutually signaling and interpreting gestures. Indeed, the systems of symbols and matrix of social structures have a life of their own, being driven by dynamics that can overwhelm individuals; and yet, it is people who occupy positions in social structures, play roles, hold symbols in their heads, and sustain the culture and structure of a society. Thus, the process of interaction undergirds the majestic structural edifices and cultural constructions.

It is often difficult to make the connection between micro-level interaction and macro-level structures and cultural systems. We know that they are connected—the micro is not possible without the existence of the macro, and vice versa—but the mutual influence of the two levels is often hard to discern and dissect. This problem is often termed the problem of micro-macro "linkage" or the micro-macro "gap" (J. Turner, 1983; Alexander et al., 1986). Yet, for our purposes, we need only recognize that the processes outlined in this chapter are what sustain the structures and symbols of the social world. Without the ability to use gestures, to role-take, to role-make, to present self, to manage impressions, to present fronts, to use staging props, to mutually typify, to construct and shift frames, to use rituals, and to use remote others and reference groups as a frame of reference, the structures of society (groups, organizations, communities, categories, strata, and institutions) and the symbol systems of culture (language, technology, stocks of knowledge, values, beliefs, norms) could not exist. Conversely, these structures and symbol systems constrain and guide the course of interaction.

SUMMARY

1. Interaction involves the mutual signaling and reading of gestures and the adjustment of responses to the emission of gestures. Human interaction, according to G. H. Mead, also involves the capacities for mind (thought, deliberation, and covert rehearsal of alternatives) and self (seeing oneself as an object).
2. In Erving Goffman's analysis, interaction occurs on a stage, both a frontstage and backstage, and uses physical props to orchestrate a personal front as part of a more general process of impression management. Goffman also developed the notion of

"frame" as a part of impression management, whereby individuals signal what is to be included and excluded as a relevant consideration during the course of interaction.

3. Ethnomethodologists stress that much of humans' sense for order is sustained by implicit "folk methods" which are implicitly used by individuals to preserve the presumption that they experience the social world in similar ways.

4. Interaction occurs in social structures, where considerations of roles become important. People manage their emission of gestures to make roles for themselves, and they actively read the gestures of others in order to discover the roles that others are trying to establish. This process is possible because individuals carry in their stocks of knowledge inventories of roles which they draw upon in making a role for themselves and in interpreting the gestures of others. Individuals also seek to verify and reverify one anothers' roles.

5. Many interactions proceed in terms of mutual typifications in which individuals view one another as categories and adjust their responses accordingly.

6. Interaction depends upon rituals, or stereotyped sequences of gestures, that signal the opening, closing, framing, and other aspects of the interaction process.

7. Interaction involves awareness of, and adjustment to, the expectations of others and group perspectives not physically present in a situation. Such reference groups and remote others often guide and direct the behaviors and responses of individuals.

8. Interaction, social structure, and culture are interrelated. Each could not exist without the other.

KEY TERMS

backstage   Erving Goffman's term denoting areas of privacy where the self-conscious manipulation of gestures can be relaxed.

ethnomethods   A concept introduced by Harold Garfinkel to denote the implicit interpersonal signals emitted to create the presumption that people in interaction share a common view of reality.

frames/framing   The term employed by Erving Goffman to denote the process of using gestures to include (or exclude) certain matters as in (or outside) the interaction.

front   Erving Goffman's term to denote the use of gestures to present oneself in a particular way and in an identifiable mode of action.

frontstage   Erving Goffman's term denoting situations where individuals consciously manipulate gestures in ways designed to elicit desired responses from others, especially with respect to one's sense of self.

impression management   Erving Goffman's term to denote the deliberate manipulation of gestures and physical props in order to project a particular image of oneself to others.

interaction   The process of individuals mutually emitting gestures, interpreting these gestures, and adjusting their respective courses of action.

mind   G. H. Mead's term to designate the process by which individuals covertly rehearse alternative lines of conduct, anticipate or imagine the consequences of each of these potential lines of behavior, and select that line of behavior most likely to facilitate cooperation.

physical props   The use of objects, including the body and its spacing relative to other bodies in the environment, in order to signal a line of conduct.

reference group   Perspectives of groups, both those in which one is participating and those which are remote, that are used as a frame of reference for self-evaluation and for guiding conduct.

rituals/interpersonal rituals   The process of using highly stereotyped sequences of behavior to mark the opening, closing, and course of interaction.

role-make   A concept introduced by Ralph Turner to denote the process of emitting gestures in order to create a particular role for oneself in a situation.

role-take   A concept introduced by G. H. Mead to denote the capacity to read the gestures of others and, thereby, to sense what they are likely to do in terms of their dispositions to act and the cultural symbols relevant to a situation.

self/self-conception   The capacity to see oneself as an object in a situation and to carry cognitions, feelings, and evaluations of oneself as a certain type of person who is deserving of particular responses.

typifications   A concept introduced by Alfred Schutz to denote the process of categorizing others as an instance of a general class or type which, in turn, enables individuals to respond in stereotypical ways and, thereby, to reduce the interpersonal work in interaction.

CHAPTER 6

Socialization

We all become human by interacting with others, and out of this interaction we acquire a personality, learn how to fit into society, and order our lives. This process of socialization into culture and social structure is vital to society and the individual. Without socialization we would not know what to value, what to do, how to think, how to talk, where to go, or how to respond. We would not be human. While socialization in the early periods of life is the most important, we never stop being re-socialized throughout our life course. Such socialization helps us make the transition to new life situations; without it, we would be rigid robots and victims of our early life experiences.

INTERACTION AND BECOMING HUMAN

In 1920, Rev. A. L. Singh confirmed a rumor that had circulated among villagers in rural India: the existence of children living with wolves (Brown, 1972). Setting up an observation post outside a large cave in an abandoned anthill, he and a few villagers observed a mother and her cubs, two of whom looked but did not act human. The local people were afraid to excavate a place where such "ghosts" resided, but Rev. Singh eventually found workers willing to open up the anthill. The mother attacked the workers and she was killed, but once inside, the diggers found four little creatures—two wolf cubs and two little girls. One of the children was about eight years old, the other about eighteen months. They were wolfish in appearance and behavior. They had hard calluses on their knees and palms from walking on all fours. They moved their nostrils to sniff food. Eating and drinking involved lowering their faces into the food. They ate raw meat and hunted wild animals. When brought back to civilization, Kamala and Amala shunned other children and in fact, preferred the company of the dog and cat. When sleeping, they rolled up together on the floor.

It was never known how these children got into the wolf den, but what is revealing is how well they adjusted to being wolves. Cases like this underscore the degree to which our social experiences influence what we become. We do not fall out of the womb fully "human." We must be taught what to be, how to behave, and how to think. If you are raised by a wolf, you will become more like a wolf, even though your physiology is not well suited for it and, in the end, you will die because of it. Raised by human parents, you become human—a direction more suited to your biological equipment.

Our biological makeup, then, does not ensure our humanness. Cases of children isolated from humans at birth clearly document the need to learn how to be human. Take the case of "Anna of the Attic," an illegitimate child whose grandfather had kept her alive in the attic but had deprived her of all human contact (K. Davis, 1940, 1947). When found by social workers, Anna could not walk or talk, and because she did not respond to human gestures, she was initially thought to be blind and deaf. Before she died four years later, she had made considerable progress in learning how to move and communicate, but it was clear that she would never be normal. Another case of an isolated child, Isabelle, demonstrates that when isolation is not so complete, early deficiencies can be overcome through intense training. Like Anna, Isabelle was illegitimate, and she had been isolated by her mother who was a deaf-mute. She had not learned how to use conventional language, but unlike Anna, she had learned how to communicate; she communicated with her mother through a series of guttural, croaking sounds. Hence, later she was able to become almost normal when given special training.

The conclusion to be drawn here is that our most basic human capacities—discriminating sounds, seeing and using gestures, walking, talking, responding to others—are to a great extent learned. Our genetic endowment provides the capacity to learn these behaviors, and may even direct us to learn them, but it does not guarantee their emergence and development. We become human through interaction with others in a variety of cultural and social structural contexts. The interactions influencing the development of those capacities that allow us to participate in society are termed *socialization*. We carry into this world a genetic heritage—a human physiology, cognitive capacities, emotional propensities, and perhaps some basic drives for food, companionship, and later, sex—but just *how* this heritage is manifested is in large part the result of our interaction with others in social and cultural contexts.

SOCIALIZATION AND SOCIETY

Each of us is made unique by **socialization**—that is, by our biography of specific interaction with others in a cultural and social context. This biography may be what interests us most about socialization. We all want to know what made us into the person we are. Far more important sociologically, however, is the socialization experience of whole populations. What is it that people have *in common* by virtue of socialization? For a society can only be sustained if its new members acquire capacities that enable them to participate fully in the society. As functional theories would stress, our unique qualities are far less important than what we share: the capacity to function in the same society (Parsons, 1951).

What are these capacities (J. Turner, 1985c, pp. 100–104)? One essential capacity is the acquisition of **motives** that direct us to occupy positions and to play essential roles. We all must be willing to play such roles—as worker, father, friend, mother, citizen, etc.—if a society is to be sustained. Alienation, disaffection, and dissatisfaction are, of course, prevalent in large and complex societies. And if significant numbers reveal these attributes and fail to perform basic roles, society begins to crumble or at least change.

Another capacity is cultural (Parsons, 1951). All of us must, to some degree, share commitments to common values, beliefs, and institutional norms, or we must agree to disagree and separate ourselves into different subcultures. But a society composed of too many highly diverse subcultures is likely to reveal conflict and tension, as people clash over their respective views of what is right and wrong, of what should and should not be done, and of what actions are proper and improper. Thus, to some degree, each of us must be guided from within by common cultural symbols—what we can call **cultural directives**. Only in this way can our interactions proceed, on the basis of similar moral assumptions, commonly accepted beliefs, and agreed-upon norms.

Yet another capacity is to see ourselves as an object, or to have a conception of ourselves as a certain kind of person, as interactionist theories stress (Mead, 1934; James, 1890). If we lack a **self-conception,** our behaviors will not reveal consistency and we will have no stable object or point of reference to assess and evaluate with cultural symbols (Rosenberg, 1979; Epstein, 1980; Gecas, 1982, 1985; Bandura, 1977). People without a stable sense of self seem, even when they abide by the norms, "flighty" and "flaky." There is a lack of an inner compass guiding their actions (Gecas and Schwalbe, 1983). In addition to a more stable self-conception, we also carry a more *situationally based sense of self* (Goffman, 1959). We see ourselves somewhat differently in varying situations, but we are not chameleons. Our more stable sense of self places limits on how we think about ourselves in life's diverse contexts. Moreover, sustaining this self-conception becomes a powerful motivational force in human interaction, giving our behaviors a direction and pattern that facilitates the responses of others to us (Gecas, 1986, 1989, 1991; Miyamoto, 1970; J. Turner, 1987).

Still another crucial capacity stressed by interactionist theories is a collage of **role-playing skills** and abilities. All of us must have the ability to read the gestures of others and role-take with them. We must be able to role-make for ourselves, to assert through the orchestration of gestures the role that we are playing (R. Turner, 1962). We all must be able to move back and forth between front- and backstage areas (Goffman, 1959). We must be able to use, implicitly, a variety of folk methods or tacit understandings in our relations with others (Garfinkel, 1967). We must be able to frame and to categorize others and situations (Goffman, 1974). Without such minimal capacities, we cannot interact with others (J. Turner, 1988).

Yet another personal capacity revolves around **emotions**. Much research has been done on the basic or primary emotions possessed by humans at birth (Kemper, 1987; Ekman, 1982; Plutchik, 1962; Plutchik and Kellerman, 1980). While some disagreement exists, the emotions of anger, happiness, sadness, fear, and surprise appear to be inborn. What is remarkable, however, is the elaboration of these basic emotions into many additional ones (see Table 6-1). Humans thus acquire a complex array of emotional states through socialization. The reason for so many emotions is that they facilitate fine-tuned interaction (Turner and Molnar, 1993). If we can display and read many diverse emotions, we can signal our moods and intentions, and others can respond to us in appropriate ways. Imagine a social world where the only emotions that we could read were the primary ones—fear, anger, happiness, sadness, and surprise. Such a world would lack the subtlety and the emotional richness of our daily lives, but more importantly, it would be very difficult to construct and sustain the complex, fluid, and robust interactions, social structures, and cultural symbols that order human society.

From a sociological viewpoint, it is the acquisition of these capacities through interaction with others that allows us to participate in ongoing patterns of social organization. Each of us reveals a unique profile in terms of our motives, cultural directives, self-conceptions, role-playing skills, and ability to display emotions. But to a minimal degree, we all must have these basic capacities if society is to exist. This is what is sociologically important, for the job of the sociologist is to understand what makes social relations and social organization possible. The dynamics of socialization as it leads to the acquisition of these basic capacities are thus critical to understanding not just ourselves as individuals but also the operation of society.

TABLE 6-1. The Diversity of Human Emotions

PRIMARY EMOTIONS	Happiness	Fear	Anger	Sadness	Surprise
SOME VARIATIONS OF PRIMARY EMOTIONS	satisfaction pride love	anxiety apprehensiveness aversiveness	contempt distaste aggressiveness	resignation ennui sorrow	startlement amazement astonishment

SOME COMBINATIONS OF PRIMARY EMOTIONS	Happiness
	  (plus another)
	gratitude (fear)
	hope (fear)
	wonder (fear)
	vengeance (anger)
	nostalgia (sadness)
	joy (surprise)
		Fear
		  (plus another)
		awe (happiness)
		guilt (anger)
		envy (anger)
		worry (sadness)
		panic (surprise)
			Anger
			  (plus another)
			snobbishness
			  (happiness)
			shame (fear)
			hate (fear)
			jealousy (fear)
			depression (sadness)
			rage (surprise)
			bitterness
			  (sadness)
				Sadness
				  (plus another)
				yearning
				  (happiness)
				hopefulness (fear)
				grief (anger)
				boredom (anger)
				crestfallen
				  (surprise)
					Surprise
					  (plus another)
					delight
					  (happiness)
					shock (fear)
					disgust (anger)
					disappointment
					  (sadness)

THE PROCESS OF SOCIALIZATION

When we were born, we were narcissistic blobs, and we were not highly social. We wanted this and that, and we wanted it now. If we did not get it, we would cry and scream. Yet, immediately after each baby is born socialization begins to tame this narcissism, because the infant finds itself in a social structure—hospital, home, family—where it *must* interact and get along with others—nurse, mother, father, and others. Thus begins a lifelong process of interaction in an ever-increasing variety of contexts, and it is out of these interactions that a profile of motives, a system of cultural symbols (language, values, beliefs, norms), a self-conception, a distinct role-playing style, and an array of emotional capacities are developed.

Several rather obvious, but nonetheless critical, principles operate during socialization. One is that early socialization has more influence on the formation of our human capacities than later socialization. The philosopher John Locke argued that the newborn is like a "blank slate" on which first experiences make indelible marks. This is clearly an overstatement, because an infant is hardly "blank." Indeed, infants must possess a series of biological tendencies and capacities which are "hard-wired" into its biology. Thus, we may be a "narcissistic blob," but we are not blank. For at a minimum, we have biological needs and drives, complex neuronets, numerous glands for hormonal secretions, repertoires of primary emotions, minimal needs for affiliation, and many latent biological capacities which will eventually become manifest (see Figure 6-1). And because we must meet our needs and realize our capacities through the responses of others, we must interact with others. As we learn to interact, we read the gestures of others, we get our first self-images in the looking glass (Cooley, 1909). We begin to feel the expectations of others and experience our first contact with cultural codes; we begin to develop our own ways of gesturing and role playing so as to get along with others; we begin to channel and direct energies toward others in ways that will eventually become stable motivations; and we begin to expand our emotional horizons. Since we have had no previous social interactions, we do not have any legacy of role-playing style, sense of self, motives, culture, or emotions beyond those we are born with to filter these early social contacts. And so they have a disproportionate influence on the kinds of basic capacities that we will develop.

Another basic principle of socialization is that interaction with significant others—people who are emotionally important to us—is more influential than interaction with ordinary individuals (Sullivan, 1953). At first, of course, parents and relatives are our significant others. As we learn to role-take and role-make with them, we assess ourselves in the mirror provided by their gestures and begin to assume their perspective and, hence, the cultural codes that they personify. Furthermore, we acquire a style of role playing and presenting ourselves so as to get along with them and we direct our motivational energies in ways that enable us to meet their expectations. And we learn to manage our emotional displays. Later in life, we acquire many significant others—peers,

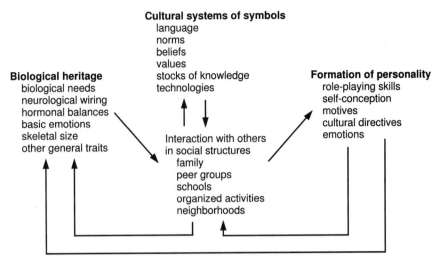

FIGURE 6-1. The interplay of biology, culture, interaction, and social structure

teachers, lovers, spouses, our own children, employers, and even media person-alities—but they never have quite the same influence as the significant others with whom we first interacted.

A third principle is that interaction in primary groups—groups where people know one another and feel a closeness and intimacy—is more crucial in the formation of personality than contact with others in secondary groups—groups in which interaction is less immediate and more formal (Cooley, 1909). It is not that secondary groups do not have influence on how we behave and play roles, how we think of ourselves, how we interpret cultural codes, how we channel motivational energies, and how we display emotions. But the influence is never as great as that of our family, close friends, and other groupings where we have *face-to-face*, close contact with others.

Yet another principle is that long-term relations with others have more influence on personality than short-term interactions. True, individuals can come into our lives briefly and exert an enormous influence, but our feelings about ourselves, commitments to cultural codes, style of playing roles, and channeling of emotions and motivational energy are most typically shaped by long-term relationships.

Thus, early primary group interactions among significant others with whom relationships endure are the most influential in the development of personality. These ideas may seem obvious, but they are not trivial. For these principles have operated for all of us and help account for who and what we are.

The development of our basic capacities to participate in society does not occur in a short time, nor does it ever truly end. But by the time a person is an adolescent or teenager, many basic capacities have begun to crystallize. The individual is constrained by a stable self-conception, is likely to possess a particular role-playing style, is guided by a particular profile of values, is committed to certain beliefs, is aware of most crucial norms, and is able to mobilize motivational energy and emotions in habitual ways.

We must be careful not to view these capacities as too fixed, or crystallized. For after adolescence, there are new significant others who come along at crucial times. There are new groups with which to affiliate. There are lasting friendships and affiliations that have yet to be made. Still, to some degree, these later significant others must take us as we already are. One is no longer the "blob" to be molded at will; and hence, motives, cultural codes, self-conception, emotional tendencies, and role-playing style are unlikely to change dramatically. Change will probably be gradual, at times imperceptible. This is why someone whom we had not seen for many years seems very much the same as before.

A great deal about humans as social beings can be learned by examining efforts to change them and by looking at cases where people do seem to undergo dramatic transformations. Indeed, there is a vast industry—clinical psychology, psychotherapy, psychoanalysis, group therapy, and hundreds of applications of ideas in these fields—devoted primarily to changing people. Some change is possible in these efforts—more so in some capacities of individuals than others. Much change can occur in cultural values and beliefs; and people can become more aware of crucial norms. It is also possible to alter emotional propensities and role-playing style by dramaturgical coaching. Thus, individuals can become somewhat different with conscious effort. They can become better role takers and role makers; they can change their beliefs and their capacity to abide by norms; and they can better-regulate some emotions. If these kinds of changes are sought, then various programs do help. If, however, people want to change their self-conception and motives, then a long and difficult journey lies ahead. One does not so easily eliminate deeply held self-feelings with short-term coaching, nor does someone suddenly change motives from, for example, a strong need for affiliation to a need for power or achievement. Change here will be slow and in most cases not so dramatic.

Yet, in real-life situations fundamental changes sometimes occur. For example, an ex-alcoholic is often a very different person after treatment, because he or she had previously sunk to such depths of maladjustment—loss of job, family, friends, and self-esteem. And starting from this devastated personal landscape, rehabilitation does indeed create a new self-concept and new motivations. But few humans would willingly strip themselves bare in this way; and thus, our old self-conception and motives resist transformation. They place constraints on what we can do to ourselves.

These situations tell us something about adult socialization. As we move into various new phases of life—and into new jobs, families, workplaces, communities, clubs, and organizations—it is our role-playing style and cultural directives that are the most likely to be altered. Our self-conception will, of course, be changed somewhat, depending on our successes and failures as well as on our satisfaction with others, but not to the same degree as cultural codes and role-playing styles. Our motives and emotional propensities may shift around somewhat as our lives run their course, but again not dramatically. Only with real physical decline do motives begin to change, and even then, old desires and passions often persist.

From the standpoint of maintaining social order, it is probably best that personality is not wholly fluid. And it is significant that role-playing abilities and cognizance of cultural codes are the most readily changed. For if people could readily change their self-concept and motives, it would be hard for others to respond to them. There would be no consistency in their actions, making it difficult for others to adjust. But if people can change and even improve their role-playing abilities, then their interaction is facilitated and cooperation is more likely. If they can also acquire new cultural directives, this too can facilitate interaction with others, integration into the existing social order, and adaptation to new social contexts. And if they can better signal and control their emotions, then this will further cooperation and adaptation.

Changes in role-playing abilities and cultural directives do not always promote social order, of course. Just the opposite is often the case, as people who were once straight become increasingly deviant or as individuals who once accepted the social order rebel against it. Yet, our more flexible capacities are also the most crucial to making adjustments and readjustments to social situations, and this fact is very significant. For it means that people are capable of flexibility in their relations with other individuals and in their involvements in collective enterprises, while those components that are least flexible—self and motives—provide a sense of stability and continuity both for the individual and for those in his or her environment, even in the face of readjustments to changing circumstances. Thus we can, in a sense, maintain our core compass and at the same time alter our more peripheral course. Without this dual capacity, social change in human affairs would be even more awkward and traumatic than it already is.

STAGES OF SOCIALIZATION

Many efforts have been made to describe the stages of socialization in more detail than I have done thus far. The goal of these efforts is to mark important turning points in a person's development in the life course. Each approach has its own set of stages and phases, and so it is difficult to draw any firm conclusions. Yet, a review of several prominent approaches can perhaps provide a sense for the complex transformations that each of us has, and will have, experienced.

George Herbert Mead's Stage Model

Since Mead (1934) unlocked the mysteries of human interaction, it should not be surprising that he also couched his ideas in a developmental way. For Mead, the newborn must survive in a world requiring cooperation with others, with the result that a child learns those behaviors which facilitate cooperation. Once biological and neurological maturation is initiated, the first process is learning what gestures mean, and then using them to signal one's own needs and, at the same time, to read the gestures of others to determine their likely responses. At first this ability to perform what Mead termed *role taking* is very limited because *mind*—or the ability to think, weigh, and rehearse alternatives—is limited, and *self*—or the capacity to see oneself as an object—is not well developed (see Key Terms at the end of Chapter 5 for details on these processes).

This early phase Mead termed the **play stage** of development, because a child can only take the role, or read the gestures and assume the perspective, of one other at a time. He illustrated this stage by reference to very young children in a sandbox; they will, he observed, tend to pair off because they cannot effectively read the gestures of more than one other at a time, nor can they adjust their responses to more than one other.

With practice, biological maturation, and further development of mind and self, a second stage is reached. This is the **game stage,** and Mead's example was the players on a baseball team. They can simultaneously role-take with all the other positions and, thereby, assume the perspective and likely responses of others. Moreover, they can see themselves as an object from the point of view of multiple others; and they can reflect and think in ways that promote positive self-evaluation and cooperation with others. When children reach this stage, the scale and scope of their interactions are greatly expanded and the stage is set for the rapid development of increased role-taking facility, increased self-awareness, and increased capacity to think and rehearse covertly lines of conduct.

The final stage is what Mead termed role taking with the **generalized other,** or as he sometimes termed the process, role taking with a "community of attitudes." The idea here is that children can now assume not only the role of immediately present others, but also the generalized perspectives guiding interaction (what we might term today the values, beliefs, norms, and perhaps emotional moods). They can use this perspective to assess and evaluate themselves as objects and to guide their deliberations about the most appropriate courses of action.

When individuals reach the stage of the generalized other, they possess the basic skills needed to function in society: They can read and use gestures, or role-take, with a single individual or simultaneously with multiple others in an organized setting; and they can plug themselves into the system of cultural symbols and use this as a frame of reference for self-evaluation and for regulating conduct.

Jean Piaget's Model of Cognitive Development

The Frenchman, Jean Piaget, was one of the foremost psychologists of this century. Watching his own children, he became fascinated with how they organized their experiences; and in later experiments, he confirmed that there are clear turning points in the cognitive development of children (Piaget, 1948, 1952). Each of these turning points, or stages, marks a qualitative jump in the child's ability to represent the objects of its world in terms of symbols and to manipulate these symbols. These stages underlie those discussed by Mead, for the ability of an infant and later a child to develop the capacity for cooperation in society hinges on its cognitive development.

Stage 1 Piaget termed the **sensorimotor stage,** lasting from infancy to about two years. During this stage children live in a world of direct sense impressions, but at the very end of this early period, they come to see that objects do not disappear when no longer seen or touched. They can now hold an image of an object in their minds, and in so doing, a basic cognitive capacity for subsequent cognitive growth and socialization is laid down.

Stage 2 is the **preoperational,** lasting from about two to seven years old. During this phase children learn to see the difference between objects and the symbols used to represent them. Yet, children still have difficulty seeing the world in abstract terms, as is evident by one of Piaget's most famous experiments. In this study, Piaget placed two identical glasses of water in front of five- and six-year-olds and asked them if the amount of water in each glass was the same (they agreed that it was). Then they watched as Piaget took one of the glasses of water and poured it into a taller and thinner glass so that the water level in the glass was much higher, and again he asked them what glass held more water (most said the taller glass). Thus, the ability to hold abstractions— weight, volume, size—is limited for children up to the age of seven. They can symbolically represent their world, but they cannot easily hold and use more abstract symbols.

Stage 3, lasting from seven to around eleven years old, is the **concrete operational** where children learn to use logic and reasoning, but not abstractly. They connect events in terms of cause and effect, and they can understand events from another's point of view (what G. H. Mead termed *role taking*). But they often have difficulty discussing more abstract ideas about cause and effect as well as general types of situations divorced from specific people's responses.

Stage 4 is the **formal operational,** beginning at around twelve or the onset of adolescence. Here children can see the world in abstract terms. They can do more complicated mathematics; they can reason about general issues of morality; they can think about cause and effect in abstract terms; they can ponder types of situations without reference to people they actually know. They thus have the basic abilities to become full adults.

Piaget's emphasis on cognitive development gives us a sense for why the capacities outlined by G. H. Mead proceed in stages. The ability to use gestures and eventually linguistic symbols develops during the sensorimotor stage, as children cope with a world of others. Role taking begins when gestures can be read, but this capacity is limited because in the preoperational children cannot think abstractly. Yet the beginnings of the transition from Mead's *play* to *game* stages occur during this preoperational stage, because there is sufficient cognitive development for children to role-take with multiple others at one time and even concrete remote others (like a child's parents). Mead's view of the final stage, or role taking with the *generalized other*, requires the ability to think more abstractly about generalized perspectives, points of view, and generic situations; and so this ability may begin in the concrete operational stage but must wait for the formal operational to be fully developed.

Sigmund Freud's Model of Repressed Needs

Sigmund Freud (1900, 1938) lived about the same time as Mead, and some of Freud's ideas roughly correspond to Mead's. For example, Freud's famous distinction among the **id, ego,** and **superego** parallels Mead's notions of impulses (Mead, 1938), self and mind, and generalized other (Mead, 1934). For Freud, the human personality is a constant struggle between often antisocial impulses and needs (id) which cannot be expressed in society and internalized cultural traditions and taboos which demand that only certain behaviors be emitted (superego). The ego seeks to reconcile these by channeling impulses in ways that are acceptable to the cultural dictates as the individual has absorbed them. I should emphasize, perhaps, that Freud did not see the id, ego, and superego as "things" but as ongoing *processes* of the human personality.

Human personality development, Freud argued, revolves around a child's growing awareness that he or she must control unacceptable impulses, especially those concerned with sexuality, in light of the ever increasing demands of conscience and superego. Unlike Mead, who saw personality development as relatively harmonious, Freud recognized that unacceptable impulses and needs must be **repressed** and, thereby, pushed below consciousness by ego processes. Yet, when repressed impulses are powerful and when the ego cannot find ways to satisfy them in socially acceptable ways (in terms of the demands of superego processes), behavioral pathologies can result. The ego phases of personality employ many *defense mechanisms* to reconcile id and superego pressures—denial, blame, displacement of anger to acceptable targets, rationalizations for justifying unacceptable behaviors, and so on.

Socialization and the development of personality are thus riddled with conflict: each movement in a growing child's early life involves ever more superego constraints, ever more unacceptable drives and impulses (id), and ever more intense efforts to reconcile this conflict (ego). The unresolved conflicts that emanate from this period often haunt people as they move into adult life.

Erik Erikson's Psychoanalytic Model

Working with a psychoanalytic framework, but making it more sociological, Erik Erikson (1950) argued that socialization is a lifelong process and that it is marked by eight basic stages, each of which represents a challenge which, if met, enhances ego development and a strong sense of ego identity (that is, positive and coherent feelings about oneself during the life course) and which, if unmet, disrupts ego development and identity.

Stage 1 presents the challenge of **trust versus mistrust**. If the infant receives love and nurturance, he will develop a basic trust in others, whereas if these are not forthcoming or if they are inconsistently given, a sense of mistrust will come to dominate the child's responses. Stage 2, which runs to the third year of life, offers the challenge of **autonomy versus doubt** and shame. If the child can experience success in her efforts to learn, she will develop a sense of autonomy, self-control, and self-efficacy, whereas if the child fails in many learning situations, she will reveal self-doubt and experience shame. Stage 3, which corresponds to the four- to six-year-old period, offers the challenge of **initiative versus guilt**. If the child can enjoy success in further exploring his environment and in forming positive relations with peers, he will experience a sense of initiative, self-confidence, and pride, whereas if the child is unsuccessful in these efforts, he will experience a sense of failure, guilt, and shame. Stage 4, which runs from six to thirteen years, revolves around the challenge of **industriousness versus inferiority**. If the child can do well in groups and organizations (like school) outside the family, she comes to feel industrious, whereas if the child does not succeed, then she develops a sense of inferiority. Stage 5, which corresponds to adolescence, the challenge is one of **identity formation versus identity confusion**. If the adolescent can establish relations and enjoy successes, and thereby see himself as a certain type of person with particular skills and attributes, he comes to have a stable identity, whereas if relations and accomplishments are sporadic and punctuated with failures, then the adolescent will experience confusion and instability in his sense of identity about who and what he is. Stage 6, which is the phase of young adulthood (the stage of most of those reading this book), the challenge is **intimacy versus isolation**. If the young adult can develop stable and positive love relationships, then she will have a capacity for intimacies, whereas if such relations cannot be established, then a pervasive sense of loneliness and isolation will ensue. Stage 7, which corresponds to mature adulthood, the challenge is **generativity versus self-absorption and stagnation**. If individuals can feel that they have been active and successful in family, work, and community, they will experience generativity or a feeling that they have contributed to the well-being of others, whereas if these realms have been marked by problems and failings, then a sense of self-absorption in personal problems and/or a feeling of stagnation will emerge. And finally stage 8, which concerns the end of life, presents the challenge of **integrity versus despair**. If older people can find meaning and continuity in their life as they reflect back on it, they feel a sense of integrity, whereas if they cannot break the cycle of self-absorption and fail to contribute to others, they find themselves in a state of despair as the end of life nears.

The Movement through Life

There are other stage models that I could present, but the message is clear: We acquire what is essential to social life: cultural directives (whether viewed as "generalized others," "superego," or some other label), role-playing skills (the role taking and role making), self-conceptions and identity, emotional dispositions, and motivations. We acquire these fairly early, certainly by early adolescence, but depending on *how* we acquire them, they become useful tools or potentially burdensome personal problems. These problems are resolved or aggravated as we grow older, depending upon the emotional baggage that we carry from childhood and the number of positive experiences that we have during adulthood. Table 6-2 highlights the essentials.

Early socialization is very important because once rudimentary neuromotor

TABLE 6.2   Varying Views of the Emergence and Development of Personality

	Key Changes in Personality	Mead's Model
Stages		
Early childhood (ages 1–2)	Awareness of gestures; first capacities to role-take and see oneself as an object; contact with sanctions which personify values, beliefs, and norms; domination by biological motives; some elaboration of primary emotions.	*Preparatory stage:* neuromotor development as a precondition for mind, self, and role taking
Young childhood (ages 3–6)	Language use and increased facility at role taking with not only individuals, but also with remote, multiple, and generalized others; self-images begin to forge a self-conception; awareness and internalization of basic values, some beliefs, and many norms; emergence of socially acquired motives; and manifestation of variations on primary emotions (see middle of Table 6-1).	*Play stage:* role taking with specific others, and first self-images and minded deliberations that take others into account *Game stage:* role taking with multipleothers; increased capacity for minded deliberations; emerging self-conception
Late childhood (ages 7–12)	Increased capacity for language use and role taking with all types of others in ever more complex situations; well-developed role-playing skills; self-conception begins to reveal consistency and stability; a well-developed matrix of acquired motives that channel those which are biologically based; a large inventory of values, beliefs, and norms as well as stocks of knowledge; full range of variation in primary emotions and most combinations of emotions (see bottom of Table 6-1).	*Generalized other:* ability to role-take with cultural perspectives and use these as a basis for self-evaluation and minded deliberations over courses of action
Adolescence (ages 13–17)	Fuller capacity for language use and role taking in all types of situations; a distinctive role-playing style has emerged; self-conception is relatively stable; most socially acquired motives are in place; large inventory of cultural directives, although some beliefs undergo change from earlier childhood; full complement of human emotional states, although the manifestation of emotions reveals a distinctive pattern.	From now on, socialization involves the use of capacities for mind, self, and role taking to participate in, and sustain, patterns of social organization
Young adulthood (ages 19–35)	Most components of personality are well-set; beliefs may change; more knowledge of institutional norms is acquired; increased stocks of knowledge; increased role-playing skills, although style does not change dramatically.	
Mature adulthood (ages 36–65)	Relatively little change in personality components, although beliefs can undergo change; increased role-playing skill and stores of cultural directives are evident; self-conceptions, motives, and emotional responses may change in response to the aging process and to success or failure in key roles.	
Elderly (ages 65–75)	Motives, self-conceptions, beliefs, and emotions may change somewhat in response to shifting roles and coping with the biological process of aging.	
Very Old	Coming to terms with potential death; changes initiated above may accelerate.	

Piaget's Model	Freud's Model	Erikson's Model
Sensorimotor stage: neuromotor development for object recognition	Domination by id impulses and first contact with sanctions and constraints imposed by cultural codes	The first challenge: trust versus mistrust
Preoperational stage: capacity to use symbols to designate objects	First awareness by ego of need to control id impulses in face of cultural constraints; some degree of superego formation, although most constraint is still external	The second challenge of autonomy versus self-doubt and shame over early efforts at learning
	Ego is now actively engaged in effort to reconcile id and superego process; defense mechanism of ego are now developing rapidly if this conflict proves too burdensome	The challenge of initiative and confidence versus guilt and failure in further explorations of the environment
Concrete operational stage: capacity to use logic and reasoning about objects		Meeting the challenge ofindustriousness versus inferiority as participation in groups and organizations increases
Formal operational stage: capacity to reason and think abstractly	A clear pattern of ego reconciliation of id and superego processes is evident; ego-defenses are well in place; and if such defenses are too great, behavioral pthologies are evident	Dealing with the challenge of identity formation versus identity confusion as one records successes or failures in their interactions and dealings with others
	If ego has been successful in resolving conflicts without elaborate ego-defenses, then a stable identity and capacity for personal growth is possible; the opposite is true if ego-defenses are elaborate and persisting conflict between id and superego exists	Meeting the challenge of intimacy versus isolation in terms of the ability to acquire stable and positive love relationships
		The challenge of generativity versus self-absorption and stagnation in response to success or failure in contributing to the well being of others
		The challenge of integrity versus despair as one reflects back on their lives and either breaks or maintains the sense of self-absorption and despair of adulthood

and perceptual abilities develop, young children read gestures, role-take, get their first self-images, experience their first contact with cultural codes, channel their motivational energy, and deal with their own and others' emotions. With further cognitive development through what Jean Piaget called the concrete and formal operational stages, the growing cognitive abilities of young children facilitate the development of mind, self, ego, and superego as these operate to enhance role-playing skills, to develop particular patterns of motivational energy, to internalize and use cultural codes, to crystallize a particular self-conception, and to organize a syndrome of emotional responses. Just how these develop depends upon experiences in interacting with others, perhaps those outlined by Erikson in his review of the challenges with which individuals must cope.

By late adolescence, some stability in the way these components of personality affect one another may have developed, although the conflicts and ego defenses emphasized by Freud can operate to keep a person in an emotionally unsettled state. But for most people, a pattern of stability in role-playing style, in motives, in self, in values and beliefs, and in emotional tendencies emerges; this stability gives the person equanimity and social relations continuity.

STABILITY AND CHANGE IN THE SOCIAL ORDER

One reason for the relative stability of these personality components, once formed, is that these capacities are integrated into one another. Our self-conception is the result of evaluating ourselves in terms of cultural codes; our role-playing style and role taking with others are greatly influenced by our self-conception and cultural codes; our emotions are tied to our interpersonal experiences, motivations, self-evaluations, and cognizance of cultural codes; our motives are guided by cultural codes and emotions, and in turn, our interpretation of these codes and emotional states is influenced by our motives; and finally, our role-playing style is also greatly influenced by our motives and emotions, as we selectively role-take and role-make in efforts to consummate our needs. Our capacities thus constitute a system whose interrelations resist dramatic change.

We all need this integration because, without it, our emotional lives would be tumultuous. Many people do reveal inconsistency in these traits, and they lead miserable lives. For example, their ability to play roles and evaluate themselves positively may fall short of their cultural directives. Or, their role making may be inconsistent with their sense of self. Or, their motives may be inadequate to the cultural expectations that they place on themselves, and as a result they feel and must deal with negative emotions like anger, hurt, and shame. We have all known individuals in such situations, and to a degree we all reveal such incompatibilities.

Some inconsistency in our basic human capacities can be endured, but if the inconsistency is great, change in personality is likely or emotional problems can ensue. The converse is also true: Relative consistency among these capacities is a force that resists change. If self, cultural directives, motives, emotions, and role playing are in reasonable harmony, we are unlikely to change, unless we find ourselves in dramatically new social situations requiring changes. Typically, we seek out and interact in situations where we feel comfortable and experience positive emotions. We attempt what we can achieve. We selectively filter our inconsistent inputs from others. And we avoid situations where our cultural codes are inappropriate. As a consequence, we find comfortable social niches for ourselves and our lives become predictable—even boring. This is the appeal of vacation spots like Las Vegas and Atlantic City; they allow you, if only briefly, to get "out of your rut." But society as a whole depends on such ruts, because as people find niches that are compatible with their personality, social life becomes predictable. Predictability, routine, and perhaps boredom are the binding stuff of social order (J. Turner, 1988).

And once in place, this compatibility between our social niches and personality becomes yet-another force working to maintain the stability of personality so essential for continuity of social order. In societies where people feel out of their niches, their personality is under great strain to change or, as is also the case, people feel pressure to change the "system" to fit their needs, aspirations, self-feelings, and abilities. For example, revolutions in a society often come when a period of "rising expectations" (cultural beliefs that life is getting better and should continue to get better) is followed by a downturn or leveling off in people's social and economic conditions (Davies, 1969). Here, the inconsistency between cultural codes, on the one hand, and people's sense of self-worth, their motivational needs, and role-taking skills, on the other, is sufficient to move them against the social order. When such dislocations between personality and social conditions hit large numbers of people, then change in social structures is as likely as alterations in personality. Social movements, revolt, and protest require a large number of people who cannot find social niches compatible with their human capacities (R. Turner and Killian, 1978; Smelser, 1963). Just as consistency among our traits and harmony between these traits and the social conditions are the stuff of social order, inconsistency and lack of harmony are the impetus behind social change like revolutions.

SUMMARY

1. Socialization is a particular type of interaction—one which shapes the nature of human personality and, in turn, human behavior, interaction, and participation in society. Without socialization, neither humans nor society would be possible.
2. In general terms, the basic components or capacities of personality relevant for understanding human behavior in society can be labeled (a) motives, (b) role-playing skills and style, (c) cultural directives, (d) self-conceptions, and (e) emotions.
3. As a general set of guidelines, interactions which are initiated early and which are long-term, in primary groups, with significant others will have the most influence in how these components of personality are forged and developed.
4. These components have been variously conceptualized by different thinkers, most of whom see socialization as occurring in stages of development marked by important points of transformation. Depending on the interest and focus of the analyst, these transformations vary: (a) For George Herbert Mead, they revolve around the development of ever more ability at role taking, as this leads to the formation of abilities for

mind and self; (b) for Jean Piaget, these capacities are ultimately based upon cognitive development revolving around object recognition, concrete symbolization, and abstract symbolization; (c) for Sigmund Freud, these components of personality will reflect the ongoing struggle of ego to reconcile id and superego processes; and (d) for Erik Erikson, these components will be forged out of a long series of challenges that each individual faces in the course of a lifetime.

5. Personality tends to stabilize, to some degree. This fact gives each person some equanimity in his or her life, while facilitating the maintenance of social order.

KEY TERMS

autonomy versus doubt   The second stage in Erik Erikson's development scheme, running to the third year of a child's life, during which a child's degree of success in learning gives it either a sense of autonomy or doubt and shame.

concrete operational stage   The third stage of cognitive development in Jean Piaget's scheme, lasting from seven to eleven years of age, during which children learn to use logic and reasoning, although abilities to employ abstract reasoning remain limited.

cultural directives   The profile of values, beliefs, norms, and other symbol systems that individuals use in guiding their behaviors and interactions.

ego   Sigmund Freud's term to denote the process of reconciling id impulses with superego constraints, often forcing the use of repression and defense mechanisms.

emotions   The moods or states of individuals revolving around, and involving elaborations of, such primary states as anger, fear, sadness, happiness, and surprise.

formal operational stage   The fourth and last stage of a child's cognitive development in J. Piaget's scheme, lasting from twelve years of age to adolescence, during which the ability to use abstract representations of the world develops.

game stage   George Herbert Mead's second stage in the socialization of children, during which they develop the capacity to role-take with several others simultaneously, to read their perspective, to evaluate oneself from this perspective, and to cooperate in groups of others.

generalized other   G. H. Mead's term denoting the community of attitudes or perspective of social groupings. The capacity to role-take with varieties of generalized others marks the third and final stage of childhood development because it is now possible to assume broader cultural perspectives and use these for self-evaluation and regulation of behavior.

generativity versus self-absorption and stagnation   The seventh stage in E. Erikson's developmental scheme, lasting through mature adulthood, during which success in family, work, and community lead to a feeling of being able to give to others, or if not, to self-absorption and stagnation in life.

id   S. Freud's term for impulses and needs, many of which cannot be expressed in society because they violate taboos and conventions.

identity formation versus identity confusion   The fifth stage in E. Erikson's developmental scheme, lasting for the duration of adolescence, during which the ability to establish relations and enjoy success leads to a sense of identity or, if such relations do not emerge, to confusion about who and what one is.

industriousness versus inferiority   The fourth stage in E. Erikson's developmental scheme, running from six to thirteen years, during which the degree of success in groups and projects provides a sense of industriousness or failure.

initiative versus guilt   Third stage in E. Erikson's developmental scheme, lasting from four to six years of age, during which success in exploring the environment and in forming positive relations provides a sense of initiative or failure, shame, and guilt.

integrity versus despair   The final stage in E. Erikson's developmental scheme, corresponding to old age, during which individuals see meaning and continuity in their lives, or experience despair.

intimacy versus isolation   The sixth stage in E. Erikson's developmental scheme, lasting through young adulthood, during which stable and positive relations produce a capacity for intimacy.

motives/motivation   An individual's level of energy, and nature of energy, devoted to occupying positions and playing roles in society.

play stage   G. H. Mead's first critical stage in the socialization of children, during which they acquire the ability to use, and interpret, gestures with at least one other person.

preoperational stage   The second stage of a child's cognitive development in J. Piaget's scheme, lasting from two to seven years of age, during which children learn to use symbols to denote objects, although the capacity for use of abstract symbols remains limited.

repressed/repression   S. Freud's term denoting the process by which unacceptable impulses (id) are pushed below consciousness by ego processes seeking to conform to superego demands.

role-playing skills   An individual's ability and capacity for role taking and role making in interaction with others.

self-conception   An individual's view of himself or herself as a certain type of person with particular attributes and, hence, deserving of certain kinds of responses from others.

sensorimotor stage   The first stage of a child's cognitive development in J. Piaget's scheme, lasting to about two years of age, during which children learn to retain images of objects in their environment.

socialization   Those interactions instilling in individuals the basic components of personality that are necessary for their participation in society.

superego   S. Freud's term denoting the morality of society as it has been absorbed by an individual.

trust versus mistrust   The first stage in E. Erikson's developmental scheme, lasting to two years of age, during which a child's experiences with love and nurturance provide it with a sense of trust or mistrust of others.

CHAPTER 7

Groups and Organizations

The group, composed of just a few people in interaction, is the basic unit of human organization. But as the scale of society has increased, groups are linked together to form more complex organizations—such as factories, bureaucracies, and offices. Much of our daily life is spent in groups; indeed, try to imagine anytime where you are not in a group or thinking about people in one. The workers pictured above constitute a group, but as the enclose of their setting illustrates, they are also part of a larger organizational structure in which they work. It is this lodging of groups in larger, more inclusive structures that enables humans to construct elaborate and complex societies.

When we occupy a position, play a role, experience emotions, evaluate ourselves, and invoke cultural symbols, we do so in a social structure. The most elemental structure is the **group,** consisting of just a few positions and considerable face-to-face interaction among those playing roles and taking cognizance of relevant cultural symbols. In turn, groups are sometimes lodged in **organizations,** composed of many different kinds of positions coordinated to accomplish certain goals. This coupling of groups and organizations is not inevitable, however. Family and friendship groups often operate outside of a more inclusive organization; and much activity in organizations—for example, as a client or customer—does not usually involve group memberships. Yet, as populations get larger and as the scale of social life increases, organizations begin to penetrate more and more of our daily lives. In the process, organizations create new groups and, at times, they gobble up many of our old groups. We may not like this trend, and many seek to escape it by forming new groups outside the tentacles of organizations; but still, we implicitly recognize that without organizational structures, virtually all aspects of our lives—jobs and income, education, health, safety—would not be possible or viable. Thus, since so much of our daily existence occurs inside groups and organizations, their analysis is a topic worthy of further inquiry.

GROUPS

The Effects of Group Size

Groups are often labeled **primary** and **secondary**. This distinction follows from the effects of increasing the number of members in a group (Hare, 1992). For, as more people are added to a setting, it becomes increasingly difficult to know everyone or to interact directly with them. The result is that secondary groups become less cohesive, less intimate; they become more formal with explicit norms; and they become difficult to sustain for long periods of time (imagine, for instance, being stuck in a large sociology class all day). Such groups are thus created for some relatively short-term purpose, such as giving a lecture or watching a concert. In contrast, when groups are smaller, they have the potential for greater intimacy and cohesion because their members can interact face-to-face and get to know one another. Intimacy is not inevitable, however, especially if members of a small group do not spend much time together. Hence, a primary group emerges when rates of interaction and feelings of intimacy have been given time to develop—as is the case for your family and close friendship cliques.

Many groups are somewhere between primary and secondary—work groups, friends in a dorm or sorority, or a small class. These are relatively small groups, and one can often sense the movement to a more primary pattern. But equally often, this movement does not go all the way for lack of duration or because the activities of the group (such as competition for promotions, for grades, for popularity, and the like) get in the way—a fact that conflict theories always emphasize. We have no name for these in-between groups, except their designation as groups. But the effects of size destroy the possibility of a great intimacy, and even when size does not get in the way, the nature of the larger organization in which the group is lodged frequently inhibits intimacy, closeness, and cohesion.

The Power of Groups

The more primary a group, the greater its capacity to influence us along many dimensions. One line of influence is our self-conception because we see ourselves reflected in the gestures of others who are important to us. Another is our values and beliefs because we tend to take on the cultural symbols of groups in which our sense of self and identity is implanted. Still another is our role behavior and motivations because we conform to the norms of primary groups and because we take on their values and beliefs and, as a consequence, adjust our general role-playing style and demeanor. Yet another line of influence is our feelings and emotions because our emotional states will tend to ebb and flow with our experiences with those who have become important to us.

It is perhaps disturbing to recognize that groups have this kind of power—especially in a society where cultural values emphasize self-reliance, self-determination, rugged individualism, and personal autonomy. But if we are honest with ourselves, the point is obvious: Self-conception, values and beliefs, moods and emotions, motives, demeanor and role-playing style are dramatically influenced by group affiliations. Take any group in which you feel some closeness to its members and think about your self-feelings, emotional states, demeanor, beliefs, motivations, and values. These will be greatly shaped by your membership in this group, although your past group memberships—family and close friends, for instance—will also have exerted and, as we will see shortly, still exert considerable power over you. Thus, we are not interpersonal chameleons; we do not change every aspect of our being with each new group. Our present group affiliations will have to overcome the effects of our past affiliations or, as is more often the case, blend into these effects of past group attachments.

Group Dynamics

Since groups are so much a part of our lives, we should understand some of the basic processes occurring in groups. Let me briefly discuss the most important.

Leadership

Groups which must get something done tend to develop two types of leaders, what Robert Bales (1950) termed **task leaders** and **socioemotional leaders.** At times, of course, the task leader is appointed by virtue of the larger authority system (a teacher's assistant, for example, if you are in a sociology course with discussion sections). Task leaders seek to direct others in the group and to coordinate their activities in order to achieve the group's goal. But task leaders also create tensions, and so, socioemotional leaders emerge to ease the tension—some with a joke, a wry comment, or soothing words when feathers get ruffled. At times, a particularly adept leader can play both roles, being a task master and, at the same time, able to ease tensions and keep emotions under control. This process of leadership formation becomes readily apparent, once we are looking for it. Observe what occurs in a study group, a dorm meeting, a work meeting, or any situation where the group is trying to get something done; chances are this division of leadership along task and socioemotional lines will be very apparent.

Decision Making

We might think that leaders would make bolder decisions than the group as a whole, but in fact, collective decisions by the group tend to be more decisive than those by an individual (Kogan and Wallach, 1964; Janis, 1972). The reasons for this phenomena are twofold: First, when an individual alone must decide, fears about making a mistake or being wrong invite caution, whereas a group decision deflects responsibility to more individuals, thereby making them bolder; second, in cohesive groups, members often withhold criticism of one another, and as a result, they may be less critical of bold suggestions, thus leading the group to act more decisively.

Indeed, this latter process often leads to what has been termed **groupthink** (Janis, 1972, 1982) where individuals reinforce one another so much that they lose touch with reality and become too bold or grandiose. For example, many of Adolf Hitler's mistakes in World War II can, I suspect, be seen in groupthink terms, as close advisors reinforced one another's pronouncements to the point that strategically bad decisions were made. Much of America's continued involvement in the Vietnam war was, no doubt, the result of groupthink processes among top-level military brass and advisors to the President; they simply lost touch with the reality of the war and the strength of the Vietcong. Many of the disastrous decisions made in American corporations during the 1970s and 1980s were, no doubt, driven by groupthink rather than the external realities of an ever more competitive world economic system.

Whether bold or timid, decisions within a group tend to go through a sequence of events. Initially, information gathering occurs; next, evaluation and assessment ensue; tensions begin to rise as members line up on one side or the other; a decision is then made; and finally, efforts to restore harmony by socioemotional leaders become prominent. If you have ever been in a decision-making group, you will have noticed the sense of euphoria, joking, and other tension-release processes at the end of a meeting. Such socioemotional work smooths over tensions and creates a more pleasant atmosphere if the group must meet again.

Cohesiveness and Solidarity

Groups vary considerably in how much attachment members have to one another and to the group. In cohesive groups, where people feel solidarity, members are more secure, and they are more likely to conform to the norms of the group. What conditions produce these effects (Shotola, 1992; Kellerman, 1981)? One is small size because solidarity is created by high rates of face-to-face interaction which are only possible with smaller numbers (Collins, 1975). Another is a sense of threat from the outside, for people band together when they feel besieged (Simmel, 1956). Yet another force is the similarity in backgrounds of members, for it is far easier to develop strong attachments to those who are like you. And a final force promoting solidarity is a high rate of positive sanctioning (as opposed to negative sanctions) for conformity to group norms, for if people experience rewards for conformity, they develop emotional attachments to those offering these rewards (Coleman, 1991).

Think about any group in which you experienced solidarity, and it will be evident that these forces are at work. An athletic team, a fraternity or sorority, a close set of friendships, or a family all tend to reveal at least some of these forces, and as a consequence, they reveal cohesion and solidarity. Such groups have the most power over us because our membership in them is so rewarding.

Expectation States

When members of a group play their roles in a particular way, these performances create expectations that future role behaviors will also be enacted in this manner (Berger et al., 1974). We can feel these expectation states by the looks and anticipation of others or by their disappointment if we do not live up to their expectations. This pressure pushes us into continuity in role performances, and it is one of the great powers of groups over us.

But we do more than create expectations inside the group as a result of our actions and interactions; we always bring with us to a group characteristics from outside (Berger et al., 1977; Berger et al., 1980; Webster and Foschi, 1988). These characteristics often generate expectations about what a person can, or cannot, do in the group, as well as how much prestige and influence a person should have in the group (Berger et al., 1985; Berger et al., 1989). These are sometimes termed our **diffuse status characteristics** and include such features as age, sex, race/ethnicity, level of education, appearance, perceived intelligence, and other highly visible characteristics which members of the group can use to guide their responses. As people bring these external features to group settings, they set up expectation states. For example, men and women have very different expectations leveled on them in groups, as do older people, minorities, and others who can be clearly distinguished. If you doubt this, examine a group of individuals with different diffuse status characteristics and then ask what your reaction would be if the women started to play roles like the men, or vice versa, or if any of the participants began to act out of character. Your reaction should reveal your expectation states for these individuals.

Referencing

As I mentioned in Chapter 4 on social structure, groups serve as a frame of reference, or **reference group,** for us, providing a perspective for orienting our thoughts and actions. This process operates not just for a group in which we are presently interacting but also for groups in which we are not interacting, or even for groups in which we have never been members. In fact, most of the time we employ the norms, values, beliefs, and other cultural symbols of several groups simultaneously in a situation. We are, for example, aware of the norms and other expectations of the group we are in, but at the same time, we may also invoke the symbols of other groups, such as our family, close friends, or groups to which we aspire.

To understand our behavior, then, it becomes necessary to know the configuration of reference groups we are invoking (Merton and Rossi, 1957; Kelley, 1958). For, our large brains and corresponding cognitive abilities (Piaget, 1948) allow us to role-take with others far removed from the present, using our attachments or hopes for attachments to these others as guidelines for our conduct (Mead, 1934; Shibutani, 1955). Thus, reference group processes greatly expand the nature of membership in a group and the processes by which groups exert influence upon us. If you take any group situation, and ask yourself which groups are serving as a frame of reference, you will be surprised, I think, that more than immediate others are exerting pressure on you. The power of distant reference groups, then, is always there, subtly pushing on thoughts and behaviors.

In sum, we can view groups as the most elemental social structure. It is their immediacy that gives them such power. Yet, groups are limited by several constraints, because they create what the German sociologist Niklas Luhmann (1982) has called "bottlenecks." These bottlenecks stem from the fact that, in a face-to-face group, only one topic can be addressed, and only one person can speak at a time. If you doubt this, just watch what happens in a group where several people try to talk all at once, each introducing a new topic; chaos is the usual result, until someone reins everyone in in ways that limit the topic and that allow speakers to take turns. The necessity for sequential interaction in a small groups means that there are severe restrictions on how much groups can accomplish by themselves and on how fast they can proceed in performing tasks. As long as tasks are simple, groups are sufficient for organizing people. But, as the scale of tasks magnifies, how are the inherent limitations of groups to be overcome? The answer resides in connecting groups together in some way so that each performs a limited range of tasks which are coordinated with those of other groups. What emerges from such efforts are **complex organizations**.

COMPLEX ORGANIZATIONS

Early Complex Organizations

Early human populations organized themselves in a very simple way: a few nuclear families (that is, mother, father, and children) moving about in a band, gathering and hunting. Most activity in these simple societies was conducted by individuals alone, or in the family unit. And so it was for most of human history (Lenski, Lenski, and Nolan, 1991; Maryanski and Turner, 1992). For reasons that are not fully understood, however, people began to settle down around 10,000 to 12,000 years ago; and as they did so their numbers increased greatly. Small groups cohabiting in small bands were no longer sufficient to organize the increased numbers of people, and so, nuclear kinship units were connected together to form extended units (clusters of nuclear families related by blood or marriage) which, in turn, were grouped into lineages (clusters of extended families linked by blood or marriage ties). Then, as the scale of society increased, lineages were used to build clans (clusters of lineages) which could, if necessary, be linked together into moieties (clusters of clans).

You can easily see what humans were doing: They were taking their basic group unit—the nuclear family of parents and their offspring—and creating a more complex pattern of social organization. Using blood and marriage ties in this way, it is possible to organize very large numbers of people—perhaps as many as a few million but more typically a few thousand. Yet, at some point in history new kinds of complex organizations were created in order to deal with larger numbers of people and more complex tasks; for there are limits to organizing people by blood and marriage ties. The outcome of this limitation was for humans to begin building **formal organizations**, linking together nonkinship groups in hierarchies of authority.

Formal Organizations

Max Weber's Ideal Type Portrayal

The German sociologist, Max Weber (1922), who was one of the founders of modern sociology, constructed an "ideal type" of *rational* bureaucracies. He recognized, of course, that this ideal type was a kind of fiction, but he felt that it could serve as a common yardstick for measuring different types of formal organizations. Here is what Weber saw as the underlying features of rational bureaucracies: First, all bureaucracies have an explicit division of labor, with each position or office having a delimited set of responsibilities. Second, the norms governing behaviors for any position, as well as for relations between positions, are explicit, clear, and codified in writing. Third, different positions are ordered hierarchically, with those positions and offices higher in the authority ranks supervising those below them. Fourth, role enactment by incumbents in positions is emotionally neutral and disinterested, with individuals repressing emotions and passions as they play their assigned roles. Fifth, people are assigned to positions for their technical competence rather than personal considerations. Sixth, positions and offices are not owned by their incumbents but by the larger organization. And seventh, employment constitutes a career in which individuals move up the hierarchy in terms of some combination of merit and seniority.

Sounds a bit cold and impersonal when stated this way; and indeed Weber worried about this aspect of bureaucracy and its affects on social life in modern societies where bureaucratization was a clear trend. Weber probably worried too much because people usually find a way to make life more bearable and pleasant with bureaucratic structures (Maryanski and Turner, 1992). But still, given the formality and impersonality of bureaucratic structures, why did humans create them? Why "cage" oneself, to use Weber's metaphor, in such a world of hierarchy, constraint, and impersonality?

The Emergence of Bureaucracy

Functional theorizing provides perhaps the best answer. When populations get large *and* begin to engage in large-scale tasks, such as public works, military defense or conquest, and internal political administration and control, needs or requisites for more complex organizational structures emerge. How could the great pyramids in Egypt be built? How could Roman legions conquer most of Europe and Northern Africa, and much of the Near East? How can thousands of workers be organized in corporations? By fits and starts, populations confronted with large-scale tasks gradually developed organizations that, with time, approximated Weber's ideal type. War was perhaps the biggest impetus as large armies were mobilized, but large-scale public works and governance of vast territories and big populations were also crucial. Two innovations were particularly critical along the way (Weber, 1922): (1) the development of money and (2) the expansion of markets. For, once workers can be paid by a reliable currency (and we must remember that this was, and is today in many countries, a big obstacle to development) and thereby sell their labor in a market and use their income in other markets to buy goods which they could no longer produce for themselves, the stage is set for bureaucracies—*if* there is a need for large-scale mobilizations of people for various tasks.

The late Talcott Parsons (1966, 1971), the preeminent functional theorist of this century, argued that societal evolution and development depended upon the creation of bureaucratic structures. At first these structures did not resemble Weber's ideal type because family ties and other personal considerations often outweighed technical competence in the selection and promotion of individuals. Until this obstacle to "rationality" could be overcome, full modernization was not possible. Indeed, in much of the world today, many critical aspects of Weber's typology cannot be realized, with the result that societies remain arrested at a premodern phase.

Types of Formal Organizations

Amitai Etzioni (1961, 1964) once provided a useful typology of formal organizations in modern societies. One type is **voluntary organizations** in which members can freely enter and leave the organization. Members in such organizations are not paid, although when the organization gets large, there is a salaried professional staff which is organized bureaucratically. In America, voluntary organizations are highly visible, pulling members into their fold for a wide variety of reasons—for example, as a way to organize leisure time activities, as a means for pursuing a social or political cause, as a special interest group (National Rifle Association and Sierra Club, for instance), as an adjunct to another organization (such as the PTA for schools), as a way to facilitate communication and perhaps economic/political action among those in a social category (such as the NAACP or the National Organization for Women), as a means for bestowing charity (the United Way, a skid-row mission), and so on for many other needs, interests, and goals.

Another organizational type in modern societies is the **coercive organization** which separates members from the society and tightly regiments their activities under the ever present threat of physical coercion. Prisoners, patients in mental hospitals, or draftees in an army are all part of a coercive organization whose professional staff is organized bureaucratically. Such organizations are usually very hierarchical, with clear lines of authority for regulating activity and, if necessary, administering coercion.

A third major type of organization is the **utilitarian organization** where people enter the bureaucratic structure for some practical reason and where, in rational choice theory's terms, they have calculated the costs of entering with the rewards to be received. Private corporations, universities, unions, and government agencies are the most common type; and in a modern society, they dominate our lives. Indeed, try to think of daily life without job, retail stores, education, or government services.

This typology of three organizational types—voluntary, coercive, and utilitarian—is a kind of ideal type itself. There are often elements of the other types in any one. For example, elementary and secondary schools are coercive in the sense that we were required by law to attend, but they are increasingly utilitarian for as one goes up the educational ladder, people calculate the benefits of more education. Or, to take another example, voluntary organizations—say, some religious sect—can become highly coercive toward their members once they have joined. And, there can be an element of voluntarism and utilitarianism in coercive organizations, as is the case when one joins the armed services or checks themselves into a mental hospital. Etzioni's typology, then, just gives us a rough sense for variations in the kinds of bureaucratic organizations that are used to organize members in an organization. We might now ask: What accounts for the prevalence of any one type, or different forms of a given type? An answer to this question resides in the ecology of organizations.

The Ecology of Complex Organizations

Ecological analysis emphasizes that organizations exist in a resource niche—a particular set of clients, members, customers, government subsidies, or any resource that enables the organization to survive. Organizations are also viewed as potentially being in competition with each other for the resources available in a niche. Indeed, whole *populations* of organizations, much like species in the biological world, emerge to exploit resource niches and then die or at least decline in numbers when that niche is overexploited (Hannan and Freeman, 1977, 1984, 1986, 1987, 1988, 1989). For example, the number of labor unions and membership in them grew when workers in America opposed the abusive practices of many companies (the pool of disgruntled workers being the resource niche of labor unions), but as labor-management relations became less confrontational and as the economy shifted to a more white-collar profile, the resource niche of labor unions shrank, with the result that the number of unions and the percentage of workers who belong to unions decreased in America, and dramatically so. The same processes are seen, from an ecological view, to operate for all types of organizations.

An important part of ecological analysis is the notion of **niche density,** which is the total number of organizations in a niche. When density is high—that is, when there are many organizations trying to secure resources of a certain kind—competition in the niche increases, and some organizations "die" or are folded into more successful organizations. For example, at one time there were many different labor unions which competed so intensely that, eventually, some died and most merged into large confederations—the AFL and CIO. Take another example, such as retail stores; here, the competition among large department stores has been intense, with many disappearing or moving to a new resource niche. J. C. Penney, for instance, used to sell everything from lawn mowers, furniture, and appliances to underwear and dresses, but it found that it could not compete effectively with Sears, Kmart, Walmart, and big discount stores (including many generalized retailers which "died" in the competition, such as W. T. Grant and Zodys). So, it moved to a more upscale niche, abandoning general-purpose retailing for an emphasis on middle-level clothing and accessories.

Thus, competition increases with density, with some organizations surviving and others dying or being forced to seek resources in different niches. This process occurs not just with retail stores, but other types of organizations as well. For example, potential members are a resource niche for voluntary organizations; and as their density increases with respect to members with a certain level of income, education, and other characteristics, some will have to move to a new niche consisting of members with different levels of income, education, and other features (McPherson, 1981, 1983, 1988, 1990). The same is true of agencies in government which seek resources from tax revenues; if too many agencies compete for resources of a given kind—say, those dealing with health—then some will die, or be consolidated with others.

The total level or amount of resources in a niche is also important. If resources increase, then competition will decline until more organizations move into the niche and increase its density. If resources shrink, then competition will be intensified and some will die or move to new niches. A good example is the defense industry in America after the collapse of the Soviet Union. The total level of resources for military hardware has decreased, forcing many companies into bankruptcy or into new niches (geared to nonmilitary domestic production).

Ecological analysis thus views a society, and the world economic system for that matter, as a series of resource niches consisting of money, members, clients, customers, or any resource that can sustain an organization. High levels of resources in these niches allow new organizations to be born, until their density increases competition, causing some to die or seek new niches. Hence, the distribution of organizational types in a society reflects the number of resource niches, the density in these niches, the level of competition for resources in a given niche, and the rates of death for organizations.

The Internal Dynamics of Organizations

Ecological analysis tells us much about why different types of organizations come into existence, but it does not explain with any detail what goes on *inside* organizations. Whether or not organizations survive is, to a great extent, tied to how they operate. We should, therefore, review some of the internal dynamics of organizations.

The Informal System

As symbolic interactionist theories would emphasize, people construct their social relations, even when there are severe bureaucratic constraints. Humans are not robots or cogs in cold, impersonal bureaucratic machines; they create social relations alongside and often in defiance of the formal structure of positions, rules, and authority. This process of generating a set of more personal and informal relations is often termed the **informal system** (Roethlisberger and Dickson, 1939).

At times the informal system works to the advantage of the organizations, as is the case when employees bypass cumbersome rules which impede efficiency. At other times, the informal system works against organizational functioning by creating networks of informal ties which keep people from doing their jobs. For example, we have all encountered people in organizations who seem too busy chatting or gossiping with one another to pay much attention to their jobs, but perhaps equally often we have found employees who use their informal networks in an organization to assist us and to cut through a lot of "red tape."

The structure of an organization, then, is much more than the positions and lines of authority on an organization chart. Superimposed on this formal structure are informal relations which supplement and, at times, supplant the formal system of positions, norms, and authority. To appreciate how an organization is actually structured and operates thus requires understanding of both its formal and informal systems.

Authority and Conflict

Conflict theories stress the significance of inequality in generating tensions and confrontations (Collins, 1975). Since organizations are hierarchies of authority, there should always be conflict because power is distributed unequally. In fact, the informal system is often fueled by resentments of people in lower-level positions against those with authority (Dahrendorf, 1959). In a sense, the informal system becomes a way to preserve one's personal dignity (and self-conception), while at the same time enabling one to resist quietly or get back at people in higher-level positions.

Differences in authority also create conflicts over "turf" within an organization. Those who have certain responsibilities and authority resist giving them up to those who might take them over. Indeed, a great deal of infighting occurs in organizations as people and officers make claims to authority, only to find themselves in conflict with others making similar claims. We have all probably been caught in such a battle, as different people assert their "rights" to deal our problems; or we may have found ourselves in a situation where one person has encroached on another's job and has been reprimanded for this encroachment. One can just feel the tension in such situations, indicating that positions and formal rules do not always eliminate conflict. Indeed, they often aggravate it;

and so, it is in the nature of a hierarchy that conflict should take up a considerable amount of the time and emotional energy of those working in an organization.

Tasks and Authority

The nature of an organization's tasks and the kinds of technology it must use greatly influence the nature of its structure, especially the levels of hierarchy (Perrow, 1967, 1986). As a general rule, when tasks involve machines and workers, hierarchy increases because workers and machines need to be tightly coordinated. Yet, too much supervision can create resentments of workers against their supervisors: this was the case with the automobile industry in America until better efforts were made—as in the Honda and Saturn automobile plants—to decrease levels of supervision *and* better coordinate machines and workers. Conversely, the more that tasks require the coordination of skilled workers to produce a unit item (like a custom yacht) as opposed to a mass-produced item (like a small car), the more informal is the coordination of workers and the less is the need for supervision. The greater quality of such "craft" production is the motivation behind the effort by larger mass-manufacturing firms to use "teams" of workers who informally work together without being closely watched by a supervisor to produce units (like transmissions or engines for cars) which are then inserted onto the assembly line.

When service is the task of an organization rather than a physical good or product, then hierarchy is reduced because moment-by-moment supervision is less essential. Instead, supervision involves the review of paper and information after it is produced, just to make sure work was done correctly. As a result, authority hierarchies are, to a degree, reduced.

Control and Authority

In addition to its tasks, the type of organization—whether a voluntary, utilitarian, or coercive type—greatly determines how control of its members is achieved (Collins, 1975). If an organization is a utilitarian one, using only wages and salaries to motivate workers, then considerable supervision is necessary to ensure that workers "earn their money." However, if the commitments of workers come from a sense of professionalism, supervision is less necessary because "pride" in work is a good substitute for authority and supervision. Voluntary organizations, as well as work involving a high degree of skill and training (medicine, law, university teaching, etc.), can usually dispense with much supervision because of worker commitments to their jobs. Efforts to couple less skilled wage labor with a sense of professional commitments to norms indicating what constitutes a "good job" have not always been successful, as the struggles in the last decades of the U.S. auto industry have illustrated, but if it can be done, less hierarchy and supervision are necessary.

In coercive organizations, however, considerable hierarchy and supervision are always essential to ensure that people are doing what they should, because in such organizations—such as prisons and mental hospitals—conformity to rules must be forced, with the threat of coercion. Such organizations are never very effective, although armies can become efficient "fighting machines." In the case of an effective army, though, it is the building of informal commitments to norms and the pride of the soldiers (not the authority hierarchy or threat of a court martial) which make them effective.

Organizational Culture

The nature of tasks, authority, and control greatly influences the culture of an organization, or the symbol systems (values, beliefs, and norms) guiding role behavior (Smircich, 1983; Pondy, 1983). If workers resent supervision and are motivated primarily by wages, then the culture of an organization will emphasize "just doing one's job" without great emotion or commitment to the organization. In contrast, if commitments to the goals of an organization motivate workers, the organizational culture will stress worker efforts above and beyond their specific tasks. Or, if members simply try to avoid coercion by figures of authority, then it is likely that two cultures will emerge, an authoritarian one guiding the efforts of those who supervise to get conformity to their dictates and a subversive one emphasizing doing just enough publicly to avoid coercion but a great deal privately to subvert the efforts of an organization. Prisons are a good example of this last type of culture where the guards and administration have an entirely different culture than the inmates who have a vast system of informal practices, norms, and beliefs that defy all authority.

The culture of an organization has become a prominent issue because of foreign competition to American corporations. U.S. manufacturing firms, for example, have a long history of antagonistic relations with workers, fostering a culture of "just doing one's job" among workers who have no commitments to the organization and who, as a result, perform shoddy work. Changing this culture has proved difficult, although American manufacturing corporations must do so if they are to survive. Yet, rather than change the way it does business, a corporation often just exports its jobs overseas to foreign factories where workers are more docile. In contrast, among high-technology companies, American corporate structure is most effective because it creates strong commitments of workers to the goals of the company, thereby securing extra effort and high-quality work while reducing the need for supervision and too many levels of authority.

Parkinson's Law

Workers always try to appear busy in order to justify their jobs, even if such efforts are merely wasting time (Parkinson, 1957). This situation becomes a source of vast inefficiency for an organization because it must often pay people to do unnecessary work. But, there is always the dilemma of how to determine what is necessary and unnecessary, especially when workers will go to great lengths to justify what they are doing. Thus, Parkinson's law states that "work expands to the time available for its completion"; and this fact poses a dilemma of determining *how much* time is needed for various tasks. The operation of Parkinson's law is often what makes large bureaucracies—whether governmental or corporate—so cumbersome, inefficient, and wasteful; and yet, it is always difficult to define *which* positions are unessential and whose jobs should be eliminated. This dilemma genders a great deal of political rhetoric about "eliminating waste," but just *where* and *how* to do so is always more difficult to do than the rhetorical promises of politicians and corporate managers.

The "Peter Principle"

Another source of inefficiency in organizations stems from the tendency of organizations to promote people to "their level of incompetence" (Peter and Hull, 1969). If workers do a good job at one level, they are usually promoted to a more demanding (and, of course, better-paying) job; at some point in this process, workers may be moved to a position whose demands exceed their competence. Yet, rarely are people demoted back to jobs within their realm of competence. If this process occurs again and again across a wide range of workers, the organization can become loaded with incompetents. By itself, this creates inefficiency, but oftentimes, organizations have to hire new people to "work around" or "assist" the incompetent—a practice which only burdens the organization even more.

Ritualism

Because formal organizations have explicit rules guiding worker performance, they tend to encourage rigid conformity to these rules, even when such conformity subverts the goals of the organization. Such "ritualists" tend to be older employees who have done their job, day in and day out, in a certain way, and as a result they become so accustomed to their routines that they lose sight of the goals of their organization and blindly conform to the rules (Merton, 1968). They go "by the book," revealing a trained incapacity for flexibility and innovation; and if the informal system in an organization is dominated by such ritualists, then the organization becomes inefficient, ineffective, and, if you have to deal with it, maddening and frustrating.

Alienation

Many jobs are, let's face it, repetitive and boring. They do not need or require our creativity or innovation. We stay in the job for the money, and little else. Such work is alienating; and bureaucratic organizations are by their nature structures in which a great deal of routine, repetitive work must be done—whether shuffling paper or sitting in front of a monitor on a computer. It is often difficult to make work less alienating because of its very nature; and thus a problem for all large-scale complex organizations is to keep too many from being disaffected, putting in just enough effort to pass the grade but little else.

The Changing Structure of Organizations

The organizations of modern life are changing in some dramatic ways. Part of the reason for this is technological; another part is due to efforts to overcome the problems and dilemmas discussed above; and still another force is the quickening and intensifying competition of a world economic system. On the technological side, often in response to lower-wage labor in other parts of the world, the application of knowledge has created industrial robots which can now do much of the dull, repetitive work in manufacturing; as a result, organizations can give manual workers potentially more interesting jobs, although much labor will remain dull and repetitive; or as has often been the case, organizations simply eliminate workers' jobs. Over the last twenty years, new applications of technological knowledge have created new kinds of jobs revolving around information and servicing; and as a result, much of the labor force sits in front of a computer terminal or wears a phone set. These jobs are, however, often as boring as the manufacturing jobs in factories that they have replaced; and in America, they tend to pay less than older types of manufacturing jobs. Moreover, as fewer workers are needed in manufacturing, sales and services jobs have also increased, but their organization is often tedious. A sales clerk in a department store or a worker in a fast-food outlet is probably stuck in a job that is as routine as those in factories but without the pay of the older industrial jobs. Thus, it is not clear that technological changes have created organizations that are dramatically less bureaucratic than those in the past. At the high-technology end—computer programing, engineering, corporate research and development, medicine and biotechnology, university education and research, and the like—organizations clearly provide more interesting and challenging work; and to the extent that more high-technology sales and service jobs in organizations allow for initiative and creativity, they too are probably more gratifying. But the impetus to change from technology as this is fueled by intense global competition has not, as of yet, changed the nature of much work for most people.

Efforts in a competitive world economy to restructure organizations—both corporate and governmental—have been as important a source of organizational change as technology. Better-quality goods and services, delivered quickly and inexpensively, require that work be reorganized in ways that increase commitments to the organization while reducing excess levels of authority and the problems that such authority engenders—alienation, ritualism, and conflicts. Thus, organizations of the future will seek to create a cohesive culture emphasizing pride in work in order to reduce direct supervision and to encourage innovation and initiative. Whether or not this will occur on a broad scale is difficult to know, but there are limitations on how far these trends can go because people will still have to work with machines and provide menial services.

SUMMARY

1. Much behavior and interaction occurs within a social structure, or organized networks of positions, norms, and roles.
2. The most basic type of social structure is the group which, depending on its size, can range from primary to secondary. Primary groups are more intimate and cohesive, involving more conformity to norms, than secondary groups.
3. Groups have power over people, constraining and constricting the images of self, the values and beliefs, the emotions, the motives, and role-playing style of their participants.

4. Groups are highly dynamic structures, revealing a number of basic processes: (a) leadership and the emergence of task and socioemotional leaders, (b) decision making and development of consensus and groupthink, (c) cohesiveness and solidarity as these emerge from high rates of interaction, similar backgrounds of members, and external sources of threat, (d) expectation states or the use of external characteristics of members or past performances to anticipate what individuals are to do in the group, and (e) referencing or the use of outside groupings as a frame of reference for guiding thoughts and responses in a particular situation.

5. As the scale of society gets larger and the tasks more complex, groups are connected together to create organizations which reveal formal roles, a clear division of labor, hierarchies of authority, control of emotions, technical competence of incumbents, organizational control of offices, and career movements up the hierarchy.

6. There are various types of organizations: (a) voluntary organizations, where people freely join to pursue certain goals and interests, (b) coercive organizations, where individuals are physically forced to remain separated from the rest of the population, and (c) utilitarian organizations, where members rationally calculate the costs and benefits of being a member.

7. One key dynamic of organizations is ecological: organizations exist in a resource environment and must often compete with other organizations for resources leading to patterns of growth and decline in various types of organizations in a society.

8. Another set of dynamics is internal, revolving around a series of processes: (a) development of informal ties within the formal hierarchy, (b) conflict stemming from inequality in the distribution of authority, (c) task activities as these reflect the technologies and products produced, (d) control and authority revolving around patterns of external supervision and worker commitments, (e) cultural processes in which values, beliefs, and norms create a particular "ethos" in how work is to be done, (f) "Parkinson's law," or the expansion of work to fill the time allocated, (g) "Peter's principle," or the promotion of workers to their level of incompetence, (h) ritualism or the performance of work without consideration of the goals of an organization, and (i) alienation arising from dull and routine work tasks.

9. The nature of organizations has, in recent decades, changed enormously under the impact of technology and world economic competition, causing the loss of many manufacturing jobs and the increase in lower-paying sales and service jobs.

KEY TERMS

coercive organizations   Those bureaucratic structures in which members are forced to remain isolated from the society.

complex organizations   Social structures which combine more elementary groups in order to form larger and more inclusive units with specific goals and purposes.

diffuse status characteristics   Those features reflecting an array or set of status positions occupied by an individual which an individual carries into a group and which serve as a basis for members' responses.

formal organizations   Those goal-directed structures in which status positions are organized in offices and hierarchies, in which names are codified and explicit, and in which roles are played dispassionately.

groups   Small social structures composed of only a few different status positions, small numbers of incumbents, relatively dense ties among positions, and clear cultural expectations about role behaviors.

groupthink   The process in group decision making in which members reinforce one another to the point that the decision does not bear a close relationship to the realities of the situation.

informal system   The system of ties that people develop within the formal structure of an organization; such ties often supplant, but always supplement, formal lines of authority.

niche density   In organizational ecology, the total number of organizations of a given type seeking the same or similar resources.

organizations   Goal-directed social structures revealing hierarchies of positions, linked together by authority and clear norms, with increasing numbers of incumbents at the lower levels of the hierarchy.

primary groups   Small face-to-face groups in which people feel more involved, more intimate, and more cohesive.

reference group   Perspectives of groups, both those in which one is participating and those which are remote, that are used as a frame of reference for self-evaluation and for guiding conduct.

secondary groups   Large groups where face-to-face interaction among all members is not possible, resulting in a corresponding decrease in intimacy, cohesiveness, and duration.

socioemotional leader   An individual who seeks to smooth out tensions that arise as the members of the group seek to realize the group's goals.

task leader   An individual in a group who directs and coordinates other members' activities in order to accomplish the group's goals.

utilitarian organizations   Those bureaucratic structures which people enter on the basis of calculations of costs and benefits.

voluntary organizations   Those bureaucratic structures which people may freely enter and leave.

CHAPTER 8

Inequalities: Class, Ethnicity, and Gender

Some people get more than others in societies—more money, more prestige, more power, more life, and more of everything that humans value. Such inequalities create divisions in society—divisions with respect to age, sex, wealth, power, and other resources. Those at the top in these divisions want to keep their advantage and privilege; those at the bottom want more and must exist in a state of constant anger and frustration. Indeed, imagine what the poor person above must be thinking; is she dreaming of what might be, or is she angry over what she cannot have. Inequality is thus a tension-producing machine in human societies. It is the source of energy behind social movements, protests, riots, and revolutions. Societies can, for a time, keep a lid on these disruptive forces, but if severe inequalities persist, tension and conflict will punctuate and, at times, dominate social life.

115

When some social categories of individuals consistently get more of what is valued in a society than other categories, a system of inequality exists. For, valued resources—power, material wealth, prestige and honor, health, educational credentials, and other resources—are rarely distributed equally. Some get more than others, and their respective shares of resources help maintain their distinctiveness and visibility as a category. Men and women, for example, are "different" not only because of their biology, but also because of their varying shares of resources which magnify or at least confirm their biological differences. Ethnic subpopulations are "different" not just because of their cultural traditions but also because of their varying slices of the resource pie. Unskilled manual workers are distinct from skilled white-collar workers, not just because of the nature of their work, but also because they receive different amounts of critical resources.

You are, of course, acutely aware of these divisions in a society. You sense the frustration and anger of those ethnic groups who do not have much, and if you are part of a different group, you avoid places where you will stand out. If you are a woman, you experience quiet anger at the advantages men have in the labor market and houses of power; and if you are a man, you know that change in the distribution of resources is occurring and you will have to share jobs, income, prestige, and authority more equally with women. And when you encounter individuals of a different social class, there is a tension beneath the pleasantries stemming from the fact that one of you has more than the other. Inequalities, then, are an important dynamic in any society, and hence, they are worth understanding in more detail.

CLASS STRATIFICATION

What Is Stratification?

Stratification is the general term used to describe a society which (1) distributes income, power, prestige, and other valued resources to its members unequally; and (2) creates distinctive classes of members who are culturally, behaviorally, and organizationally different (J. Turner, 1984a). The *degree* of stratification is determined by *how* unequally resources are distributed, *how* distinctive social classes are, *how* much mobility occurs between classes, and *how* permanent classes are. A **caste system** like that in India is one where there is a high degree of stratification because people are born into a class or "caste" which receives vastly different shares of resources than other castes and from which it is difficult, if not impossible, to move. An **open-class system,** like those in the western democracies, is one where class boundaries are fuzzy and changeable and where some mobility from class to class is possible. Indeed, as a member of a society with a more open class system, you are now working to improve the class position given to you by your family, or you are trying to hang onto a class position. And you work hard in school and worry about your performance, because you know educational credentials will determine, in large part, your job, income, prestige, and power in American society. The stakes are high, and this is why colleges and universities are tense and serious places beneath the surface frivolity.

Analyzing Stratification

Because stratification is such a central dynamic in human societies, it has been a topic of theoretical concern since sociology's beginnings. Let us see, therefore, how sociologists have sought to conceptualize stratification, starting with the conflict theories of Karl Marx and Max Weber.

Karl Marx on Stratification

Marx presented a simple, and perhaps too simple, conflict theory of stratification (Marx and Engels, 1848). In Marx's eye, those who own the means of production in a society—that is, the resources and capital used to produce goods and commodities—are able to control the house of power, cultural symbols, work activities, and lifestyles of others. There is, then, in all societies a basic tension between owners and nonowners—whether peasants and lord, or capitalist and workers. Because those who own or control the means of production have power, they are able to manipulate cultural symbols, creating ideologies justifying their power and privileges while negating the claims of others to property and power. And if need be, they can physically coerce and repress those who challenge their control. Yet, Marx argued that the basic **conflict of interests** between those with and without property and power would inevitably create the conditions for a revolution by those who had little control of their work activities, negligible property, and virtually no power.

How was a conflict of interest to become an open conflict which would redistribute resources and alter the nature of the class system (and, in Marx's naive utopia, do away with all class distinctions)? For Marx, the answer was this: Those who owned and controlled the means of production would act in ways to "sow the seeds of their own destruction" by creating conditions that enabled the less advantaged to, first of all, become aware of their own interests in redistributing property and power and, secondly, to become politically mobilized to change the system (Marx and Engels, 1848). For example, in his analysis of capitalism, Marx (1867) viewed the owners of the means of production—**the bourgeoisie**—as driven by competition with one another in the pursuit of profits and as acting in ways that would raise the consciousness of the workers—**the proletariat**—thereby enabling the workers to see their true interests clearly despite the veil of ideology propagated by capitalists and to mobilize power to realize their interests in changing society. For example, the bourgeoisie were driven by competition to concentrate labor in towns and factories, to make them alienated appendages to machines, to disrupt their routines and lives through layoffs, and to force them to live in squalor and filth by keeping wages as low as possible (Marx and Engels, 1848). Under these conditions, workers could communicate their grievances and begin to break through the ideologies of the bourgeoisie (indeed, Karl Marx saw his and Frederick Engels' *The Communist Manifesto* as the decisive demystification of bourgeoisie ideology). Then, once workers were aware of their true interests, they could organize and take power from the capitalists.

Actual events never quite went as Marx predicted, but we should be careful in rejecting all of Marx's ideas. For he had some basic insights into stratification: Stratification is to be understood in terms of economic organization, especially the relation of people to the means of production. Those who own and control property, especially the means of production, have power to control the lives of others in disadvantaged classes. Class stratification inexorably generates conflicts of interests that become the focal point for conflicts which redistribute money and property. The great revolution by the proletariat did not sweep the industrial world, and where it did occur, it was initiated by peasants more than the urban proletariat and it hardly created a classless society. Yet, there is a fundamental set of insights in Marx's analysis that should not be lost.

Max Weber on Stratification

Weber (1922) was a lifetime critic of Marx, but he too proposed a conflict theory of stratification. The main difference between their respective theories was that Weber saw stratification as multidimensional. Inequality revolves around three dimensions: classes, status groups, and parties. **Classes** are created by people's relationship to markets—for jobs and income, for purchasing of consumer goods, and for creating a level of material well-being. This notion is similar to Marx's ideas about classes being determined by the relation of their members to the means of production, but it is different in its recognition that many distinct classes can exist and that ownership of property is only one basis for generating a social class. Society does not, therefore, inevitably polarize into the "haves" and "have-nots"; it can reveal a more textured and varied class system. **Parties** are the organization of power, but unlike Marx, these do not bear a direct relationship to property and the means of production. Members of a society can have power without great property, and vice versa; and power is often used for purposes other than the goals of the propertied classes (for example, the military and its elite members are rarely owners of the means of production or holders of great amounts of property; the same is often true of influential politicians). **Status groups** are social categories and network ties among those who share similar cultural symbols, tastes, outlooks and lifestyles; and who, as a result, can command a certain level of deference, honor, and prestige. Although status groups may reflect their members' shares of property or power, they are an independent basis of stratification (for example, elite college professors often have group affiliations with powerful and propertied people, but they themselves rarely have great amounts of property or power). Thus for Weber, stratification involves more than hierarchies of classes reflecting the economic order; stratification also revolves around hierarchies of power and status group membership.

Yet, when analyzing conflict, Weber's theory is similar to Marx's (J. Turner, 1991, 1993b). There may be constant conflicts within and between different classes, parties, and status groups, but when great societywide conflicts emerge, they are the result of (1) a high correlation of membership in classes, parties, and status groups (that is, elites in one are also elites in the other two), (2) great discontinuity in the resources of those who are high and low in these consolidated hierarchies, and (3) little chance or opportunity for mobility to higher positions in these three hierarchies. When all these conditions prevail, a **charismatic leader** can emerge to articulate a revolutionary ideology and to mobilize the downtrodden in the pursuit of conflict and redistribution of property, power, and prestige. Here Weber sounds like Marx, but with some important qualifications. First, high correlation of membership in classes, status groups, and parties is not inevitable, as Marx would have asserted, nor does great discontinuity of resource shares or low rates of mobility always occur. Second, even when all conditions are present—high correlation of membership, great discontinuity, and low mobility—a revolution does not necessarily follow. For, chance and fortuity determine whether a charismatic leader can emerge and be successful.

The Functions of Stratification

Marx and Weber both saw stratification as creating tensions and, at least potentially, producing conflict between those with various shares of resources. There is, however, another way to look at stratification: as an integrative force in society. For Kingsley Davis and Wilbert Moore (1945), as well as other functionalists (Parsons, 1953), inequalities can be related to critical functional needs or requisites in society.

The famous, and often-criticized, "Davis-Moore hypothesis" argues that if a position in a society is functionally important *and* difficult to fill because of the skills required, it will receive greater resources—money, power and influence, and prestige (Davis and Moore, 1945). Both conditions—functional importance and difficulty in filling the position—must be present. For example, the position of garbage collector is functionally important (just imagine a world without garbage collectors) but unskilled and easy to fill; therefore, it will not receive a great many resources. In contrast, a doctor is both a functionally important and high-skill position, and hence according to the Davis-Moore hypothesis, it must be highly rewarded. Inequality is, therefore, a way of motivating qualified people to undergo the training and sacrifice necessary to do functionally important and skilled work in a society.

Functional theories have, however, been resoundingly criticized for an obvious flaw: They make the existing inequalities in a society seem correct and legitimate, as if those with resources always deserve them because of their skill and functional importance. In fact, critics argue, people gain resources by luck, abuse of power, corruption, tradition, and other processes that have little to do with functional importance or talent (Tumin, 1953, 1967).

Evolutionary Theories

Some more recent theories have tried to understand stratification in a more long term historical perspective, going back to hunters and gatherers and then moving forward to ever more complex societies. Gerhard Lenski's (1966) theory argues that stratification is the result of increasing economic production which creates a surplus of wealth beyond subsistence needs. As surplus grows, the ability to support nonproductive individuals increases; some are able to mobilize power to usurp this surplus, thereby creating privilege for themselves. Thus, privilege and power are connected: those with wealth can mobilize power to enhance their wealth; and on the other side of this equation, those with power can use it to extract surplus to gain wealth and prestige. But with industrialization, this long-term historical process is reversed, at least to a degree. For those without privilege begin to mobilize and oppose the abusive use of power and the hording of economic surplus (much as Marx would have predicted); and they force the organization of power to be more democratic, often without a great revolution (as Marx would not have predicted). The result is for some redistribution of wealth through a progressive tax system which places higher taxes on the wealthy (or at least tries to do so, except the wealthy always try to weasel out of this burden). These revenues are then used to provide education, health, welfare, and job opportunities for the less privileged. But this process only goes so far because people fight against taxes and manipulate public opinion to convince the less privileged that high taxes are not in their best interests.

If you think about your own hostility or that of your parents to taxes, you can see how successful this manipulation has been. It is one of the reasons that the United States has the most inequality in the modern industrial world *and* the lowest tax rates of all industrial countries. We can see the results of these facts by now exploring stratification in America in more detail.

Stratification in America: A Brief Look

Let us recall our definition of stratification: the unequal distribution of valued resources and the creation of social classes or categories of people who, by virtue of their shares of these resources, reveal distinctive cultural symbols, demeanor, tastes, and lifestyles. And let us also remember that there are degrees of stratification in terms of how unequal resources are distributed, how distinctive are class categories, how permanent these categories are, and how much mobility between them occurs. With these considerations in mind, we can construct a brief picture of stratification in America.

Inequality in Resources

While "money isn't everything," a cynic might conclude that "what money isn't, it can usually buy." While status group membership and the mobilization of power can operate somewhat independently of money, a rough indicator of the degree of inequality in a society is its **wealth distribution**. In the United States, this distribution (1) takes all people with money or property that can be converted into money, (2) rank-orders all persons from highest to lowest, (3) divides this ranking into equal-size statistical categories—usually the top 20 percent, the second 20 percent, the third 20 percent, the fourth 20 percent, and the bottom 20 percent—and (4) then asks the question: How much of all the total wealth in a society does each of these ranked 20 percent categories, or wealth fifths as they are usually called, have? Calculating these figures is complicated and not done very often, but the answer frequently comes as a shock to Americans. As Table 8-1 reports, the top 20 percent of holders of wealth have most of

TABLE 8-1. Wealth Inequality in America: What Percentage of All Wealth Did Each Wealth Fifth Receive?

Wealth Fifths	1962	1983
Top fifth	76.0%	74.7%
Second fifth	15.5%	14.2%
Third fifth	6.2%	6.9%
Fourth fifth	2.1%	3.0%
Bottom fifth	0.2%	0.1%

Source: 1962 data from Turner and Starnes (1976); 1963 data from Wolff (1987). Both sources rely upon data supplied by the Federal Reserve Board.

all wealth in a society—cash, stocks, bonds, houses, cars, jewelry, or anything that can be converted into money; the next highest 20 percent, or the second fifth, has some of the wealth; the third fifth somewhat less; the fourth fifth very little; and the bottom fifth virtually none. Thus, 20 perent of Americans have most of the wealth; the rest have little wealth—perhaps a house (which is mortgaged) and a pension fund if one is lucky. And, as a recent government report on wealth distribution documents (Federal Reserve System, 1992), the top 1 percent of wealth holders has a net worth greater than 90 percent of the population combined. We have many of the props of wealth—cars, stereos, phones, TVs, and perhaps a home of our own. But in reality, at least half of all Americans have little; they can borrow on their future wages to buy comfort, but this does not lead to the accumulation of much wealth.

Income distribution is somewhat more equal, as can be seen in Table 8-2. The top 20 percent control almost half of all the income in a given year (which is then used to accumulate wealth year after year). The second income fifth receives about a quarter of all income, and the rest goes to the remaining 60 percent in the proportions listed in Table 8-2. These data are easier to collect (right off IRS tax forms) and, hence, are reported every year (U.S. Bureau of the Census, 1991). The last decade has seen the largest jump in the share of the top 20 percent in the history of the government reporting of these figures (J. Turner, 1993a). Inequality thus increased in America during the 1980s and early 1990s.

TABLE 8-2. Income Inequality in America: What Percentage of All Income Did Each Income Fifth Receive?

Income Fifths	1960	1970	1980	1990
Top fifth	42.0%	43.3%	44.2%	46.6%
Second fifth	23.6%	23.5%	24.8%	24.0%
Third fifth	17.6%	17.4%	16.8%	15.9%
Fourth fifth	12.0%	10.8%	10.2%	9.6%
Bottom fifth	4.9%	4.1%	4.1%	3.9%

Source: U.S. Bureau of the Census, 1983, 1991.

Prestige is also a valued resource; and like any resource, it too is distributed unequally. In Table 8-3, the prestige rankings in the United States of various occupations is reported. As is evident, occupations receiving high income and requiring high levels of education are the most prestigious. Those in such positions can thus command deference and honor from others.

Power is another valued resource because it gives some the ability to control, or at least to influence, the actions of others. Yet power is a very illusive resource because those who have it often use it subtly. Moreover, power is often lodged in organizations, such as unions, corporations, and interest groups; and as a consequence, the actual hold on power is more ambiguous. Does the chief executive and top lieutenants have more power than, for example, the clients of the organization? Thus, we cannot construct a table outlining the distribution of power, as is possible for income and prestige. Power is much more elusive, and finding it has been the subject of great controversy in sociology (Alford and Friedland, 1985). Some argue that there is an elite controlling much power (Mills, 1956; Domhoff, 1967, 1978) and using this power to influence major decisions. Others argue for more pluralism and see power as less concentrated and dispersed across many diverse individuals and organizations (Dahl, 1961). Such controversy exists because, once again, power is often hidden or diffused in ways that make it difficult to know who has how much power. But in general terms, those who have wealth, who control large organizations, and who are represented by large organizations will have power (Turner and Starnes, 1976; Turner and Musick, 1985).

Class Formation

How many classes are there in America—that is, people who share a given slice of the money and prestige pie and who, thereby, reveal common attributes?

TABLE 8-3. Differences in Prestige Scores for Selected Occupations

Rankings of Selected Occupations	Prestige Score
Physician	82
Professor	78
Judge or lawyer	76
Dentist	74
Minister	69
Secondary school teacher	63
Librarian	55
Bank teller	49
Machinist	48
Plumber	41
Carpenter	40
Waiter	20
Maid	18

Source: National Opinion Research Center (NORC), 1982.

How clear are their boundaries? How much mobility from class to class occurs in a lifetime, or between generations? And how enduring are the classes? Some of the answers to these questions are easier than others to provide. Let us take them in order.

How many classes are there? An answer depends upon how fine-tuned we want to be. A rough approximation would distinguish the following: elite (wealthy, powerful, and prestigious), highly affluent (accumulated wealth and prestige from high-income professions or businesses), upper-middle white-collar (high-salaried professionals or successful businesspersons who have accumulated some wealth), solid middle white-collar class (respectable income, some wealth in pension fund and home equity), lower white-collar middle class (modest income, few accumulated assets, perhaps home equity), upper blue-collar class (respectable income, some wealth in pension funds and home equity), middle blue-collar (modest income, few accumulated assets), and impoverished (low income, unemployed, unemployable with no assets). As an important note, this last class of impoverished people is the largest of the industrial world—numbering 35 to 50 million people and engulfing 13 to 14 percent of the American population (J. Turner, 1993a; Ropers, 1991; Sherraden, 1991).

The differences in these classes revolve around several factors. One is whether one works with their hands (blue-collar) or does nonmanual work (white-collar); this factor is very important, and we can always see rather easily the differences in white- and blue-collar people's demeanor, lifestyles, and other characteristics. Another dividing point is the level of income and the capacity to accumulate assets from one's income; people who have assets act and think differently than those who do not. And the less money you have, the greater is the difference between you and those with some assets. A final point of division is how much power and prestige you have, as a result of your income or the nature of your work. People with power and prestige act and think differently than those without these assets.

These class lines are fuzzy, indicating that there is no hard divide or discontinuity between them. This observation answers the second question posed

TABLE 8-4. Percentage of the American Population Officially Defined as Poor, 1960–1990

Year	Poor
1960	22.2%
1965	17.3%
1970	12.6%
1975	12.3%
1980	13.0%
1985	14.0%
1988	13.1%
1990	13.5%

Source: U.S. Bureau of the Census, 1991.

above. Turning to the third question, there is some mobility between these classes, but not great leaps. Statistically, you are most likely to be mobile to the next adjacent class—either up or down. If you start in the lower middle, you might expect to make it to the solid middle, or move to an upper blue-collar job. If you start in the blue-collar classes, you can move with the acquisition of education credentials to the middle white-collar classes. But if the economy is in recession and if the government cuts programs back, then you are likely to stay where you started or even fall back down the stratification ladder—as many have done in the early 1990s in America. Most Americans remain in one social class during their entire lifetime; and if they are mobile, they do not move very far—despite a lot of hoopla about those who have gone from rags to riches.

An answer to our final question posed above emphasizes that classes in America are not completely stable because of broader changes in the economy that are altering the profile of jobs from manufacturing to service. Thus, the proportion of people engaged in blue-collar work has decreased, whereas the percentage of people in white-collar work has increased. Equally significant, there has been a dramatic increase in low-wage service jobs (fast-food employees, for instance). Elite classes remain fairly stable, with some fluctuations in the composition of the highly affluent and upper-middle classes. As you read these words you probably seek to stay in these last two classes, or make it into them. If you started nearby, you have a chance (if you get the right credentials, and a lot of them). But, the changes in the economy that increase the number of low-wage service and clerical jobs, while decreasing the higher-wage skilled and semiskilled blue-collar jobs, place you in a frightful situation: Much of the white-collar work available is not high-wage or highly skilled; and hence, realizing a more privileged class standing will be difficult and involve lots of competition.

ETHNIC STRATIFICATION

Interwoven with class stratification is ethnic inequality. That is, some people of a particular ethnic background are disproportionately likely to be members of particular social classes. And, since much of this differential placement of ethnic subpopulations is into lower social classes, it is not surprising that class conflict can become supercharged by ethnic antagonisms between those who have and those who want resources. You can sense this fact every day, as you move about and deal with people from different ethnic backgrounds. You may see yourself as a tolerant and fair person, but you cannot help but feel a subtle tension between you and members of other ethnic populations. This tension is not just the result of cultural differences (say, languages and beliefs), variations in behavior (speech styles, ways of carrying oneself), and organizational differences (diverse patterns of group affiliation); it is also the result of differences in money, power, and prestige that become associated with these cultural, behavioral, and organizational differences. If you are low in these differences because of your ethnic background, you may show a subtle hostility and carry a chip on your shoulder;

if you are high, you sense this hostility and perhaps you deny a distant sense of fear. Since so much of our lives in American society involves ethnic relationships, and conflicts, we need to know more about this phenomenon.

Race and Ethnicity

The term **race** is used to denote what are perceived as biological differences: skin color and facial configurations, for example. But we mean more than just biology; for if we did not, we would make racial distinctions between the tall and short races, the gray- and brown-eyed races, and similar biological differences. In fact, we should probably never use the term "racial group," because it has no scientific basis. Where, for example, is the cutoff line in terms of biology between being "black" or "white," "Asian" or "Caucasian"?

When we use the term "race," then, we really mean **ethnicity,** or those behavioral, cultural, and organizational differences that allow us to categorize members of a population as distinctive (Turner and Aguirre, 1994). Yet, when ethnic distinctions are associated with superficial biological features like skin color or eye configuration, they become convenient "markers" of ethnicity. And they often become a basis for escalated prejudice and discrimination which, in turn, increase *ethnic stratification*, or the disproportionate allocation of various ethnic populations to particular social classes.

Prejudice and Discrimination

Prejudices are beliefs about members of an ethnic group who are perceived to possess undesirable qualities (Allport, 1954, 1979). Think of ethnic epithets, and the connotations they carry, as clear indicators of prejudicial beliefs—"nigger," "wop," "pollack," "beaner," "chink," "buddha head," "spick," "coon," and so it goes. Prejudicial beliefs are, therefore, a prominent part of American culture, as well as the cultures of other societies.

Discrimination is the differential treatment of others because of their ethnicity, and most particularly, it is the denial of members of an ethnic population equal access to valued resources—housing, jobs, education, income, power, and prestige. Prejudice often fuels discrimination; and acts of discrimination are frequently justified by prejudices. Yet, a one-to-one relation between prejudice and discrimination is often hard to discern. For example, in a classic study during the height of prejudice against Asians in the period before World War II (La Piere, 1934), hotel and motel owners were asked if they would rent to an "Asian," and a high proportion indicated that they would not; yet, when an Asian couple was sent to a hotel, they were given a room. This kind of disjuncture between prejudice and discrimination led Robert Merton (1949) to distinguish among (1) the "all-weather liberal" who is unprejudiced and does not discriminate, (2) the "reluctant liberal" who is unprejudiced but in response to social pressures will discriminate, (3) the "timid bigot" who is prejudiced but in response to social pressures will not discriminate, and (4) the "all-weather bigot" who is prejudiced and discriminates. In America, there has been clear movement over the last forty years away from the all weather bigot toward the "all-weather liberal," but the "reluctant liberal" and "timid bigot" may still make up the majority of the population.

You might now ask yourself: Which one am I? The answer is probably more complicated than Merton's typology. You may hold some prejudices, but try not to discriminate because of them. And you may inadvertently discriminate without prejudice or because of unacknowledged prejudices.

While individual prejudice and single acts of discrimination are interesting to observe and think about, especially with respect to our own thoughts and needs, what is sociologically more interesting is **institutionalized discrimination** in which there is a consistent and pervasive pattern of discrimination, legitimated by cultural beliefs or prejudices, and built into the structures of a society. At times, institutionalized discrimination can be explicit and obvious, as has been the case for blacks during and after slavery, for here there was a clear denial of access to citizenship rights like voting, jobs, education, health, and housing which was legitimated by highly prejudicial beliefs. The Civil Rights Movement and the Civil Rights Acts of the 1960s were the culmination of efforts to break down such institutionalized discrimination, but today such patterns persist in less obvious form. That is, institutionalized discrimination is more subtle and complicated. For example, blacks suffer today in crime-ridden and drug-infested ghettos because of the past legacy of discrimination, but they are now blamed by many whites (a prejudice) for not escaping these conditions; moreover, they are seen as getting preferential treatment for jobs through affirmative action which has led to pressures for reducing affirmative action and other policies designed to help blacks. The end result is that many blacks remain poor, subject to prejudices against the "lazy, welfare-dependent poor" who do not deserve assistance; such prejudices are then used to legitimate cutbacks in formal assistance while encouraging informal discrimination. You may hold these more subtle and complicated prejudices, but you should recognize them for what they are. Thus, the critical point here is that institutionalized discrimination has become more complex, and is a pervasive feature of American society and, for that matter, *all* societies with distinct ethnic groups.

The Dynamics of Ethnic Stratification

The central dynamic of ethnic stratification is, therefore, discrimination by one or more ethnic groups against targeted ethnic groups. But this simple observation begs several important questions: How does one ethnic population come to have the power to discriminate? And why do its members want to discriminate? The answer to these questions forces us to examine the interrelation among a number of crucial forces (J. Turner, 1986b; Turner and Aguirre, 1994): (1) the *relative resources* of ethnic groups, (2) the *identifiability* of ethnic groups as targets of discrimination, (3) the *level* and *type* of discrimination, (4) the *intensity* of prejudicial beliefs, and (5) the *degree of threat* posed by one ethnic group to another. Let me examine each of these forces.

Relative Resources

Ethnic groups possess different amounts of resources—money, power, prestige, work skills, and educational credentials. These differences are, of course, often the result of past discrimination, and so once a group is down, it is often hard for its members to overcome the effects of past discrimination—as is the case for many African Americans and Native Americans today. Differences in resource levels are also due to other forces—for example, the history of an ethnic population in another society and the demographic profile of those members who migrate to another society.

In general terms, the more resources an ethnic group has, the better able it is to fight off the full effects of discriminatory efforts by a more dominant group. Thus, when blacks came to America as slaves, they had few resources to fend off their continued enslavement, whereas today many Asian and Indian immigrants come with money, entrepreneurial skills, pooled family labor, credit associations among fellow ethnics, and educational credentials which are used to achieve access to valued resources, even in the face of discrimination. In being able to secure access to resources—say, professional jobs and successful family businesses—they can eventually come to acquire other resources, such as housing in integrated neighborhoods and community political power (Turner and Bonacich, 1980). In contrast, those who have few financial, educational, or political resources are less able to begin this process of ratcheting up their resources. Many African Americans and Native Americans in the United States are in this plight of lacking an initial resource base with which to overcome the legacy of past discrimination as well as the persistence of subtle, informal discrimination in the present (Turner, Singleton, and Musick, 1984).

Identifiability

To be a target of discrimination, you must be visible and distinctive in some way. If members of an ethnic population look different in terms of surface biological features, such as skin color and facial features, they are easier targets of discrimination. Thus, it is easier to target dark skinned and Asian ethnics than other ethnic populations. White ethnics in America, for example, had a great advantage over other ethnics because they could learn English and blend into the population within one or two generations. In contrast, African Americans stand out, thereby making them easy victims of discrimination.

Cultural characteristics such as language and religious beliefs, behavioral demeanor, and organization into distinctive kinds of groups can also make people targets, especially if associated with some physical distinctiveness. Thus, Mexican Americans in the southwest, Puerto Ricans in the northeast, and to a lesser extent, Cubans in Florida can become targets of discrimination because of language and perhaps Latin cultural demeanor, in addition to some distinctiveness in their skin color.

Once victimized by discrimination, biological distinctiveness is maintained because of intraethnic marriage and reproduction, while distinctive cultural, behavioral, and organizational patterns are sustained by high rates of intraethnic interaction and ghettoization in particular neighborhoods and by a general defensiveness against a society in which one does not feel welcome. The ironic result, of course, is for ethnics to remain easily identifiable and, hence, targets of further discrimination. This cycle can become truly vicious, especially for ethnics who have few resources other than their common plight with which to fight off the consequences of discrimination. It should not be surprising, therefore, that those ethnics in America who are easily identified, who lost most of their financial resources or never had them to begin with, who had their cultural heritage stripped away, and who possess few organizational structures in which to take refuge have been the most likely to remain in this vicious cycle.

The Level and Type of Discrimination

The level of discrimination has varied enormously in the history of human societies, from genocide where ethnics are killed off through expulsion and, when these extreme forms of discrimination are not possible, through segregation in a ghetto and a narrow range of jobs. Jews in Germany, Native Americans in the United States, and Indian populations in meso-America have all suffered from efforts at genocide. And more recently, the "ethnic cleansing" policies of Serbians in what used to be Yugoslavia is yet another example of an effort at genocide in a territory. More typical, however, is discrimination involving physical segregation and economic isolation of a subpopulation. Such is possible, of course, only as long as members of a population remain distinctive and identifiable.

One type of ethnic minority is lower class. Here disproportionate numbers of a population are isolated in slum housing tracts and pushed into the lowest-paying occupations such that they are in the poverty classes of a society. African Americans have suffered this fate in the United States. Another type of ethnic minority created by discrimination is the *middleman minority* where members are segregated but, at the same time, allowed to occupy a narrow range of entrepreneurial and professional economic positions which give them some affluence. For example, Jews in feudal and early modern Europe often occupied high positions in banking and finance; and many Asian immigrants in America today have moved into small-business niches.

What determines which type of a minority an ethnic population will become? One important condition is the resources—money, entrepreneurial know-how, educational credentials—that a population can mobilize. When ethnics have some resources, they can more readily move into intermediary minority positions and live a more middle-class lifestyle. But resources are not the only factor; another is the absolute size of an ethnic population. A small minority with resources can more easily find intermediary niches than a large one, for the simple reason that there are not enough small-business positions for a large population. A large ethnic population will, therefore, be pushed to lower classes, especially if their resources are limited and, as a result, their ability to fight off discrimination is low. African Americans have suffered this fate: They are too large a group to fill middleman minority positions, and they have insufficient resources to overcome discrimination (Turner and Bonacich, 1980). Indeed, what often happens is that members of a large minority who can mobilize resources—

say, educational credentials—move into middle-class positions, leaving behind their fellow ethnics. For example, many blacks in America have made dramatic strides in moving to the middle-classes in the post-Civil Rights era, but the fate of the vast majority of blacks in the lower classes has remained the same, or worsened over the last twenty-five years. Black America itself is thus divided by large class differences (Wilson, 1987).

Degree of Threat

Whether large or small, why would one group bother to discriminate? Are humans just brutes who do not like others who look and act differently? Part of the answer to this second question may be yes, but a more significant part is that discrimination is stoked up by fears, whether real or imagined. If one ethnic population sees itself threatened by another, it will discriminate. The basis of the threat can vary—loss of jobs or high wages because others will work for less, loss of cultural traditions, loss of political power, loss of neighborhoods and housing, and so on. When a population feels economically, socially, and politically threatened, it discriminates, and the more threatened it feels, the more intense and severe is the discrimination.

A large, identifiable ethnic group is more threatening than a small one because it can "overrun" jobs, schools, politics, and housing. African Americans were kept enslaved probably beyond the economic viability of the plantation system because their numbers came close to equaling those of whites in the deep south (Singleton and Turner, 1975); hence, white blue-collar and farm workers feared for their jobs, politicians their power, and all their "southern way of life." In the late nineteenth century and early parts of this century, each wave of new white immigrants to America threatened the previous wave who had just begun to feel secure; hence, Germans discriminated against the Irish, the Irish against Italians, Italians against Poles, and all white ethnics against blacks when the latter began to migrate to the northeast in the early decades of this century. Today, immigrating Mexican Americans have similarly generated fears among Anglos as their numbers have grown. These kinds of fears about the effects of an ethnic group on another may or may not be accurate; but more often than not, they are inaccurate, and they are often fueled by political leaders for their specific purposes—as did Hitler with Jews in Germany or as certain American politicians have done with respect to blacks and Hispanics in America.

Prejudicial Beliefs

When fearful, people erect negative stereotypes about those who pose or, more typically, are perceived to pose a threat (Feagin, 1991). The greater the fear, the more negative the stereotypes. Blacks in America, for example, have had to endure incredibly vicious stereotypes as less than human, as childlike, as Sambos, as sexually aggressive, as welfare cheaters, and so on. To a lesser degree, each wave of European immigrants suffered from negative stereotypes—dumb Pollacks, greasy and dishonest Italians, corrupt and drunken Irish, and so on—but they all had the advantage over blacks of being white and, hence, less identifiable once they shed some of their European culture.

Negative stereotypes escalate fears which, in turn, justify more intense discrimination. Thus, cultural beliefs are an important dynamic because they codify a group's sense of threat and, at the same time, arouse further this sense of threat, while legitimating acts of discrimination. Of course, other beliefs can operate as a counter force against prejudicial beliefs, as has been the case in America where beliefs in equality have always posed a challenge to prejudicial beliefs and negative stereotypes of ethnics.

Ethnic Discrimination in America

We now have the conceptual tools for analyzing ethnic stratification in America. Those most disadvantaged ethnics—that is, those disproportionately in the lower and poverty classes—have been the most biologically distinct, the lowest in most crucial resources, the victims of the most intense discrimination, the most threatening because of their large size, and the subjects of the most negative stereotypes and prejudices. The more advantaged ethnics, or those who have been able to move into the mainstream, have been less identifiable, relatively higher in resources, victims of less intense discrimination because of their small size and/or their resources (which could be used to fight discrimination), less threatening, and subject only to moderate (but not vicious) stereotyping.

Take any ethnic population in America—Poles, Jews, African Americans,

FIGURE 8-1. The mutually reinforcing cycles of ethnic inequality. Some of the mutually reinforcing processes in ethnic inequalities are outlined below. The double arrows and the positive signs are intended to emphasize the closed nature of the cycles and the difficulty of breaking them once they get established. For example, prejudice, discrimination, threat, and continued identifiability feed off one another; one increases the other, and vice versa. It is the mutually escalating nature of the cycles denoted by the arrows in this figure that increases the ethnic dimension of class stratification and, in the long run, makes ethnic stratification such a volatile dynamic in human societies. Think about the fate of various American ethnics caught in these cycles.

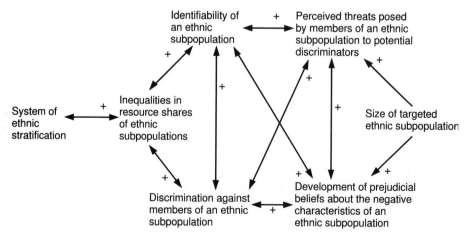

Mexican Americans, Cubans, Native Americans, Vietnamese, Koreans, Japanese, Chinese, and so on—and study each with respect to the forces of identifiability, resources, threat, prejudicial beliefs, and discrimination. If you do this, you will be able to see why you and others stand at particular points in the class system in the United States. It is an exercise worth performing because with the collapse of the Soviet Union, the United States is now the most ethnically diverse society in the world. Hence, much of your life will be entangled with these dynamics of ethnic discrimination.

GENDER STRATIFICATION

Sex and Gender

In all societies, humans categorize one another as male or female; and on the basis of this distinction, cultural beliefs and norms indicate what positions men and women should occupy and how they should play the roles associated with these positions. There has been in the course of human evolution enormous variation in what is defined as appropriate for men and women, a fact indicating that distinctions between the sexes are more sociocultural than biological. This process of culturally defining the appropriate positions and roles for each sex is termed **gender differentiation**; and this concept should be distinguished from **sexual differentiation** which denotes the biological differences between males and females.

The two notions of sex and gender, however, are not so easily separated because much of what a population comes to see as the "natural" biological propensities of the sexes is culturally defined and enforced through sanctions. The only clear biological differences between men and women are genetically caused differences in hormonal secretions and their effects on the development of the sex organs and other anatomical features (skeletal size, percentage of body fat, and musculature). There may be other genetically based differences, but there is no unambiguous evidence for these. Moreover, even the most unambiguous differences become so elaborated and impregnated by cultural beliefs and norms, as well as roles and practices within social structures, as to make the line between sex and gender unclear.

The socially constructed basis of sex is dramatically illustrated by cases where the biology of a person's sex is ambiguous. For example, in one study, children born with the organs of both sexes (termed *hermaphrodites*) took on the sexual characteristics—attitudes, demeanor, and sexual preferences—which reflected their socialization by parents as either male or female (Ellis, 1945; Money and Ehrhardt, 1972). In another illuminating case, a young and seemingly normal girl who had the external sex organs of a female and who had been raised as a female underwent a voice change at puberty; a closer medical examination revealed that "she" was chromosomally a male. Informed of this, she "went home, took off her girl's clothing, and became a boy, immediately beginning to behave like other boys" (V. Reynolds, 1976, p. 125).

From a sociological view, then, we are best to concentrate on **gender processes,** or those cultural and social forces that affect the positions occupied and the roles played by men and women. I will concentrate on gender stratification because it is a topic which directly affects all of our lives.

The Dynamics of Gender Stratification

When the positions occupied by men and women habitually carry with them different amounts of income, power, prestige, and other valued resources, a system of **gender stratification** can be said to exist. Since humans abandoned hunting and gathering some 12,000 to 18,000 years ago, gender stratification has existed in all known societies. And this system has favored males who have been more likely to occupy positions and play roles bringing the most power, material wealth, and prestige. How are we to explain this situation?

Functional theories would seek to answer this question by emphasizing that a sex-based division of labor was more likely than any alternative to meet the survival needs of early human populations. It is more efficient, and hence more adaptive, in a simple society to have women perform those activities around child rearing and domestic activity, while having men leave the camps to hunt for game and, later, to fight in conflicts. For, women must bear and nurse the children, and their domestic activities would seem to flow "naturally" out of this biological "fact" of human life. In contrast, men cannot nurse a child and are, on average, about 15 percent to 20 percent bigger than women; and thus, it is more "natural" for them to leave camps to hunt and perform other tasks that cannot be done by nursing females. Once this division of labor existed, it became elaborated and expanded, bringing inequality between the sexes.

There is some merit in this argument, but it is seriously flawed. First, women in many traditional societies do most of the heavy work *and* raise children (Lenski, Lenski, and Nolan, 1991). There is no reason, once the nomadic hunting-and-gathering way of life was abandoned and people settled down, why men could not do the same and use their talents for raising children and performing domestic chores. Second, if women's roles are so functionally important, why do they command so much less prestige, power, and wealth now that the hunting-and-gathering era is past? Thus, we need to look elsewhere for a more complete understanding of how gender stratification has persisted.

One place to look is conflict theory where the emphasis is on power (Collins, 1975; Collins and Coltrane, 1991). Because men are somewhat larger and stronger than women, at least on average, they have used this capacity for coercion to create and sustain a gender-based stratification system. Thus, over the long course of history, men and women have competed for scarce resources, with men ultimately holding a decisive coercive edge. The underlying coercion involved has, of course, become masked by cultural beliefs and norms which make it seem "natural" that men should dominate access to valued resources. And only in very recent history has this cultural mask been pulled off, leading to a growing social movement in much of the industrial world to redress the inequality between men and women. Yet, there are still powerful forces operating to sustain gender stratification, even in societies like the United States where efforts to undo the legacy of the past are under way. What, then, are these forces? Some are cultural; others are institutional. Let us look at both.

At a cultural level, beliefs have worked against women, emphasizing their nurturant and domestic character (J. Turner, 1977). Such beliefs have been translated into normative expectations about the proper positions (domestic) and role behaviors (passive, nurturant) for women. Such cultural symbols persist because the young are socialized by their families, schools, peers, and media to accept them. When a baby is born, its sex is the first thing the parents wish to know because it dictates how they will respond to the child and what they will expect. Girls will, for example, be channeled into "soft" demeanor, boys into "hard" and more aggressive behavioral modes; girls will be encouraged to practice in their play activities "female" roles (mother, nurse, and housewife), whereas boys will be encouraged to adopt "male" roles. With this channeling into play activities, definitions of what it means to be masculine and feminine are communicated.

These subtle messages about masculinity and femininity are reinforced by peer interactions and experiences in schools. In America, for example, boys are encouraged to play competitive sports involving aggressiveness and physical contact; whereas, despite some changes, girls are channeled into less competitive and less physical sports or, even more significantly, into observer/cheerleader roles where they are mere adjuncts to male activities. Peer interactions reinforce these differences in school and family socialization, as do the media (books and television). The end result, as interactionist theories would stress, is that boys and girls (and later men and women) come to define themselves in masculine and feminine terms and to seek out positions in social structures that reinforce these definitions. Such efforts are reinforced by the broader institutional structure in America, and elsewhere in the industrial world.

If one looks at the economy, there is a clear split between women's work (secretaries, nurses, school teachers, librarians, and low-wage service jobs) and men's work (skilled blue-collar labor, doctors, administrators, and higher-wage professional jobs). For instance, in rough percentages for Americans, 99 percent of the secretaries, 93 percent of the bank tellers, 88 percent of the billing clerks, 83 percent of elementary school teachers, 80 percent or so of librarians, 70 percent of the sales clerks, 60 percent of the social workers, 36 percent of college teachers and professors, 14 percent of lawyers, judges, and physicians, 5 percent of the dentists, a little over 4 percent of the engineers, 2 percent of the carpenters, and less than 1 percent of the plumbers are women (U.S. Department of Labor, 1991). The pattern is clear; and if you are a woman, you should be aware of the obstacles that you will confront in moving into male-dominated jobs and professions. And if you compare the jobs dominated by women on the prestige rankings reported in Table 8-3 (and the associated power and income of these jobs), it is evident that women are disadvantaged in America.

In the American political arena, matters are even worse. Women secured the right to vote only about 75 years ago; women hold a small proportion of seats in the House of Representatives and just a few in the Senate; and over 90 percent of the presidential appointments to all high-level judiciary and administrative jobs go to men. Thus, high-income and high-power positions are overwhelmingly held by men; and when women work in government, they are still disproportionately in lower-pay and lower-prestige "women's jobs" (secretaries, file clerks, and the like).

Domestically, well over 60 percent of women now work (U.S. Bureau of the Census, 1991), but virtually every study on the family division of labor reports that women still do most of the traditional work in American households—washing dishes, cleaning clothes, vacuuming, shopping, and other inside-the-house chores (Turner and Musick, 1985). In other modern, industrial countries the same pattern prevails and, in fact, is even more pronounced. In the long run, perhaps, the ever-increasing percentage of women in the labor force may break this traditional division of labor down, because as women work and make concrete financial contributions to the household, they will acquire more say in how chores are divided. But, even with their financial clout, plus serious efforts by women's groups to raise both men's and women's "consciousness," the traditional division of labor prevails in all western, industrial societies. Again, if you are a woman, this is a situation about which you should be aware.

Thus, despite considerable publicity given to changing "sex roles," men still control the high-income, high-power, and high-prestige positions; and they still are able to weasel out of much domestic labor, even when their wives work. How is this possible? The answer resides in the socialization of men and women into beliefs about femininity and masculinity, and in discriminatory practices in the labor markets. These are subtle forces, but their effects are profound.

There are, however, signs of change. Women are now securing, in dramatically increased numbers, college degrees in traditionally male-dominated fields—business management, computer science, dentistry, engineering, law, and medicine. Moreover, antidiscrimination laws have reduced discrimination against women in traditionally male-dominated blue-collar jobs, although men still overwhelmingly hold these positions. There are also signs of growing women's participation in politics, especially at local and state levels; eventually such increased participation at these levels will produce viable candidates at the national level, as is evident by the number of women candidates for Senate races in 1992. The long-term effects of these changes will, no doubt, alter cultural beliefs about the appropriate roles for both women and men, while changing balances in the domestic division of labor. But these will be relatively slow changes because old systems of cultural symbols, socialization practices, informal employment practices, and political activity are difficult to alter.

Much like ethnic stratification, a gender dimension to stratification is sustained by mutually reinforcing cycles. Women are identifiable; they pose threats to male domination of key roles; they are subject to prejudicial beliefs about their "biological" makeup; they are exposed to a wide array of discriminatory practices. And beliefs and demeanor are sustained by differential socialization. Figure 8-2 delineates the mutually reinforcing nature of the cycles involved. How are such cycles to be broken? The most important force has been women's

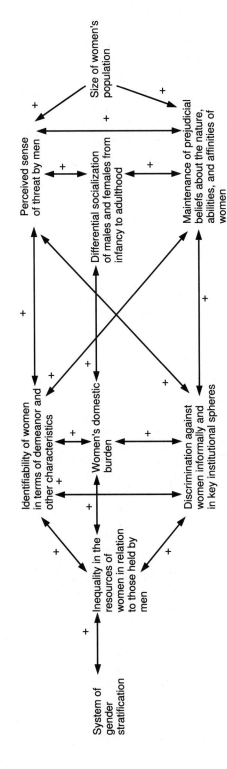

FIGURE 8-2. The mutually reinforcing cycles sustaining gender inequalities and gender stratification

increasing participation in the labor force, where they secure resources as bread-winners, which gives them power to redefine gender identity and to shift some of the domestic burden. In turn, the growing anger of women, coupled with their large size as a subpopulation, have led them to mobilize to change prejudicial beliefs (about the nature of women and their qualities) and to initiate political action to reduce discrimination. Thus, the positive and mutually reinforcing cycles outlined in the figure above are being broken; and a new era of gender relations in America is beginning.

SUMMARY

1. Inequality in a society revolves around the differential distribution of valued resources to various categories of individuals—class, ethnic, and gender being three of the most important.
2. Class stratification exists when income, power, prestige, and other valued resources are given to members of a society unequally and when, on the basis of this inequality, various subpopulations become culturally, behaviorally, and organizationally distinctive.
3. The degree of stratification is related to the level of inequality, the distinctiveness of the classes thereby formed by such inequality, the amount of mobility between classes, and the permanence of classes.
4. A number of approaches to the study of stratification exists: (a) the Marxian approach emphasizing the ownership of the means of production as the cause of class stratification and mobilization to conflict and change in patterns of stratification; (b) the Weberian stressing of the multidimensional nature of stratification (revolving around not just class, but party and status groups as well); (c) the functional approach arguing that inequality reflects the reward system for encouraging individuals to occupy functionally important and difficult-to-fill positions; (d) the evolutionary arguing that the long-term trends toward increases in inequality after hunting and gathering have been reversed somewhat in modern societies.
5. Stratification in America is marked by high levels of inequality with respect to material well-being and prestige. Inequality in the distribution of power is more ambiguous. Fuzzy boundaries between adjacent social classes exist in America. Mobility is frequent, but most people do not experience great mobility in their lifetime.
6. Ethnicity is the identification of a subpopulation as distinctive in terms of surface biology, resources, demeanor, culture, or organization; and ethnic stratification exists when some ethnic subpopulations consistently get more of the valued resources in a society than other ethnic subpopulations.
7. Ethnic stratification is created and sustained by discrimination which is legitimated by prejudicial beliefs. Discrimination and prejudice are fueled by the (economic, political, social) threat that a target ethnic group is perceived to pose, while being sustained by mutually reinforcing cycles revolving around ethnic identifiability, threat, prejudice, and discrimination.
8. Gender is the differentiation of males and females in terms of culturally defined characteristics and structural positions occupied. Gender stratification exists when men and women in a society consistently receive unequal shares of money, power, prestige, and other resources.
9. The gender dimension of stratification is sustained by mutually reinforcing cycles of

socialization, gender identity, and gender-related beliefs which, in turn, become the basis for discrimination and prejudicial beliefs fueled by males' sense of threat.
10. Gender relations are changing in America, as these mutually reinforcing cycles are being broken by women's participation in work and politics and by assaults on gender beliefs that place women at a disadvantage.

KEY TERMS

bourgeoisie, the   In Karl Marx's analysis, those who own and control the means of production in capitalist societies.

caste system   A stratification system with clearly marked class divisions, in which people are born into a particular class and have little chance for mobility to a different class.

charismatic leaders   Max Weber's term for those who, by virtue of their personal qualities, can mobilize subordinates in a system of inequality to engage in conflict with superordinates.

classes   For Max Weber, those who share a common set of life chances and opportunities in markets; for Karl Marx, the divisions in a society reflecting ownership of the means of production; for more general analysis, the differences among subpopulations by virtue of their respective share of valued resources.

conflict of interest   Karl Marx's term for the basic tension and incompatibility of goals between those who control resources and those who do not.

discrimination   The differential treatment of others, especially those of an ethnic group or a gender category, so that they receive less valued resources.

ethnicity   Those behavioral, cultural, and organizational characteristics that distinguish subpopulations in a society.

gender/gender differentiation   The process of culturally defining the appropriate positions, roles, and demeanor for men and women.

gender processes   Those cultural and social forces that affect the positions occupied and roles played by men and women in a society.

gender stratification   The situation where the positions typically occupied by men and women habitually receive different levels of valued resources.

income distribution   The percentage of total income held by different percentages of the population, usually calculated in terms of income fifths.

institutionalized discrimination   Patterns of systematic discrimination against an ethnic subpopulation, a gender category, or some other cohort of people that are legitimated by cultural symbols, carried out informally and formally, and built into the structures of a society.

open-class system   A stratification system with less clearly demarcated classes and with opportunities for mobility from class to class.

parties   For Max Weber, the organization of power as a distinct basis for inequality and stratification of individuals who bear varying affiliations and access to organizations holding or seeking power.

prejudices   Beliefs about the undesirable qualities of others, especially those in an ethnic group.

proletariat, the   Karl Marx's term for those who do not own the means of production in capitalist society and who must, therefore, work for those who do.

race   Perceived biological distinctiveness for categories of individuals.

sex/sexual differentiation   The biological differences between males and females.

status groups   Max Weber's term for subsets of individuals who share similar lifestyles, who form ties because of shared culture, tastes, and outlooks, and who, by virtue of these, can command a certain honor and prestige.

stratification systems   Structures revolving around (1) the unequal distribution of valued resources to the members of a society and (2) the distinctive categories thereby created by virtue of the shares of resources held by different subpopulations in a society.

wealth distribution   The percentage of total wealth held by different percentages of the population, usually calculated in terms of wealth fifths.

CHAPTER 9

Institutions

To survive, humans had to create ways of dealing with the basic exigencies of biological and social life. They had to secure enough food and sustenance, to provide safe ways to bear and raise children, to govern themselves and manage conflict, to educate each generation, to alleviate anxiety and tension in people, to develop knowledge and understanding, and to heal the sick. Each of these exigencies unleashed the creative power of the humans, fostering and then elaborating upon the basic structures—termed social institutions—that help meet the basic contingencies of human existence. As societies become large and complex, most institutions are lodged in ever larger social structures housed in buildings like those pictured above. Only the family remains free from this kind of monolithic constraint.

In order to survive in their environment, the first humans *had* to do certain things or die. A functional theory would call these "survival requisites," but whatever we want to call them, humans needed to secure food and shelter, find ways to regularize sex and mating, protect and socialize children, band together in ways that would reduce conflict and tension, and develop cultural symbols to regulate their affairs and to overcome their anxieties about life and death. Those human or protohuman groups that could not meet these minimal requisites perished. Thus, the emergence and development of humans as a species was tied to how our distant ancestors organized to survive. A small and simple band of families wandering a territory, gathering and hunting as they needed, was enough for at least 30,000 years of our history. But, when humans settled down, populations began to grow, and as a result, new problems of survival emerged: how to coordinate and control larger numbers of people, how to develop better ways of securing food and shelter for the expanding population, how to reduce conflict over scarce resources, how to protect the population from enemies, and so on (Maryanski and Turner, 1992). Again, from a functionalist perspective, these new problems can be viewed as survival requisites which *had* to be met if the population was to sustain itself. And, as the scale and complexity of human societies increased over the last 12,000 years, new problems emerged, creating needs (at least in people's minds) for matters that *had* to be resolved.

These kinds of fundamental problems faced by humans are the essence of social institutions. Basic institutions—economy, family and kinship, and religion—were there when humans first organized; later, new institutions were added to deal with the new exigencies and contingencies of life—polity or government, law, education, medicine, and most recently, science. Institutions thus deal with what are perceived by people to be basic problems and conditions of social life, but once created, these institutions have a life of their own as they become impregnated by cultural symbols and as they become situated in social structures (J. Turner, 1972).

WHAT IS A SOCIAL INSTITUTION?

A **social institution** can be viewed as a special kind of social structure whose status positions are organized around what are seen by members of a society to be important societywide problems. The norms guiding role behaviors in these positions are general and well known to members of the society, and the incumbents feel a moral imperative as they play roles because the norms are infused with values and beliefs about what is right and wrong, good and bad (J. Turner, 1972). If you think about key institutional positions that you are most likely to occupy presently—student, child to your parents, spouse, parent to your children, worker, voter, member of church—they all have this special quality: They are perceived as critical to resolving important problems; they are guided by general and well-known norms; and they are infused with values and morally loaded beliefs. Just how these positions are organized varies from society to society, but institutional structures are constructed from positions lodged in groups which, as the scale of society gets bigger, are pulled increasingly together into organizational structures and networks of organizational structures that cut across the entire society.

This may all seem a bit abstract, and so it is time to examine the nature of specific social institutions. In this way, this definitional work can take on more meaning. And equally important, we can come to appreciate that institutions are interrelated; the structure and events of one has effects on the others, and vice versa.

KINSHIP AND FAMILY

The first enduring social structure in human evolution was, no doubt, a system of kinship. The operation of other early institutions—economy, education, and religion—was initially folded inside relations among parents and their children. And, only later in human history did other institutes become distinct and differentiated from these bonds of kinship. To say that family was the first enduring structure signals that it was important to the viability of human social organization. From a functional perspective, kinship and family relations meet certain basic survival requisites (J. Turner, 1972): (1) regularizing sex and mating, thereby avoiding much of the potential conflict and tension over this most basic activity; (2) providing for the biological support of each member of the society, and especially the newborn and young who are a society's future; (3) creating a stable unit of socialization so that the young can acquire the culture and role-playing skills essential to adult life; (4) supplying an atmosphere of social support for the young and adults alike; and (5) regularizing and systematizing the placement of young adults into crucial productive (economic) and reproductive (childbearing, child rearing) positions in society. From a functional perspective, if these needs are not met, the survival of the species becomes problematic; and in the simple societies of the first humans, blood and marriage ties represented the easiest route for building viable social structures. Thus, the **institution of kinship** is the organization of marriage and blood ties into structures that ensure regularization of sex and mating, biological support, socialization, social support, and social placement.

Basic Elements of Kinship

Kinship is a system of norms about some very fundamental matters, and as I noted above, these norms are infused with strongly held values and beliefs. The rules of kinship thus carry special significance for the members of a society.

One cultural norm is about **marriage** which is, after all, what creates and sustains family and kinship systems. In many societies when and whom to marry have not always been a matter of free choice. In many kinship systems, marriage must occur outside of a larger kin unit or community (a rule of **exogamy**) and at times into another specific group (a rule of **endogamy**); and always, marriage has been guided by **incest rules** forbidding sexual relations and marriage among parents and offspring, as well as most close relatives (Murdock, 1949, 1965).

Another kinship rule which has a great impact not only on marriages but also on virtually all other aspects of kinship is *descent*. The rules of **descent** specify whose side of the family is to be more important. Three basic options have existed in the history of human societies: (1) **patrilineal descent,** where the male side of the family is more important, with wealth and authority passing through the male line (son-father-grandfather-uncles, etc.); (2) **matrilineal descent,** where the woman's side of the family is more important and where property and authority pass through the woman's *male* relatives (not through the woman herself or her female relatives); and (3) the one with which you are most familiar, **bilateral descent,** where both sides are equally important and, at the same time, neither has great influence.

Another set of kinship rules revolves around where and with whom the married couple will live after marriage. These are termed **residence rules,** with several patterns dominating the history of kinship: **patrilocal,** where the couple lives with or near the male's family; **matrilocal,** where the couple resides with the woman's relatives; **avunculocal,** where the couple lives with the male's mother's brother; and again the one with which you are familiar, **neolocal,** where there is free choice about where to live. In general, descent rules determine residence rules, but not always, with the result that matters can become awkward when power, property, and authority (the descent rule), on the one hand, do not correspond to where people live (the residence rule), on the other. Still, over 70 percent of the societies that have been known were patrilocal (Murdock, 1949).

Other important kinship rules include those with respect to authority, which until recently gave men power over women; those about the household division of labor which, again, have favored men; those about family size which dictate the relatives who are to live with a married couple; and those about dissolution which specify how a marriage is to be terminated.

The first societies of hunters and gatherers had a very simple system, much like the one we know in the United States (Maryanski and Turner, 1992): bilateral descent, with no elder or relative having any authority over the couple; neolocal residence, where people are free to choose the place and persons with whom they will live; incest prohibitions as well as exogamy (usually specifying that you had to marry outside your band); at times, endogamy (indicating in which other band you would marry); clear division of labor (men hunt, women gather and prepare food); relatively egalitarian authority (both men and women have equal authority, or shared authority); small family size of just mother, father, and offspring; and easy dissolution of the marriage.

Yet, when human populations first began to grow during horticulture and, for a while, in early agrarianism, rules of kinship were *the* most important organizing principles, and they made family and kinship a much more complex phenomenon. Kinship became, in essence, the functional equivalent of bureaucratic organizations; and thousands upon thousands of people—indeed in some cases, millions—could be organized by a descent rule as it dictated the nature of other kinship rules. Most of these horticultural societies were not so large, though they could become so with kinship rules. In broad strokes, here is how one builds a larger social structure with kinship rules: The descent rule, along with marriage and residence rules, allows for the building of ever-more-inclusive kinship units, starting with the **nuclear unit,** the married couple and their children, moving to the **extended unit,** which links together several nuclear units, then to the **lineage,** which is the linking together through marriage and blood ties of extended units, next to the **clan,** which consists of linked lineages, and finally to the **moiety,** which links clans. There are many subtle variations, and most societies were not as neat and clean as this scenario implies. Yet kinship can be used as the organizational backbone of a society when its members cannot construct bureaucratic social forms.

Max Weber (1922) once worried about the constraints of "the iron cage" of rational bureaucracy on the human spirit, but it is unlikely that this modern cage is anything like the cage of kinship (Maryanski and Turner, 1992). Just imagine getting married, moving in with your husband's parents (patrilocality) and being under the authority of all elder male kin in the lineage and perhaps the clan and moiety (patrilineal descent), with authority residing with males and with the division of labor forcing all females, who have been thrown together from other descent lines, to try to get along and work together at gardening and domestic chores while the males go off to war or do various handicrafts. Sounds like a nightmare to me, at least if you are a woman, and humans got out of this kind of system as soon as they could, even if they had to subordinate themselves to the state and political authority.

It is in the more elaborate forms of kinship that the greatest inequalities can be found; and as conflict theorists would emphasize (Collins, 1975; Collins and Coltrane, 1991), the differences in power and authority of males and females create tensions which periodically explode, but more often are controlled by powerful norms and beliefs about "the woman's place" in the family, by the potential for coercion by the male (and his relatives), by day-to-day interpersonal sanctions, and by rituals. In such a situation, a woman has few resources to mobilize, especially if surrounded by her husband's relatives (as in a patrilocal system). Her life is better if she can be around her relatives (as in a matrilocal system) because she can draw upon them for support. One resource women have is sex, which they can deny to men or ritualize in ways that they gain resources or limit the power of men (Collins, 1975). Another crucial resource for women is the use of cultural symbols that have often been employed to create a "mystique" about the nature of women which, in turn, can be used to control husbands (Collins, 1975). But throughout human history, ever since humans left the relative equality of the hunting-and-gathering way of life, women have been at a disadvantage. And we live with the legacy of this disadvantage today, as was evident in one section on gender in the last chapter. The resentment by women to their subordination has always been present, though repressed and submerged by cultural beliefs and sanctions. As women have begun to work in great numbers and to acquire material resources, however, these resentments are coming out and forcing a rebalancing of power relations in the households of the modern world (Chafetz, 1990). Nowhere is this trend more evident than in the United States.

Kinship in America

Perhaps this history of kinship seems remote, but it is relevant to understanding kinship in America and, hence, the current situation or future prospects for each of us. Structurally, our kinship system is bilateral, neolocal, and nucleated, with considerable ambiguity over authority and the division of labor between men and women. This structure of a relatively isolated unit with changing and ambiguous norms about the division of labor and authority is inevitably going to reveal conflict and increased rates of dissolution (J. Turner, 1977). Let us examine this situation in more detail.

Industrialization completes the nuclearization of the family. Large extended families never were particularly pleasant, despite all the romanticism about the old days, and so people got out of them whenever possible. Agrarianism began the process; industrialization completes it because extensive kinship ties are a hindrance in an industrial system where people move about, leave their homes to be educated, pursue independent careers, and try to enjoy the good life.

But isolated nuclear families face a number of dilemmas. One is the expectations which guided the formation of this family unit in the first place. In the United States powerful beliefs about *romantic love* dominate mate selection (J. Turner, 1977, pp. 72–78): One is supposed to marry on the basis of mutual attraction and compatibility (rather than fecundity, money, family ties, and other less romantic considerations); such attraction extends to love and sex, with the couple becoming an emotionally bonded pair; and this compatibility is to persist, even in the face of problems, because "love conquers all." Of course when this **romantic love complex,** as it is sometimes called, is stated in this way, it is easy to snicker. But, if we are honest with ourselves, some version of these ideas has guided, or is now guiding, mate selection.

Thus, American couples enter marriage with expectations —typically very unrealistic ones—about what will occur. Moreover, living together before marriage does not appear to help the future stability of the marriage. For example, in a recent study in Sweden where living together is common, women who cohabited with their spouses before marriage were 80 percent more likely to get divorced than those who did not live with their husbands before marriage (Bennett et al., 1988). A similar finding emerged in a recent study in the United States. Now obviously something is amiss here, and it is this: Those who live together are often afraid of commitments and have other doubts about marriage; and so, we might expect them to get divorced more often. Yet, those who do not live together before marriage will tend to enter the marriage with unrealistic expectations, setting the stage for dashed hopes and anger.

These romantically in love couples must confront the full weight of ambiguous norms about authority and the division of labor. And if children enter the picture, this normative confusion becomes even more unclear. Who does what in the care of the child? Who has the say—over what issues? These questions are not easily answered, especially if the wife is working or if she sacrifices/interrupts her career to raise children. If you add to this mix concerns over finances, fatigue from work, and accumulated resentments in trying to make things run smoothly, the potential is there for marital tension leading to divorce. Higher

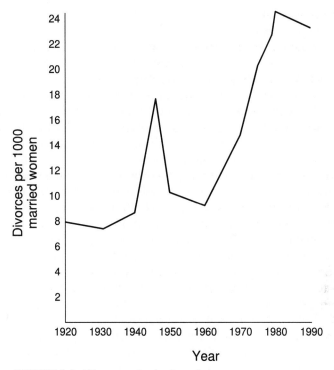

FIGURE 9-1. Divorce rates in America

divorce rates are, therefore, inevitable. But how high? And is the institution of kinship in America collapsing?

   Divorce rates are difficult to calculate for the simple reason that, in order to do it accurately, one would have to let people live their whole married lives before knowing for sure if they will get divorced. Thus, the figures bantered in the media—50 percent of couples get divorced!—are very problematic, if not just plain wrong. One of the most useful statistics is the number of divorces per 1000 married women over 16 years old; at least this figure offers some basis for comparison across time. In reviewing Figure 9-1, in 1920 there were 8.0 divorces per 1000 married women; in 1940 this figure was 8.7; by 1946, it was 17.8 (all those quick marriages before and during the war began to come unglued); by 1950, it was back down to 10.3; and then it began to rise: 14.9 in 1970, 20.3 in 1975, 22.8 in 1979, 24.6 in 1980, and 23.3 in 1990. But is this a 50 percent figure, as you have heard? Again there is no way of knowing, but one effort to get a better figure involves using a national survey that would ask people age 50 years or older about their divorce history, under the assumption (not always true, of course) that they are past the prime years for divorce. Then data for different years can be compared—in this case 1972 and 1990 (Stark, 1992, p. 390); 21.3 percent of those responding in 1972 indicated that they had been divorced or legally separated, whereas among the fifty-plus group in 1990, 26.6 percent reported divorce or legal separation. Thus, divorce had risen, but not that dramatically; and it is nothing close to the 50 percent figure. But still, these data are for older people and do not tell us much about the likelihood for success in marriage of younger couples just getting started.

Eighty percent of those who get divorced remarry, and so, people want to be married in a nuclear family unit. But there is a fluctuating trend toward one-parent families, partly as a result of divorce but also significantly among unmarried mothers. The figure is now 25 percent of all babies born in America are to women who are not married. Thus, these children will grow up under difficult circumstances, as their mothers seek to cope with the stresses of supporting and raising children. Add to this number the children in stepparent families and divorced single-parent households, and we can see that children and their parent(s) must deal with a great deal of strain in their households—as perhaps some of you may have experienced firsthand. Virtually every study of these households reports terrible strain on both parent(s) and children. Parents in such families report wanting to be away from their children, and feel much happier when children are grown and gone (White and Booth, 1985). Surprisingly, even steadily married couples experience a significant increase in happiness when their last child has moved out (White and Edwards, 1990), indicating that talk of the "empty nest" syndrome is greatly exaggerated, at least in most cases.

In sum, then, kinship in America is subject to enormous strain, leading to increased, though hardly crisis level, divorce rates. Part of this situation is inevitable in a time when romantic love expectations must confront the ambiguity of key kinship norms; and part of it is the result of women's changing roles as breadwinners and their resentment of traditional patterns of subordination to men. Other sources of strain on families, such as the high proportion of children born outside of marriage present more difficult problems for the mother and children because of the financial and emotional pressures that result when there is only one parent from the very beginning. If there is a crisis in the family, then, it is this rather than the divorce rate (whatever that may actually be).

ECONOMY

A truly fundamental problem for humans is securing resources from the environment, converting these into usable commodities, and then distributing them to the members of a society. From a functional perspective, then, if humans do not secure food, convert it into something edible, and distribute it to all, people and society do not survive. And so, because the economy is so fundamental to life, it should not be surprising that all other institutions will be greatly influenced by its structure and dynamics.

Basic Elements of All Economies

All economies operate in terms of some very basic elements (J. Turner, 1972). There is **technology** which, as we saw in Chapter 3 on culture, is knowledge about how to control and manipulate the environment. This knowledge must be combined with (1) **labor,** or the persons performing economic activities, and (2) **capital,** or the implements, such as machines and tools, used in economic activity as well as the money to buy these implements. **Entrepreneurship** is the organizational capacity to coordinate technology, capital, and labor in order to gather resources, produce goods and services, and distribute these to members of the society. An **economy,** then, is the organization (entrepreneurship) of technology, capital, and labor in order to gather resources, produce goods and services from these resources, and distribute these goods and services to members of a population.

Types of Economies

A majority of the approximately 40,000 years that humans have existed as a species were spent in a hunting-and-gathering economy, where small bands of 30 to 50 individuals wandered over a territory gathering indigenous foods and hunting game. The technology was simple—knowledge of plants and hunting; capital consisted of spears and perhaps a bow and arrow; labor was divided along sexual lines with women gathering and men hunting; and entrepreneurial functions were performed by the band and families in the band, or by the individuals working alone. Such economies did not produce much, but neither did people work very hard—perhaps 15 hours a week. The anthropologist, Marshall Sahlins (1972), once called hunters and gatherers "the original affluent society" because life was relaxed and leisure dominated over work.

When members of the few remaining hunting-and-gathering populations have been asked why they never took up gardening and farming, their answer is that they do not want to work so hard. We are, perhaps, rather lazy animals at heart; and from the archeological record, it is clear that hunters and gatherers of the past also knew about planting with seeds, because they would often throw some seeds out when breaking camp with the hope that they could later "harvest" the food when returning months later. But they avoided settling down on the land for most of our history as a species. Why? I suspect the answer has always been the same: Who wants to work that hard turning the soil, planting seeds, weeding gardens, harvesting the crop, storing what one can, and then doing it all over again year after year (Maryanski and Turner, 1992)?

At some point between 12,000 and 18,000 years ago, however, some humans did begin to work this hard. Horticultural economies thus emerged, consisting of: knowledge about seeds, plants, and cultivation (technology); digging sticks, grinding stones, and other hand-held implements (capital); gardening and harvesting, mostly by women (labor); and organization by kinship (entrepreneurship). Horticulture is distinct from agriculture because gardening is conducted without the aid of a plow and other nonhuman sources of energy, like beasts of burden and wind or water power. It is not fully known why humans took up this labor-intensive economy, but let me offer a best guess (Maryanski and Turner, 1992). Humans first settled down, at least for a time, near rivers because there were fish and lush plant life around rivers. Why move about if the staff of life is there for the plucking? With the extra food and a more sedentary life, the population began to grow; people began to exhaust local animal and plant life because they did not move on and thereby let resources replenish themselves. For, these settled populations were too large to move in the old way, and so, they began to practice horticulture. They had made a decisive step, though, for once settled, the nature of human society changes dramatically. When populations grow, new structures are required—elaborated kinship and political authority—to coordinate and control activity; and territories now have to be defended, again creating needs for political authority to mobilize military activity. The beginnings of the end for the original affluent society were thus initiated. In a few thousand years, hunting and gathering would be gone, forever.

Agrarian economies represented a significant technological break from horticulture because they possess knowledge of how to harness animal power and inanimate energy (water and wind) to basic economic processes. This breakthrough, in turn, stimulated further technological development: knowledge of metallurgy and smelting being two of the most important. As a result, capital accumulation in a more productive economy could be greatly extended: Money became widely used; and metal tools, shops, milling facilities, roadways, canals, transportation using the wheel, and a host of implements became common. Labor was ever more specialized, and new kinds of economic positions and roles—merchant, artisan, banker, and other specialties—emerged. And entrepreneurship changed dramatically because village and kin alone were no longer adequate organizing forces; they must at first have been supplemented and then successively replaced by markets, feudal political structures, merchant houses, guilds, law and contract, and units that began to look like the modern corporation.

Industrialization is the process of harnessing inanimate power to machines attended by labor in a factory. This process was initiated just a few hundred years ago, but it has transformed the world. Industrial economies have vast technologies about how to manipulate and control the environment (indeed, they can destroy it), and they constantly develop new knowledge. Capital formation involves money and numerous new ways of accumulating money (stocks and bonds, for example) to buy the implements of production; and the number and variety of tools and implements are, as we all know, astounding. Labor becomes highly specialized and increasingly skilled; and it sells itself in a market, like any other good or commodity. And entrepreneurship is accomplished by highly complex arrangements: the state and law, large-scale and complex market systems, bureaucracies and factories, and corporations as a way of pooling capital, labor, and technology in the pursuit of profits.

Postindustrial economies, like the one in which you and I participate, represent a shift in the nature of work. As technologies increase and are implemented as capital in machines and robotics, labor is increasingly organized around technological expansion, services, and market activities, and is decreasingly organized around manual labor. Hence, white-collar jobs come to outnumber blue-collar work. Moreover, markets and money become more dynamic and volatile, accelerating at a dizzying pace the flow of goods and services on a world scale. Urbanization and suburbanization increase as work is organized in bureaucratic structures that pool workers and, in the process, create new markets for service organizations that pull more workers in urban areas. The state and government increase their functions to control and regulate the complexity of the economy. And education expands as professional and technical credentials are needed for the new service-oriented white-collar jobs.

The American Economy

The American economy is postindustrial; hence, its labor force is increasingly nonmanual. And, as you know, there is a credentials race—indeed credential inflation—for individuals like you trying to become certified as competent to do certain kinds of nonmanual jobs (Collins, 1979). College students are, in essence, getting ready to sell themselves in a highly competitive labor market. Conflict theories would emphasize that this fact of life sets up an inherent tension among people, as they fight and compete for credentials and jobs in companies that seek their services for as low a wage or salary as possible.

Such jobs are located in profit and nonprofit corporations as well as governmental organizations, all of which are organized to varying degrees as bureaucratic structures. Relatively few of you will be in a family business, or working alone; you will be lodged in groups within complex organizations of some sort. Corporations in America are private, owned by families or more commonly by stockholders and, unfortunately in many cases, by anxious creditors. They compete with one another within local, regional, national, and, increasingly, world markets. One's fate in corporations—whether as a blue-collar worker or white-collar employee—will depend on how the corporation performs in these markets; and with the dramatic expansion of world economic activity and the movement of corporations to all parts of the world, economic life for most individuals will be insecure because of the intensity of the competition. If a person works in government, or perhaps as a paid professional in a voluntary organization, his or her security will depend upon either tax revenues or contributions, both of which are tied to the success of corporations in domestic and international markets and to the steady, taxable pay of their workers. Since the need for government services is constantly expanding, despite ideological preachings against inefficient government bureaucrats, a significant portion of the workforce is involved in providing government services. Yet, for the foreseeable future, the majority of the American workforce will not be employed in either large corporations or in government, but in small businesses which are particularly vulnerable to both domestic and world system competition and economic cycles.

Certain trends are clearly evident in this mix of organizational structures (Turner and Musick, 1985). One trend is toward *oligopoly* where a relatively few corporations produce a particular good or service and control the market for this good or service. Second, corporations in key market sectors are getting larger, as a result of mergers and hostile takeovers, as well as through the oligopolistic control of markets. Third, corporations are increasingly becoming multinational, seeking to maximize profits by using the capital and labor of foreign countries and by selling goods and services in these countries. Fourth, an increasing proportion of corporations has at least some foreign ownership. Fifth, many key markets within the United States—television and video products, cameras, and video games, for example—are dominated by foreign multinations; and an increasing number of markets is in danger of becoming controlled by foreign corporations. Sixth, as the proportion of white-collar as well as menial service jobs has increased, membership in unions has steadily declined, although even without this shift from blue- to white-collar work, union membership has been declining even among blue-collar workers. Seventh, government is a large employer and an enormously important purchaser of goods and services in markets. And lastly, as noted above, small businesses still employ a vast portion of the workforce.

These trends signal some important dilemmas and choices that Americans must make. One is the clear trend to export many blue-collar jobs to cheaper sources of labor overseas, or just across the border to Mexico or out to the Caribbean. Should this be allowed? And what can be done about this loss of jobs? Another trend is foreign penetration into American markets. Can this trend be reversed, especially as it creates balance of payments problems and, in essence, reduces the value of the dollar? But how can this problem be addressed?: through protectionism which would set off a trade war? through accepting a devaluation of the dollar and its purchasing power (and of course, the standard of living for Americans)? through government efforts to revitalize domestic production of goods and services that other nations want to buy? Yet another trend is using borrowed money for mergers and acquisitions, none of which increases the number of jobs, or the level of productivity, but which as the 1990s has discovered, sacrifices long-term profitability and viability for short-term profits. How is this problem to be handled?: through extensive government regulation? through letting the corporations fail, thereby increasing unemployment and decreasing American market shares?

These dilemmas are real. They affect each of our lives right now. And they are something with which all of us as workers and citizens must come to grips. Government is going to be a key force in addressing these dilemmas. It is, therefore, a topic which we need to examine in more detail.

GOVERNMENT

The Emergence of Polity

Why would people subordinate themselves to leaders and organizations that could coerce them? The answer is simple: They had no choice. As populations began to grow, social life could no longer be organized informally or around kinship relations. Leaders who could tell others what to do were necessary in order to coordinate activities and, if need be, to control deviance and conflict. Once this step was taken, government was born, and there was no looking back to the noncoercive relations among hunters and gatherers (Lenski, 1966; Lenski, Lenski, and Nolan, 1991; J. Turner, 1972; Maryanski and Turner, 1992; Fried, 1967; Carneiro, 1970).

The level of economic productivity, however, greatly influenced the nature of government, and how big it needs to be as well as how big it can become. Historically, much of this influence was indirect through the effects of the economy on population growth; for, as the economy encouraged or allowed a population to grow, problems of coordination and control escalated, creating the need or requisite, as functionalists would say, for political leaders and government. If these were not forthcoming or if they were ineffective, the society dissolved—a turn of events that must have occurred again and again in early human history. More directly, the level of economic surplus beyond subsistence determines how big and complex government can become; the more the surplus, the larger the government (Lenski, 1966; J. Turner, 1984a). At first among simple horticulturalists, there was not much surplus, and so leadership was limited to elders, kin, and village leaders; later with more advanced horticulture and then agrarianism, the surplus could support leaders, administrators for public services, and an army. Indeed, in agrarian systems a vicious cycle is often initiated: Government taxes the surplus to support itself and the privilege of the elite; at some point, government and elites live beyond their means and their ability to collect taxes; and then, the resentments of those who have suffered in this system burst into conflict, and the government collapses, or has to be reorganized (Goldstone, 1990). While functional theories would emphasize the necessity for government, conflict theorists would remind us that government nonetheless creates resentments and at times aggravates inequalities which further fuel resentments; and ironically, these growing resentments force the elaboration of government to control them, thereby escalating further resentments and harkening the day when these will boil over and change the nature of government. These events have also occurred again and again in human history.

Ultimately, as government grows, it becomes bureaucratically organized, and when this transformation has transpired, we can speak of **the state** (Weber, 1922). At first, the bureaucracy was merged with kinship, but as more effective and efficient administrators were needed, if only to collect taxes, and as more efficient police and armies were required to maintain order and defense, pressures built for bureaucratic structures resembling Weber's ideal type portrayal on page 103. Once any state becomes large, bureaucratic, and able to support itself, it can do more—construct more public works, engage in more war, and administer more territory. And as a result, the scale of governmental activity increases and is limited only by two forces: the capacity of the economy to support it and the willingness of the population to accept it. Neither of these forces is unproblematic, and so, as we have recently seen with the old Soviet Union, and as history tells us again and again, states often collapse and with them much of society.

Basic Elements of All Polities

As an institution, government or more generically, **polity,** contains several basic elements (J. Turner, 1972; Maryanski and Turner, 1992): First, there is **leadership,** or the ability of some to make decisions for mobilizing resources and coordinating activities. Second, there is **power** to enforce decisions, typically through persuasion and influence but, if necessary, through physical coercion. Third, there is **legitimacy,** or the existence of cultural symbols which give leaders the right to make decisions. And finally, there is the **structure of government,** or the way in which leaders, decision making, and the use of power are organized. These elements are brought to bear on certain fundamental problems of organization. One is the establishment of goals for the society as a whole, and the mobilization of individuals, organizational units, and resources to achieve these goals (Parsons, 1966, 1971). Populations which do not have goals—such as for defense, economic growth, conquest, etc.—do not need government. Conversely, the more diverse the goals and the greater the problems of coordinating and mobilizing resources to achieve these goals, the more extensive government will be. Another fundamental problem facing populations is social control and the avoidance of disorder. When populations are small, government is not needed, but as they get larger, deviance, dissent, and disagreements escalate; and it becomes necessary to use power to control these problems. Of course, the use of power itself can aggravate tensions and arouse hostilities, but without government of some sort, large societies would degenerate.

Thus, we can define government as an institution as those structures in a society that give leaders the legitimate (or at least partly legitimate) right to make decisions and mobilize power for the realization of societal goals and for maintenance of social order. The story of human development is, to an extent, about the ways different forms and types of governments have emerged, then collapsed, only to be replaced by new forms.

Types of Government

Government has, as I indicated earlier, been tied to the nature of the economy and the size of a population. In hunting-and-gathering societies, government does not exist, but in some, we can see the beginnings of government. These beginnings are in the form of what are often termed "big men" leaders who, through their personal skill and charisma, come to have the right of making and enforcing decisions for others (Earle, 1984; Johnson and Earle, 1987). Such forms of government are usually found in hunting-and-gathering populations who have settled down near waterways or on islands where they use their simple technologies to gather and to fish; they are not horticulturalists but instead hunters and gatherers who have become too large for informal social control. What emerges under these conditions are "big men," but rarely can they pass their powers on to others at their death, and so, they do not constitute a hereditary chiefdom (Johnson and Earle, 1987).

It is with horticulturalists that more stable political systems arise. When people settle down to garden in villages and use more complex kinship structures to organize their activities, elder members of kinship units become "headmen" who decide such matters as who gets what gardening plots, how the crops are to be distributed, and when to go to war. Headmen of different kin groups, such as lineages or clans, can sometimes organize as a "council" of leaders or elders, making decisions for all the kin groups in a village or even for several villages. It is from this base that a true **chiefdom** emerges in which one man (and it is always a man) comes to dominate these decisions. The chief may consult with these local headmen and councils of elders, but he ultimately is given the right to make decisions for all others under his command. Chiefdoms can become very large-scale, incorporating vast territories and subordinating villages and kin groups. With these kinds of chiefdoms, where there is an army and kin-based organization for administering decisions, we have the first inklings of the state.

The state begins the bureaucratic organization of decision making. At first, the state apparatus—tax collectors, administrators, military, and police—is under a hereditary monarch whose power is typically legitimated by religion. This form of state is not a "rational" bureaucracy in Max Weber's terms, because family ties and patronage are still prominent. It is the form of government in agrarian societies.

The modern, bureaucratic state emerges with industrialization, recruiting its members for their skill and expertise and, increasingly, democratically electing its key decision-making members. Religion recedes as the dominant legitimating symbols, being replaced by laws and, in most cases, a constitution. Modern states vary along a number of important dimensions. One is the degree to which its bureaucracy is rational, recruiting and promoting people in terms of skills and performance. Another is the degree of centralization of power and decision making. In some, power and decision making are concentrated, as in much of the Third World or in the old Soviet Union, whereas in others power and decision making are more decentralized. Still another variation is the extensiveness of state intervention into social life, with some states intervening in most spheres of social and economic life, as was the case with the now-disintegrated or disintegrating communist societies where the state owned most property and set production quotas and prices for goods and services. In contrast, other states allow considerable autonomy to social and economic actors, as is the case in the United States; and still other states fall between the American and old Soviet extremes, using state power to regulate much social life and, yet at the same time, not owning or overly regulating economic units.

A critical point of variation in modern states is the degree of democracy, or the extent to which regular and free elections determine who are to be the decision-making leaders, and for how long. In some societies, such as those in the old communist bloc countries and in some of their old members, democracy is still problematic. Leaders are not always elected on a regular schedule, and they often stay beyond their appointed time. In most Western democracies, the degree of democracy is high—so high that there is apathy about voting (especially among younger age groups). Related to the degree of democracy is the division of autonomous powers. All modern states have an executive, legislative, and judicial branch, but the autonomy of these branches varies. In some, the legislature and judiciary are heavily influenced by leaders in the executive branch, often being little more than rubber stamps. In others, there is more autonomy, with elected legislatures and judges in the judiciary having independent powers to check and balance the executive branch, and one another.

Still other variations in states are the degree of legitimacy and the need to resort to **coercion**. These two factors tend to be related: State systems with low legitimacy must rely on coercive force, or the threat of force, whereas those systems high in legitimacy can usually—though not always—achieve compliance to decisions without coercive force. But force is often necessary even in highly legitimate state systems when particular decisions—say, in America, those of school integration, busing, abortion, and other issues on which the population is polarized—are defined as illegitimate by some. Thus, states vary in what we might call "generalized legitimacy" where the basic structure and operation of the state is considered appropriate, even when there is disagreement with particular decisions.

Government in America

Government in the United States is, obviously, a modern bureaucratic state which falls on the extreme end of these points of variation. The bureaucracy is rational, despite all our grumbling about government bureaucrats; power is relatively decentralized, although, as we will see, there has been a clear trend from local communities to the state governments, from state governments to the federal government, and within the federal government from the legislative and judiciary to the executive branch; state intervention in the economy is probably the lowest in the highly industrial world; government is highly democratic; the division of powers among executive, legislative, and judiciary is still great, though declining; generalized legitimacy is high and enshrined in emotionally charged cultural symbols (the flag and the Constitution, for example), though great controversy rages on particular issues; and reliance on coercion is low, although dissent on particular social issues as well as high rates of crime have forced the use of coercive force.

There are several dilemmas and problems in this pattern of government that will, no doubt, be with us well into the future (Turner and Musick, 1985). Let me enumerate some of these. First, there is the dilemma of democracy revolving around participation in voting, influence of special interests, and effects of the media on politics. Americans are often unhappy with the political system because they do not think that their vote "counts" and that special interests disproportionately influence elections. The media nature of general elections reinforces this situation because it makes elections expensive, thereby forcing candidates to take money from special-interest groups. The result has been voter apathy—with fewer and fewer people voting in general elections. This trend has, unfortunately, the effect of increasing the power of the media and special-interest groups on candidates by forcing each candidate to mount a large media campaign to get the votes of those whose apathy can be overcome. How is this dilemma to be resolved? Increased public financing of campaigns? Elimination of all private financing? Increased media access for all candidates, or limitations on all candidates' access to the broadcast media? Increased voter participation, but how is this to be encouraged?

Another dilemma revolves around the political party system. Unlike parliamentary democracies, two large parties dominate, each with overlapping and easily altered (for mass appeal) political philosophies. Often voters feel that their choices are between two undesirable candidates, although in local elections this is less so because party affiliations are not as important (at least in smaller cities). Moreover, at times a viable third candidate can emerge in national elections—for example, in recent American history, George Wallace, John Anderson, and Ross Perot—to galvanize voter dissatisfaction, but these candidacies rarely exert enormous influence on the outcome of an election. The result is that choices for voters remain limited; and parties have unclear and highly malleable platforms as they try to appeal to the mass middle of the political spectrum, even in the face of viable third-party candidates. How, then, can more diversity in political discourse and voter options be created? Without a viable and stable multiparty system, there is no answer to this question.

There is still another problematic issue: Who has power to influence decisions? The debate in sociology has been between a (1) *power elite* perspective, arguing that a small elite group of industrialists, top-ranking military and their military-industrial-complex allies, and other elites disproportionately influence elections and decisions within government (Mills, 1956; Domhoff, 1990), and (2) a more *pluralist* perspective, arguing that no one group, amongst many competing interest groups, can dominate elections and political decisions. These positions do not have to be viewed as opposites; in fact, together they pose a profound dilemma. Power elites clearly exist, through documentation of formal and informal ties (Domhoff, 1970, 1983; Useem, 1980) at all levels of society—local, state and county, and national. They cannot dominate every decision, nor do they seek to. They can, however, influence disproportionately and often secretly critical decisions in government that affect their interests in corporate profits. Pluralist politics also exists, with the public's diverse opinions and wide varieties of interest groups also influencing decisions. The real problem is how much elite influence exists, and is the influence disproportionate in the face of the divisions of public opinion and diversity of interest groups? And can anything be done about it? As long as there is voter apathy, there is no answer to these questions; and as long as media campaigns are expensive, those who pay the bills—whether elites or special-interest groups—will often bias decision making away from the public's interests.

Yet another issue is the question of centralized power. An increasing portion of funding for local and state programs—schools, welfare, prisons, health care—comes from the federal government which gives it the power to set policies and make many decisions *for* state and local governments. This trend represents the centralization of power, ever more remote from local needs, but it also works to equalize government benefits by not letting states and local communities be too restrictive. Which is worse? unequal and, hence, unfair treatment of people at local levels? or increasing centralization of power at the national level? A related issue is not only the trend of power moving to the federal level (because "those who pay the bills call the shots"), but within federal government toward the executive branch. Increasingly, Congress *reacts to* initiatives from the President and top advisors rather than generates policies. Similarly, the judiciary has become more conservative in interpreting the Constitution, although much of this is the result of the last decades of appointments (a trend that could be reversed in future decades). The dilemma posed is that, as the executive branch initiates most key legislation and Congress can only react while being split by public opinion and influence from special interests, decision making increasingly falls to one person, the President, and the top advisors to the President. The end result is that power is more concentrated.

A final dilemma in American government is the ambivalence about regulation by government. Americans pay comparatively low taxes, the lowest in fact of the modern industrial world (except for Turkey which is, of course, not very modern); and we distrust the capacity of government to provide services in an efficient way. Yet, the governments of America's competitors in the world economy heavily intrude into both the social (save for Japan) and economic spheres, coordinating economic and social policies. And they all use tax revenues to redistribute wealth significantly (save for Japan again and France as well) and, perhaps more importantly, to encourage technological development and capital formation in selected areas within the economy. The United States has no coordinated economy policy; and it lags behind all industrial nations (save for perhaps England) in using tax revenues to subsidize technology and capital formation in key industries (defense being the only exception here). Without such subsidies American industry is less competitive, but to create them would involve raising taxes—a strategy that Americans are generally unwilling to accept even as their well-being is threatened by world economic competition.

These are some of the dilemmas faced by American government; and they are ones about which we all have well-formed opinions. What is necessary is for each of us to rethink our opinions in light of not only personal biases but also in relation to trends in the modern state and, most especially, in the new world economic order.

EDUCATION

Why Education Becomes So Pervasive

Education becomes a dominant institution only with industrialization or, as is often the case today, with concerted efforts by the governments of undeveloped or underdeveloped societies to encourage industrialization through mass education (and, I should add, political loyalty). For most of human history, however, education was informal and consisted of children simply watching their elders and, for specific skills, being instructed by their parents and relatives (J. Turner, 1972). Religious and social elites were perhaps the first to receive formal training; later more formal education was probably extended to nonelites who showed promise and to apprentices in some trades. But still, education remained recessive, lodged in kinship; and only for a relative few did explicit and formal structures exist. In traditional China, however, formal education had a much

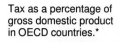

Tax as a percentage of
gross domestic product
in OECD countries.*

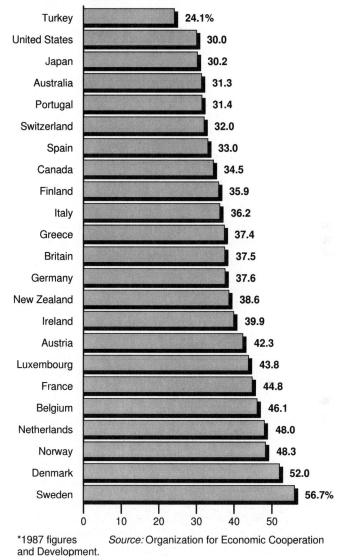

*1987 figures   *Source:* Organization for Economic Cooperation
and Development.

FIGURE 9-2. How much governments take in taxes

longer tradition and was perhaps extended to larger numbers, being the reward
for bright children of respectable families who wanted to place at least one of
their children in the Imperial bureaucracy. Thus, for most of the agrarian era,
education was primarily an institution for religious, military, and governmental
elites. It was extended to the masses only with industrialization.

Educational structures expanded because they were needed, and functionalists would argue that they have become prominent because of their major functions, including (J. Turner, 1972) socialization of necessary skills, knowledge, dispositions, and beliefs to the young; social placement of people into the society on the basis of educational credentials; cultural storage in libraries and in the minds of teachers and scholars of knowledge; and, increasingly, cultural innovation in the creation of new ideas and symbols, most particularly those with technological implications.

Other interpretations of why formal education expands are less benign. Conflict theories often argue that education in modern capitalist societies like ours is geared toward indoctrinating people into beliefs (about private property, competition, and individualism, for example) and role-playing skills necessary for a market-driven economy controlled by economic and political elites (Apple, 1982; Apple and Weis, 1983). Schools also provide the technical and administrative knowledge necessary for running a capitalist economic system; and so, education is tied to the economy in ways that perpetuate the existing class system (Bowles and Gintis, 1976; Apple, 1982).

Other conflict theories stress the importance of education for pacifying those who do not make it economically in the society; for, if schools are open to all and are the key to success in getting ahead, failure to do well in school and, hence, secure a decent job are the person's "own fault." They had their chance and did not take advantage of it. More generally, schools are seen to indoctrinate children into the values and beliefs of dominant economic, political, and status groups, forcing all to define themselves and their successes or failures by the yardstick of elites (Collins, 1976).

Indeed, some have argued that **credentialism,** or the necessity of securing degrees to gain access to jobs, forces people like you to accept what the schools demand, if you want to do well. As Randall Collins (1979) points out, these credentials often bear little relationship to technical job requirements which, for the most part, can be learned on the job. Credentials become an easy way to sort and select potential workers without great effort, and they become a way to certify that a worker is committed to the system. But credentialism is inherently inflationary in this sense: The more people who get them, the less their value in securing desirable jobs, and as a result, the more people must secure additional credentials to stand out in the job market. A high school diploma was once (and probably still is in the technical sense) enough for most routine service and bureaucratic jobs, but now a college degree is often required. And increasingly, if one wants to stand out from the pack, additional credentials are needed. However, the more credentials a person receives, the more one certifies the way the current social order is structured. If you feel that you are on an educational treadmill which is speeding up, there are good reasons for this feeling. Yet, while the extra increment of income that comes with each educational credential is decreasing, a person will still make much more money with these credentials. For example, among those at their income peak (40 to 65 years old), only 10 percent of families with less than high school degrees made over $50,000 in 1990; 28 percent of those with high school degrees did so; 30 percent with some college accomplish this level of income; 58 percent with a college degree could do it; and

65 percent with a graduate degree managed to secure this kind of income (Stark, 1992, p. 487).

Still other theories combine elements of functional and conflict arguments. John Meyer (1977), for example, argues that levels of education are the key to entrance into status groups and to the prestige and honor that they offer. A high school degree allows you to claim only a certain amount of status, a college degree somewhat more, a master's degree even more, and an M.D. or a Ph.D. allows you to be "royal" in some contexts. At each stage, the function of education is the dissemination of the proper demeanor, attitudes, and disposi-tions for all the status groups which will be open to you with a particular credential.

Meyer also emphasizes that educational structures are hardly passive, stamping people out so that they can be cogs in the existing system. Educational structures, especially colleges and universities, *create* new elite positions in the occupational sphere. Education generates new knowledge, new credentials, and new positions in the economy; and the more an economy engages in work that involves information as opposed to machines, the more the educational struc-tures have power to dictate to economic and political elites what they need—whether it be Ph.D. scientists, MBAs, or law school graduates. None of these credentials served as job requirements during early industrialism; now, they are indispensable to modern corporations.

Thus, educational systems emerge to do many things in a modern society—necessary functional things like socialize the young, place people in the economy, store culture, and innovate; and less obviously functional things like (1) generate commitments to the existing order as defined by elites, (2) blame people rather than the order for their lack of success, and (3) keep people on a credential's treadmill to certify their commitment to the society and its political economy. Moreover, as education becomes a dominant institution, it also becomes a powerful force in its own right, and it begins to define *what* credentials, knowl-edge, and positions a society *should* have.

Basic Elements of Education

Educational structures all consist of two basic status positions: teacher and student. As educational structures become large and complex, processing ever larger numbers of students, new positions are added—administrators, librarians, computer-related jobs, research, maintenance, and so on. School structures inevi-tably become bureaucratized as they get larger, and they come to form a system of bureaucracies that constitutes a career for students who move from primary, to secondary, to college, and to graduate schools. And there is an amazing consensus over the cultural symbols—beliefs and norms—about how people should act in, and react to, this system, although in America there is perhaps more controversy over these symbols than in other societies (there are good structural reasons for this, as we will see shortly).

We can thus define the **institution of education** as a system of formal bureaucratic structures designed to socialize, facilitate the placement of people into the society, to store knowledge, to generate new systems of culture. At the same time, education has many additional consequences (some intended, others not) for creating and perpetuating class and status group boundaries and for forcing commitments to the existing social order.

Education in America

Like its counterparts in the modern industrial world, the American education system is hierarchical, composed of three basic levels: the primary, the secondary, and the higher (college) educational systems; and like its counterparts in other countries, it uses a combination of grades and standardized examinations for evaluating and sorting students. But the American system is unique in several important ways (J. Turner, 1972).

One is that, unlike all other modern systems, the American system is decentralized. There is no "ministry of education" at the federal level that funds and sets the curriculum for all the schools. Instead, through a wide variety of federal programs—from school lunch programs to Operation Head Start—money comes from the federal government to local school districts, but there is no coordinated plan for these diverse monies. Moreover, about half the budget for primary and secondary schools comes from local and state taxes. This fact leads to the belief—and a very powerful one—that primary and secondary schools are *local* and should reflect local needs and interests rather than those of remote state and federal government. For, Americans believe more than any other people in the world that community sentiment and pressure should guide educational policy; and it is for this reason that local school boards are elected and adjunct organizations like the PTA are so prominent. At the higher-education level, even more decentralization and autonomy exist. Colleges and universities are funded by student tuition and fees, state and local tax monies, research grants, private gifts, interest earned on endowments, and a limited number of federal programs.

A second distinctive feature of the American educational system is that much of it is private. At the lower level (primary and secondary schools), private elite schools, schools for problem children, and church schools all exist alongside a system of public schools. Virtually all the funding for these private schools comes from tuition, donations, and perhaps interest from an endowment. At the higher level, many colleges and universities are private, with most if not all of their budget coming from tuition, gifts, and interest from the endowment. A few elite, research-oriented universities receive a significant amount of income from federal, state, and corporate research grants.

A third feature of the American system is that it tracks students within the school on the basis of grades and standardized exams, whereas in most other societies, students are sent to different types of secondary schools on separate campuses. The result is that considerable mixing of students in different tracks occurs in American schools; indeed, these are usually explicit efforts to force such mixing. In other societies, college-bound or college-eligible students are sent to their own schools, with various types of vocational training in separate schools offered to those who did not make the college grade.

A fourth unique feature of American schools is their lack of rigid barriers to college. There is a vast system of junior colleges (which do not exist in other societies) to provide the first two years of college for those who cannot afford, or who did not qualify the first time around. Moreover, the sheer scale of American higher education creates opportunities. For example, there are close to 2000 colleges and universities in America; very few other societies even approach 100. This volume of options for students with varying levels of skill and accomplishment creates many more opportunities than in other societies. Indeed, it is not an unreasonable guess that when junior and regular four-year colleges are combined, there are more higher-education opportunities in America than in the rest of the world, certainly the modern world, combined.

Higher education is also somewhat unique because much of the basic research and innovation for the society is conducted in universities, creating a large number of graduate school opportunities. In many other societies, basic research is done primarily in separate academies of science or in private industry. In America, such academies tend to be honorific organizations, with most basic research being conducted in universities, in research and development departments of large corporations, and in a few corporate laboratories, such as Bell Labs, devoted to basic research.

Many problems are perceived to exist in the American system (Turner and Musick, 1985). One is the declining test scores of children and adolescents in American schools, relative to students in the past and to students in other countries. Whether the school is the blame here ("bad teachers," "ineffective administrators," and the like) or working parents and perhaps too much television (from cartoons to MTV) is unclear. Probably all are involved, but no solutions currently appear viable, especially as tax revenues to schools level off or decline.

Another perceived problem is that the schools do not effectively reach large categories of students, especially poor and minority students. If these students cannot do well, they will not have "equal opportunities"; and while programs exist to overcome the problems (in home and neighborhood) of poor and minority children, results are mixed. With each year of school, more affluent children pull away from poorer ones on all standardized test scores, indicating that family, neighborhood, and peers have powerful effects on school performance. And as poor students get discouraged, they drop out of high schools at much higher rates, killing forever their chances for success in the society. How, then, is the school to overcome these effects? There is no easy answer.

Another dilemma revolves around the class and cultural bias of the schools: They reflect middle-class and white beliefs about what should occur. And these biases are built into the whole system of competitive grading and standardized tests with largely white, Anglo content. Critics charge that children with different beliefs, language, and life experiences can never do well in a system so rigged against them. Defenders counter that the schools reflect the nature of skilled jobs in the society, and if children are to be successful in the real world, they had better learn to perform in the schools. The dilemma is that both positions are correct, and how is one or the other side to be weighed in formulating school policy? Again, there is no easy answer.

RELIGION

Humans have great mental abilities that have enabled them to adapt and survive, but these same abilities allow us to worry about almost everything, ponder the meaning of it all, think about death, remember the past and the loved ones lost, and anticipate an unknown future. The emotions and general anxiety generated by these heady preoccupations are what led humans to create religion as a way of coping with unbridled cognitive speculation and worry. At first religions were not very elaborate, consisting of ancestor worship of dead relatives within the kinship system and appeals to the forces of nature to lend a helping hand. Hunters and gatherers had these simple religions, but the nature of religion began to change with horticulture and later agrarianism. Religion became a central institution in people's lives; specialized religious practitioners emerged; gods and supernatural forces became more powerful and numerous; and ritual appeals to these forces became more frequent and organized (Wallace, 1966). Then suddenly, in just a few centuries, the world religions—Christianity, Hinduism, Buddhism, Confucianism, and Islam—came to dominate, sweeping across great spans of territory and then sweeping away many local religions (Bellah, 1964). And today, a quick review of the front page of a newspaper informs us that religion is a highly salient and volatile force—one which is not going away as so many, including me (J. Turner, 1972), predicted just a few decades ago.

For a functionalist, this persistence of religion means that religion meets certain basic needs of individuals and society. What are some of these needs? One is the need to reduce anxiety and tension, and if people can make appeals to special forces and beings, this appears to help. Another is reinforcing crucial norms and values, for if the supernatural says this or that behavior is right and tells us to conform, we are more likely to do it, thereby facilitating the integration of society.

But as Karl Marx (Marx and Engels, 1848) argued, religion can also be a tool of repression. Elites can use it to pacify the masses by making them think that the way things are is the will of god(s) and by promising them something better in death. Marx's famous phrase—"religion is the opiate of the masses"—captures this line of argument, for if religion is functional, for whom is it functional? Who benefits? Marx's answer: It is the norms of those who enjoy privilege that are reinforced by religion; and it is the misery and anxiety of the deprived that is mollified by religion. In Marx's eye, then, religion hides the fundamental conflict of interest between those who have resources and those who do not; and it thereby legitimizes existing inequalities, making them seem correct and pulling the wool over people's real interests.

Whatever the merits of Marx's argument, there can be no doubt that religion is at the center of a great deal of conflict in the world—today and in the past. Religion is often associated with ethnic conflicts, with disputes over territory, and, as Marx stressed, with conflicts of interest over resources. Because religion charges people's emotions and puts them under the power of special forces, it becomes a volatile force in conflict, escalating the level of intensity whenever it becomes implicated. We should, therefore, know more about this basic institution in human societies.

Basic Elements of Religion

All religions have certain elements in common. One is a distinction between the *sacred* and the *supernatural*, on the one hand, and the **profane,** or secular, on the other. All religions impute special powers to objects, events, forces, and at times, persons; and these special and wondrous powers to influence daily life make them **sacred**. Most religions also postulate a **supernatural** realm, beyond the everyday, mundane world where the sacred forces, beings, objects, and events exist and operate.

The concepts of sacred and supernatural are part of more general sets of religious *values* and *beliefs*. **Religious beliefs** articulate the nature of the sacred and supernatural, often spelling out in detail diverse beings and forces as well as distinct realms of the supernatural. When sacred beings and forces are being described, this is a **pantheon,** a kind of organization chart and "who's who" of the supernatural. **Religious values** are statements, emanating from the supernatural, about what is right, wrong, good, and bad; and although other values exist in a society, these have a special quality because they are sanctioned and backed up by the sacred beings and forces of the supernatural realm.

Religious values and beliefs are connected to people and society by behavioral *rituals* and organized *religious structures* (Wallace, 1966; J. Turner, 1972). A **religious ritual** is a patterned and stereotyped sequence of actions—bodily and verbal—directed toward the supernatural and asking for its intervention in the secular, profane world. A **religious structure** is the unit within which rituals are performed, and these can vary from a gathering of aboriginals around a totem to a storefront church in America and on to the world Roman Catholic bureaucracy. Those who are members of a religious structure—whether big or small, permanent or transient, old or new—share religious beliefs and values, practice common rituals, and as a result, develop a sense of togetherness and "community."

We can thus define *religion* as the complex of structures that articulate certain values and beliefs as well as organize people's ritual practices directed toward sacred beings and forces believed to inhabit a supernatural realm. The consequences of such structures can vary from integrating a society to tearing it apart, and from alleviating people's anxieties and tensions to aggravating existing tensions over ethnicity, class, region, or religious beliefs and values themselves.

Religion in America

The United States is overwhelmingly Christian, as can be seen in Table 9-1. Some of these denominations listed in Table 9-1 are growing, others declining. Among the larger denominations, the Presbyterian Church of the United States, United Methodists, the Episcopal Church, and Evangelical Lutheran Church have all declined in membership as a proportion of the population, and dramatically so.

TABLE 9.1. Religious Affiliations in the United States, 1991

FAMILY/Denomination	Total membership	Percent of total affiliated	FAMILY/Denomination	Total membership	Percent of total affiliated
ALL RELIGIOUSLY AFFILIATED	**47,607,394**	**100.0**	Apostolic Catholic Assyrian Church of the East	120,000	
ROMAN CATHOLIC CHURCH	**57,019,948**	**38.6**	Others (13 denominations)	444,939	
BAPTIST CHURCHES	**28,463,978**	**19.3**	**LATTER-DAY SAINTS CHURCHES**	**4,370,690**	**3.0**
Southern Baptist Convention	14,907,826		Church of Jesus Christ of Latter-day Saints	4,175,400	
National Baptist Convention, USA, Inc.	5,500,000		Reorganized Church of Jesus Christ of Latter-day Saints	190,183	
National Baptist Convention of America	2,668,799		Others (2 denominations)	5,107	
American Baptist Churches in the USA	1,548,573		**CHURCHES OF CHRIST**	**3,748,887**	**2.5**
Baptist Bible Fellowship International	1,405,900		Churches of Christ	1,626,000	
Progressive National Baptist Convention, Inc.	521,692		Christian Churches and Churches of Christ	1,070,616	
American Baptist Association	250,000		Christian Church (Disciples of Christ)	1,052,271	
National Primitive Baptist Convention Inc.	250,000		**PRESBYTERIAN CHURCHES**	**3,366,411**	**2.3**
Baptist Missionary Association of America	229,315		Presbyterian Church (USA)	2,886,482	
General Association of Regular Baptist Churches	216,468		Presbyterian Church in America	217,374	
Conservative Baptist Association of America	210,000		Others (7 denominations)	256,555	
Free Will Baptists, National Association of	204,489		**EPISCOPAL CHURCH**	**2,433,413**	**1.6**
Liberty Baptist Fellowship	200,000		**REFORMED CHURCHES**	**2,205,589**	**1.5**
Baptist General Conference	133,742		United Church of Christ	1,625,969	
Other (10 denominations)	217,174		Reformed Church in America	330,650	
METHODIST CHURCHES	**13,229,155**	**9.0**	Christian Reformed Church in North America	225,699	
United Methodist Church	8,979,139		Others (4 denominations)	23,271	
African Methodist Episcopal Church	2,210,000		**HOLINESS CHURCHES**	**1,245,810**	**0.8**
African Methodist Episcopal Zion Church	1,220,260		Church of the Nazarene	561,253	
Christian Methodist Episcopal Church	718,922		Christian and Missionary Alliance	265,863	
Others (8 denominations)	100,834		Church of God (Anderson, Ind.)	199,786	
LUTHERAN CHURCHES	**8,374,898**	**5.7**	Wesleyan Church	110,027	
Evangelical Lutheran Church in America	5,238,798		Christian Congregation	108,881	
Lutheran Church—Missouri Synod	2,609,025		**JEHOVAH'S WITNESSES**	**825,570**	**0.5**
Wisconsin Evangelical Lutheran Synod	419,312		**ADVENTIST CHURCHES**	**733,249**	**0.5**
Others (10 denominations)	107,763		Seventh-Day Adventists	701,781	
PENTECOSTAL CHURCHES	**7,931,294**	**5.4**	Others (3 denominations)	31,468	
Church of God in Christ	3,709,661		**CHURCH OF CHRIST, SCIENTIST**	**700,000[1]**	**0.4**
Assemblies of God	2,137,890		**SALVATION ARMY**	**445,566**	**0.3**
Church of God (Cleveland, Tenn.)	582,203		**ROMAN RITE CHURCHES**	**345,022**	**0.2**
United Pentecostal Church International	500,000		Polish National Catholic Church of America	282,411	
International Church of the Foursquare Gospel	203,060		North American Old Roman Catholic Church	62,611	
Church of God in Christ, International	200,000		**MENNONITE CHURCHES**	**250,645**	**0.2**
Pentecostal Holiness Church International	119,073		Mennonite Church	92,517	
Others (21 denominations)	479,407		Old Order Amish Church	70,650	
ORTHODOX (EASTERN) CHURCHES	**4,659,939**	**3.2**	Others (9 denominations)	87,478	
Greek Orthodox Archdiocese of North and South America	1,950,000		**INTERNATIONAL CONFEDERATION OF COMMUNITY CHURCHES**	**250,000**	**0.2**
Orthodox Church in America	1,000,000		**BRETHREN CHURCHES**	**225,842**	**0.2**
Armenian Church of America, Diocese of the	450,000		Church of the Brethren	149,681	
Antiochian Orthodox Christian Archdiocese of North America	350,000		Others (5 denominations)	76,161	
Armenian Apostolic Church of America	180,000		**UNITARIAN UNIVERSALIST ASSOCIATION**	**182,211**	**0.1**
Coptic Orthodox Church	165,000		**EVANGELICAL FREE CHURCH OF AMERICA**	**165,000**	**0.1**
			FRIENDS (QUAKER) CHURCHES (5 denominations)	**118,070**	**0.1**
			TOTAL CHRISTIAN CHURCHES	**141,443,624**	**95.8**
			JEWS	**5,944,000**	**4.0**
			MUSLIMS	**3,000,000[2]**	**N.A.**
			BUDDHIST CHURCHES OF AMERICA	**19,441**	**(Z)**
			OTHER RELIGIONS	**200,329**	**0.1**

Source: Yearbook of American & Canadian Churches, 1991 and *The Universal Almanac, 1993*

164

Others such as Roman Catholics have been losing members, but less dramatically. Among the smaller churches, some denominations are growing rapidly: Seventh-Day Adventist, Mormons, United Pentecostal, Jehovah's Witnesses, Church of God (Cleveland, Tennessee), Assemblies of God, and, the fastest growing of all, the Church of God in Christ. These growing denominations were relatively small thirty years ago, and so with a small base of members, their rates of growth could be very high. Also, it should be noted that the figures in Table 9-1 are self-reports by each denomination of their membership, and hence there is, no doubt, some inflation of membership statistics as each denomination seeks to present itself in a favorable light.

Yet there is a pattern here: Older established and somewhat staid denominations have been losing members, whereas the evangelical religious denominations have been gaining members. The explanation resides in the early work of Richard Niebuhr (1929) who was interested in explaining why America was divided—indeed fractured—into so many denominations. Could it be simply the high levels of religious freedom of America? If this were an adequate answer, other societies would be equally fractured, and they are not. The answer, Niebuhr felt, was in the tendency of older, established churches to "intellectualize" their teachings and, thereby, make them more secular, less immediate, and less emotional. This is because more affluent people begin to join successful religions, but unlike those who are less affluent, they do not require the emotional, evangelical spirit that may have started the religion; they are, after all, more secure and less worried about their lives. For many, this tendency takes away the appeal of religion, especially for the masses who need and want religion to "solve" their immediate problems and anxieties. And so, new religions appeal to them because they can become more evangelical, emotional, immediate, while being less intellectual, cerebral, and secular. There is, Niebuhr felt, a class conflict dimension to religion in America, with older and less evangelical denominations appealing to the affluent, prompting the lower classes to look elsewhere.

Following Niebuhr's lead, others began to see that the broader secular trends of the society in many institutional spheres, especially as fueled by the growth of science as an institution, are a part of the pattern of religious fracturing in America (Stark and Bainbridge, 1980; Stark, 1981). Societywide secularization penetrates some religions, and in so doing, it becomes less salient to many who want and need religion in an immediate and emotional way. The result is that a market for religious zeal emerges—a big market—and new denominations, often using the media very effectively, emerge and win converts. Many of these fail, but as the growth figures indicate, many succeed and dramatically so. When old faiths become too secular, then, they lose members to the new, more evangelical groups; and so, we might predict that secularization of societies creates market niches for new denominations, leading to intense differentiation and competition among denominations (see the section on Organizational Ecology, pp. 105–106, for a review of the basic dynamics involved here, as organizations compete for resources).

Such has clearly been the trend in America; and it has the consequences of splitting the population in terms of *how* evangelical they are and *how much* religion will penetrate into their daily lives. And many of the major conflicts in America—prayer in schools, abortion, the teaching of Darwinian evolution in the schools—reflect this split in the cult structures, or denominations, in terms of how fervently evangelical or secular they are.

MEDICINE

For most of human history, religious practitioners—shamans, "witch doctors," and priests—were intimately involved in helping to deal with illness and disease. Appeals to sacred and supernatural forces were often all that was possible, although early humans developed many effective "folk medicines" as well. From these modest beginnings medicine gradually began to be structured as a separate institution, and with agrarianism its profile as a distinct kind of human activity is evident. The position of doctor and nurse, or their equivalents, began to emerge; and structures looking like hospitals and infirmaries became evident. In Europe, the Catholic Church often served as the locus of hospitals, with nuns doubling as nurses, indicating once again that religion and medicine often remain tied together well up to the modern era (indeed, religion is still involved in the organization of hospitals).

The separation of religion and medicine was probably more pronounced early on in societal development, as in Egypt, Greece, and Rome, but in Europe during the Middle Ages, the power of the Catholic Church made this separation more difficult. But slowly, along with the emergence of science as an institution, medicine became a distinct institution. New knowledge was acquired; hospitals were now often secular (though in many cases, disease-ridden and unsafe); and the positions of doctor, nurse, pharmacist, and other medical specialties became established and organized as a system.

We can thus define the **institution of medicine** as all those positions organized into structures which seek to develop and use secular and increasingly scientific knowledge to diagnose, prevent, and treat illness and disease among humans. At first this institution was recessive, but today, medicine is a massive institutional complex, consuming around from 6 to 9 percent of the gross national product in most industrial societies (even more in the United States).

Functional theories would emphasize that the growth of medicine occurred because of basic needs, which religion could not adequately meet, for physical health. The obvious function is the prevention and cure of illness and disease—conditions which grew ever worse as people crowded into the unsanitary urban centers of evolving societies and which, as a result, created enormous anxiety and tension. And as medicine became more established and scientific, its functions expanded to research in diagnosis, prevention, and cure of illness, to the defining of who is and who is not "sick" (Parsons, 1951), and to the provision of health maintenance for all citizens.

Conflict theorists would add some additional considerations. First, medicine becomes a focal point of class conflict because the more affluent can afford it, the less affluent cannot. Thus, health becomes one of the scarce resources that is unequally distributed; and it is not surprising that some of the most powerful political pressures in a society are toward increasing the less affluents' access to medical care. Second, there is considerable conflict within the institution of medicine over who is to dominate. For example, Paul Starr (1982) documents the transformation of medicine in America to an ever more market-driven commodity in which doctors mobilized to gain control and to endow themselves with a cultural mystique that enabled them to regulate themselves, demand client deference, control who was to become a doctor, and most importantly, acquire authority over nurses, medical research, hospital policies, pharmacists, and just about all other positions in the medical system. In so doing, they gained power, wealth, and prestige at the expense of other medical positions and, of course, their clients. Thus, in modern societies medicine becomes a principal interest group which controls an enormous amount of the GNP and which finds itself in conflict with other interests, often including the public's health. This is, at least, what a conflict theory would emphasize (Conrad and Kern, 1986).

Medicine in America represents a major social problem. It now accounts for close to 12 percent of the GNP; it is often out of the reach of poor and less affluent citizens; it is a jumble of private insurance, public assistance (Medicaid), old-age assistance (Medicare), and health maintenance organizations; it has become expensive to enter hospitals because most private ones operate at less than full capacity and because they have become competitive with respect to how much expensive high-tech hardware they can buy; major corporations are now having trouble remaining competitive in the world system because of the costs of medical insurance premiums for workers; and government budgets and deficits are now tied to the high cost of medical care for the poor and elderly.

The result of these problems is ironic: One can get the very best medical care in the world in America—if you have the money. On the other, side the United States along with South Africa is the only modern nation in the world that does not extend the right to all its citizens for quality medical care. Poor people must use public facilities—county hospitals, Medicaid clinics, hospital emergency rooms, and the like—to receive medical care which is dramatically lower in quality than that received by the more affluent whose insurance buys them access to private facilities.

These problems ultimately reside in several conditions: There is an imperfect and oligopolistic market system operating in the delivery of medical care. Doctors, hospitals, and other medical facilities have, until recently, been able to set prices, whereas their clients—patients—have not been able to shop around. Private insurance companies are often the middle broker between this medical system and their clients, thereby adding to the administrative costs of the system. And, government has been reluctant to intervene and set prices for services except for its clients—the poor and elderly—with the result that the medical system tends not to want them as clients, especially the poor under Medicaid, because they cannot pay the full fare. The result is that the United States spends more money on medical care than any nation in the world, and yet, it still does not have a system that reaches all its citizens. In recent years, however, the costs and inequities of the system are forcing change: Big corporations and their insurers are beginning to demand fixed costs and special deals for the volume clients; prepaid health maintenance organizations (HMOs) and programs are sweeping the system in an effort to fix costs; and political as well as fiscal pressures are building for some sort of national health insurance system. These are issues with which we will all grapple in the coming decade; and our health, well-being, and pocketbook will be dramatically affected by what transpires.

SCIENCE

As we saw in Chapter 2, science has become the dominant means for people in the modern world to try to understand events in the universe. Because the goals of science overlap with those of religion—understanding of the here and now, as well as of the past and future—the two were often merged together in the past. Early speculation about the stars, the sun, and the universe was often laden with religious content, but the astronomers and mathematicians in ancient societies— in meso-America through the Old World and Mesopotamia to China and the rest of Asia—also anticipated a new kind of human activity: the effort to understand the universe in terms of objective criteria. In Europe, the transition to science was punctuated by conflict; indeed Copernicus was persecuted for his assertion that the earth revolved around the sun rather than the earth being the center of the universe. In the end, what proved to be decisive for the emergence of science in the West was status competition among elites and among emerging nations. Those who had the best scientists and who could claim the most recent discoveries as *theirs* were able to claim prestige—a highly valued resource. And so, wealthy patrons financed science; and lords of the realm courted scientists to come to their kingdom. The result was a burst of creative activity, accelerating the Renaissance in Europe.

Science became further institutionalized when its utility in the development of new technologies for the economy and military was recognized. And ever since, science has been used to generate new technologies not only for economic and military activity but for virtually all social realms. And as science expanded its horizons, its structural base shifted from elite patronage to universities, government institutes, and corporate sponsors. Thus, we can visualize **science** as the organization of positions in a variety of social structures—from universities through government-sponsored academies and institutes of science to research and development units in business—that are designed to produce secular knowledge about how the universe operates in terms of the procedures of the scientific method (see Chapter 2, pages 24–28). Such activity is guided by basic norms emphasizing objectivity in the collection of data and in the assessment of theoretical laws (Merton, 1957, pp. 550–562).

There is, however, a large literature—both in philosophy and sociology— which recognizes what conflict theorists always stress: Science is an institution which serves some interests in a society more than others and which is used to benefit the more privileged in a society. Indeed some have argued that science invades other domains, objectifying and impersonalizing them in ways that dampen the human spirit (Habermas, 1970). Yet, functional theorists would argue that science meets basic needs for knowledge which can be used to better organize human efforts to survive; and it is for this reason that it has come to have such great influence on economic, political, and educational institutions.

As humans' most recently evolved institution, science is a topic worth understanding. We saw in Chapter 2 what it seeks to do, but perhaps more important is the degree to which it has infiltrated our daily lives. For while we have all become accustomed to what science provides in the way of "the good life," we should pause to think about the implications of a relentless search for new knowledge in the name of "progress," "profits," "security," and other goals. For, in any institutional sphere—economy, education, military, medicine, polity, and even religion—we can find the influence of science. In the economy, science drives a relentless search for new technologies in a highly competitive world economic system. In education, science teaching is highly prized in lower education; and much of the higher educational system, especially elite universities, revolves around scientific research; medicine is driven by scientific efforts to secure new and better "cures" for illness, a process which also drives up costs. Government finances much basic science, and its military component uses such knowledge in making new weapons. And religion often stands in an uneasy confrontation as the secular interests of science conflict with the sacred concerns of religion. Science, then, has become a major institutional force in modern societies.

SUMMARY

1. Social institutions are congeries of positions and structures that seek to resolve fundamental problems of humans as a species, and as a species that relies upon culturally mediated patterns of social organization. Because of their perceived importance, most of the general norms guiding behavior in institutional structures are well known and infused with values and beliefs.
2. Kinship is the institution that organizes relations around marriage and blood ties. Such organization is achieved through a series of norms guiding conduct with respect to marriage, descent, residence, authority, division of labor, family size, and dissolution. Such rules regularize relations in ways to resolve such fundamental problems facing humans as sex and mating, biological and social support, socialization, and social placement. Kinship in America is dominated by isolated nuclear units in which romantic love dominates mate selection and crucial norms over authority and division of labor are ambiguous and rapidly changing.
3. The economy is the institution that organizes technology, labor, and material capital for gathering resources from the environment, converting these resources through production into usable goods and commodities, and distributing these goods and commodities to members of the society. There has been a number of basic economic forms in the history of humans—hunting and gathering, horticulture, agrarianism, industrialism, and postindustrialism. The American economy is now fully postindustrial, revolving around services as much as manufacturing.

4. Government is the institution that uses power to set goals for a society and to mobilize resources for achieving these goals. When power becomes bureaucratically organized, a state can be said to exist. Modern states vary with respect to the rationality of their administrative bureaucracy, the centralization of decision-making power, the extensiveness of state intervention into domestic affairs, the level of democracy in the selection of leaders, the division of power among the judiciary, executive, and legislative branches, and the level of legitimacy attributed to government. Government in America is clearly becoming more centralized, with ever more power concentrated in the executive branch.

5. Education is the institution explicitly established as a set of formal organizations to provide socialization of necessary skills, to place people into economic positions, to store culture, and to generate innovations. All education systems reveal a set of primary, secondary, and higher-educational organizations. The American education system is by far the most decentralized and privatized of the modern systems in the world.

6. Religion is the institution that organizes ritual practices directed toward sacred and supernatural forces in the affirmation of certain beliefs. Religion appears to meet basic needs for anxiety and tension reduction in people and for reinforcing critical norms and values. Religion in America is overwhelmingly Christian, and yet within Christianity, a large number of denominations appear to ebb and flow in their capacity to attract and retain members.

7. Medicine is the institution devoted to organizing activities designed to prevent, treat, and cure illness. Medicine begins within religion, but becomes a separate and dominant institution with industrialization. Currently, medicine consumes significant portions of all modern society's gross domestic product. Medicine in America is undergoing rapid changes as the old system of private doctors, insurance companies, and government provision for the elderly and poor has become too inefficient, too unequal, and too expensive.

8. Science is the institution devoted to organizing the objective search for, and accumulation of, knowledge about the operation of the universe. Science has become a dominant institution in modern societies, penetrating all basic institutions and often standing in conflict with religion.

KEY TERMS

avunculocal rule   A residence rule specifying that a married couple and their children are to live with the male's mother's brother.

bilateral descent   A rule of descent specifying that the male's and female's side of the family and kin network will be given equal importance.

capital   The implements of economic production, and the money used to purchase these implements.

chiefdom   A form of polity in which one man comes to dominate decisions among populations organized on the basis of kinship rules.

clan   A kinship structure created when lineages are linked together by a descent rule.

coercion   The use of physical force in social relations.

credentialism   The reliance, indeed overreliance, on educational credentials for placement in the economy—a practice that stimulates credential inflation.

descent rules   Norms specifying whether the male's or female's side of the family and kin network are more important in terms of property and authority.

economy, institution of The organization of technology, capital, and labor into structures for the purpose of gathering natural resources, producing goods and services, and distributing these goods and services to members of a society.

education, institution of Formal bureaucratic structures designed to (1) socialize and facilitate the placement of people into positions in society, (2) store knowledge, and (3) generate new systems of culture.

endogamy A rule specifying that individuals must marry within another kin group or community.

entrepreneurship The organizational forms and capacities that coordinate technology, capital, and labor.

exogamy A rule specifying that individuals must marry outside a kin group or community.

extended family unit A kinship unit created when several nuclear units are joined in one household.

government, structure of The organization of leaders, power, and decision making in a society.

incest rules Norms prohibiting sex and marriage among parents and offspring, and at times other closely related kin.

industrialization The process of harnessing inanimate sources of power and machines attended by labor to the gathering of resources, the production of goods and commodities, and the distribution of goods and commodities.

institution/social institution Societywide structures that organize groups, organizations, and community with respect to basic human and organizational needs.

kinship, institution of The organization of marriage and blood ties among members of a society into structures that have consequences for regularizing sex and mating, providing for biological and social support, socializing the young, and placing the young into adult positions.

labor The persons performing economic activities.

leadership, governmental The ability of some in a society to make decisions for mobilizing resources and coordinating activities.

legitimacy The acceptance by those subject to power of the right of those using power to do so.

lineage A kinship structure created when several extended family units are linked together by descent and residence rules.

marriage rules Norms specifying who can marry whom in a society, and when.

matrilineal descent A rule of descent specifying that the woman's side of the family and kin network (especially her male kindred) are to be the most important in terms of property and authority.

matrilocal rule A kinship norm specifying that a married couple and their children are to live with the female's family and kin.

medicine, institution of Those structures in a society designed to develop and use secular knowledge to diagnose, prevent, and treat illness and disease.

moiety A kinship unit created when clans are linked together.

neolocal rule A residence rule indicating that a married couple and their children have autonomy in deciding for themselves where to live.

nuclear family unit The family unit created by the married couple and their offspring.

pantheon A set of religious beliefs specifying the inhabitants, as well as their relations and life histories, of the supernatural realm.

patrilineal descent A rule of descent specifying that the male's side of the family and kin network are to be the most important in terms of property and authority.

patrilocal rule   A kinship norm specifying that a married couple and their children are to live with the male's family and kin.

polity   The generic term for patterns of governance in a society.

power   The capacity to enforce decisions and have one's way.

profane   Denoting processes in the empirical world, in comparison with the sacred which is of the supernatural world.

religious beliefs   Conceptions about the nature of the sacred and supernatural as well as the entities and forces in the supernatural realm.

religious rituals   Stereotyped sequences of behavior designed to make appeals to the forces of the supernatural realm.

religious structure   The unit organizing rituals and sustaining religious beliefs and values.

religious values   Conceptions of what is right and wrong, as well as what should exist and occur, that are viewed as emanating from supernatural forces.

residence rules   Norms specifying where married couples are to live and reside.

romantic love complex   A set of beliefs emphasizing mutual attraction and compatibility as the basis for selecting marriage partners.

sacred   Objects and forces having a special quality because they are connected to perceived supernatural powers.

science, institution of   Those social structures designed to produce secular knowledge (in terms of theory and research) about how the universe operates.

state, the   The bureaucratic organization of the center of coercive power, legitimate authority, and civil administration in a society.

supernatural   A realm where gods and unworldly forces operate.

technology   Systems of symbols organized into knowledge about how to manipulate the environment.

CHAPTER 10

Population, Community, and Environment

The human population has been growing at an alarming rate, forcing people to live in urban areas and to suffer the consequences of pollution. Probably the most significant danger to our survival as a species is overpopulation, because more people means that resources are consumed faster, that cities become polluted and dangerous places (as is illustrated by the pollution in the sky and danger in the streets of large cities like Los Angeles), and that disease and famine become a condition of life for much of the world's population. If we consume all of our resources, if we create the conditions fostering deadly disease like AIDS or some of the older killers of humans like tuberculosis, if we overtax city facilities, if we destroy other life forms with pollution, then our chances of surviving in the future are greatly diminished.

The number of people in a society, their distribution in space, their patterns of organization, their storehouses of cultural symbols, and their effects on the environment are all interrelated. Growing numbers of people in a society have profound effects on social structures: Production expands; power becomes concentrated; inequality increases; subcultures proliferate; deviance increases; urbanization takes off; and conflict escalates. The science which studies populations—not only its size but also its characteristics, movements, distribution, and growth or decline—is called **demography** (Weeks, 1989; Menard and Moen, 1987; Almgren, 1992). In the first part of this chapter, I will examine some of the basic ways sociological demographers examine human populations.

Populations are, of course, more than a blur of people; they are *organized* and located in space. The organization of people in geographical space is, as I noted in Chapter 4, the defining characteristic of **community** structures. As populations grow, and as other social structures become necessary, communities become larger and more urban. The process of **urbanization** concentrates ever more people in space; and it is a fundamental fact of modern life, as we will explore in the second major section of this chapter.

As populations grow, they begin to have increasing effects on the environment, or **ecosystem** composed of the relations among life forms and between these forms and the physical environment. As we are constantly told, and as we can often see for ourselves, population growth, organization into industrial society, and urbanization have accelerated the discharge of waste into both local and world ecosystems, posing problems for the long-run survival of our species. This is, therefore, a worthy topic with which to close this chapter. Let me now examine where this ecosystem disruption ultimately begins: population growth.

POPULATION AND DEMOGRAPHY

Population Size and Growth

The **size of a population**—that is, the absolute numbers of people in a society—is sociologically the most important demographic feature of a society because size affects the kinds of social structures which must be created to support and organize the population. The **rate of growth** in a population, or the speed with which new people are being added, is also important since this rate determines how much burden is being placed on existing social structures and how much change in these structures will be necessary to accommodate new people. The growth rate of a population is calculated by dividing (1) the existing size of a population at the beginning of a given year into (2) the net population increase or loss (that is, new births minus deaths) at the end of the year. The resulting figure will give you a percentage per year increase or loss in a population. This percentage will usually sound very small—say a 2 or 3 percent increase—but this figure is only for one year; and if a population reveals a 3 percent growth rate, the population would double in less than twenty-five years, and it would increase many, many times over within 100 years. It is for these reasons that demographers are interested in dimensions of *birth rates* and *death rates;* the relationship between these figures determines the size of a population and its rate of growth.

The **crude birth rate** is the number of live births for 1000 members of a population in a given year. In the United States, for example, this crude rate is a little less than 16 per 1000 Americans, but it is over 50 in Kenya. Such rates give us a rough basis for comparison, but more refined calculations are usually needed. As a result, the **general fertility rate** is used as a way of factoring in age spans, usually the span of years during which women are fertile; this consideration produces a statistic which takes the total number of births per 1000 women in the 15- to 44-year-old age span, or child-producing years. By knowing the rate of actual births among those who can give birth, we have a much more refined statistic. We can make this statistic even more refined if we wish, producing an **age-specific fertility rate** of calculating the live births per 1000 in a year for particular age brackets, say 15 to 25, or 25 to 40, or for whatever our needs are. For example, we might want to compare the age-specific rate for young women in a society for different years, thereby allowing us to determine whether those in their most reproductive years are indeed having more or fewer babies.

The **crude death rate** is calculated like the crude birth rate, except this time we calculate the number of deaths per 1000 people in a population. In the United States, for instance, the crude death rate per 1000 people is less than 9, whereas for much of central Africa it is approaching 50 per 1000. One can also calculate an **age-specific death rate** in order to see the age brackets in which people are likely to die. If a society has a high figure for 50- to 60-year-olds, this tells us that many people are dying early. One of the most useful applications of an age-specific rate is the calculation of the **infant mortality rate,** which tells us the number of 1-year-olds or below per 1000 live births who die. Some African societies have rates over 200 per 1000. The rate in the United States is about 10, which sounds much better, but this rate is still higher than most other industrial nations. This rate thus tells us that in the United States, a lot of babies are dying because they do not have adequate health care.

The Demographic Transition

The relationship between birth and death rates influences, as noted above, the size of a population, as well as its rate of growth. Other factors can come into play, such as migration into or out of a society, but the birth and death rates are crucial to understanding the growth of a population. For most of human history birth and infant mortality rates were high, and the age-specific death rate would indicate that many people died early in their lives. There were perhaps as many as 3 million hunters and gatherers 40,000 years ago; this figure might have gone as high as 5 million when horticulture and then agriculture emerged on a wide scale some 8000 to 10,000 years ago (Wilford, 1981). Thus, the rate of population growth was not high—because high birth rates were accompanied by high death rates. By the time of Christ, at 1 A.D., there were 200 million people on earth; by the early 1800s this figure had jumped to 1 billion. Today, the number of people on earth has passed 5 billion, and it is growing. There has been, therefore, an accelerating rate of population growth since the spread of agriculture, as can be seen in Figure 10-1.

In his famous essay on population, Thomas Malthus (1798), argued that populations grow in a geometric, or exponential, pattern where the rate of growth is constantly accelerating (for example, 1 to 2, 2 to 4, 4 to 16, 8 to 64, etc.). Populations will, therefore, grow until they overwhelm the (economic) means of subsistence, *unless* this growth is checked by famine, disease, and war—forces which had helped stem the tide of population growth up to Malthus's time, and thereafter. But as has become evident, these forces have not been enough to serve as a check because populations continue to grow. Industrialization and the concurrent rise of medicine and science as institutions have drastically changed Malthus's calculations.

For now, death and mortality can be reduced with the applications of technologies—for example, pesticides that kill off those insects which cause disease and ruin crops; medical advances that cure illness and disease, while also reducing infant mortality; and techniques for growing and harvesting more food that can be used to support a larger population. Disease and famine were thus reduced as an effective check on population growth; and we are seeing the result in explosive rates of population growth in many parts of the world (Ehrlich and Ehrlich, 1990).

Yet, something unexpected has also been occurring: birth rates have also been declining, and in the most modern societies, they are very low and, at times, below replacement rates needed to keep a population at a given size. Malthus

FIGURE 10-1. The population bomb
Source: United Nations, 1991.

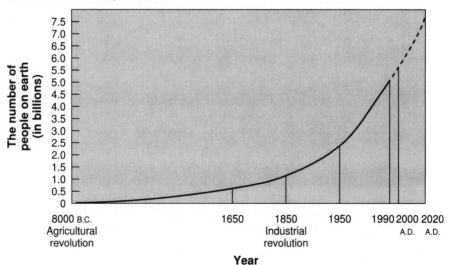

had assumed that birth rates would always remain high, but he was wrong. And his miscalculation alerts us to what is called *the demographic transition*.

The basic idea behind the **demographic transition** is this (Davis, 1945): As societies industrialize and become more modern, people begin to have fewer babies, and at the same time, new technologies decrease death rates. But there is a lag between the time the death rate declines and the time the birth rate begins to go down; and it is during this period that there is often a population explosion. People are still having many babies because of cultural beliefs and lifestyles that presumed a large portion of babies would die, that valued having large families, per se, and that needed larger families as labor and as a source of security in old age. When the infant mortality declines and older people live longer, people do not immediately lower their fertility; they keep on reproducing at the old rate, thereby increasing dramatically the size of the population. But eventually, birth rates decline as large families become a burden in nonagricultural work, as beliefs change to a more modern profile, and as people are mobile in pursuit of education and careers.

Europe went through this transition first, and twenty years ago there were great fears that the Third World would not do the same. In fact, it seemed like the death rate would decline *without* the lagged drop in the birth rate. The Third World would thus use modern technology to lower death rates, but not adopt the lifestyle of smaller families. But slowly, the birth rates of many Third World societies are beginning to decline, signaling that the world population explosion may not be as big and loud as once feared (Stark, 1992, p. 543).

Still, population will increase for quite some time, even if the birth rate dropped to replacement levels, because the large bulges of younger children produced before the birth rate declined must work their way through their

FIGURE 10-2. The demographic transition

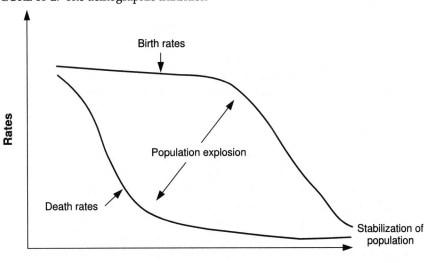

child-bearing years. The world is not free from a Malthusian catastrophe yet, but it looks much better for the human species than it did two decades ago.

Characteristics of the Population

Demographers also analyze the characteristics of a population. One of the most important characteristics of a population is its **age composition,** or the percentage of the population at various ages—say, 0 to 5, 6 to 10, 11 to 15, 16 to 20, 21 to 25, and so on up to 80+. The age composition can tell us a great deal and inform public policy. For example, if a high percentage of a population is in the younger age cohorts, then a population will grow as these people enter their child-bearing years. Or to illustrate further, if younger cohorts constitute a smaller percentage of the 20- through 40-year-olds in a population, as is the case in the United States, then the population as a whole will become older and the care of the elderly will soon be a major policy issue—as indeed it is in the United States. You will, in all likelihood, increasingly resent your social security taxes which are used to pay for the health care (Medicare) and other benefits for the elderly. And given the age composition of the population, you will have reason to be concerned because a larger burden (my generation and those right behind me) will have to be supported by a smaller and smaller group (you and those behind you).

Another characteristic of a population is its **sex ratio,** or proportion of men to women. This can become a significant concern if this ratio becomes unbalanced, as would be the case when war kills off a high proportion of the young men (as it has indeed done throughout the ages).

Yet, another characteristic is the **ethnic composition** of a population, and the various rates (birth, death, and growth) for this population. If one ethnic sub-population is growing, while others are stable, then this change is surely going to be reflected in ethnic tensions. White prejudice and discrimination against blacks and Hispanics in America are, to some extent, fueled by fears about black's and especially Hispanic's growing numbers relative to whites.

Thus, by knowing some basic characteristics of a population, we can plan—given the political will—and develop policies which take into account demographic realities. While the numbers and statistics of demographers may seem dry and dull, they have enormous implications for your well-being.

Population Movements

The size and characteristics of a population are affected by **migration,** or the movement of people into, out of, and within a society. When migration involves people coming into a society, **immigration** is occurring; when people move out of a society, **emigration** is evident; and when movement is within the regions of a society, **internal migration** is the appropriate term. The *net migration rate* is the net increase or decrease of a population per 1000 members.

Migrations occur because of a combination of push factors, or those forces prompting people to leave one area, and pull factors, or those conditions that make a destination attractive (Long, 1988). For example, most of you reading this book are the descendants of European, Asian, and Latin American immigrants who found economic, political, and social conditions in their society of origin unpleasant (the push factors) and who, at the same time, perceived the United States to be comparatively free, open, and filled with opportunities (the pull factors). The same is also true with internal migrations: first the movement westward, then the movement from colder to warmer climates where new businesses were created, then back for a while to the older regions, and now some movement again to the Sunbelt. All these movements reflect push factors (loss of a job, cold weather) and pull factors (new job opportunities, warmth). Indeed, by some projections, the populations of the northeast will grow very little, and the midwest will decline by the year 2000 as a result of internal migration patterns, whereas the south and west will continue to grow, and dramatically so, because of internal migrations as well as immigration from other countries.

Today, much of the growth in the American population is from immigration and, along with this, from the higher birth rates of many immigrants. And many of the ethnic tensions and political pressures at all levels of government in the United States today come from the turmoil created by migration of ethnic subpopulations into a region. It would, for example, be impossible to understand the social, economic, and political dynamics of the southwest without taking into consideration the immigration of Mexicans and Asians into the communities of this area. The same was true for the northeast and midwest with the immigration of Europeans between 1850 and 1920 and, to a lesser extent today, with the immigration of Puerto Ricans and Asians. Thus, migration patterns are more than a bunch of dry statistics (although, I must confess, at times it does not seem so) because these statistics give you some sense of the magnitude of the internal movements of Americans and the immigration of new ethnics. All these movements will influence your job, schooling, political standing, and many other aspects of your lives. Add to the migration patterns the rate and character of population growth and we can see how crucial the science of demography is for understanding a society.

COMMUNITY AND URBANIZATION

The Emergence and Growth of Cities

One of the effects of internal migrations and immigration is to increase the rate of urbanization, or proportion of the population living in densely settled communities (Frisbie and Kasarda, 1988). Early community structures could hardly foretell what would lay ahead as populations grew and began to migrate from settlement to settlement (Sjoberg, 1960). Early hunters and gatherers, when they began to settle and practice horticulture or fishing, created relatively small villages, but as new technologies developed, the increase in economic production could support, and indeed demand, new social constructions—markets, political systems, and religious temples—which encouraged the further congregation of some of the population into cities. This process occurred originally in Mesopotamia, the Nile Valley of Egypt, the Indus Valley of India, and the Yellow River (Huang He) Basin of China. But it was to spread to most of Europe, Asia, Northern Africa, and meso-America (Eisenstadt and Shachar, 1987).

But even as cities grew during the agrarian era, they were not large by current standards; few exceeded 100,000, and less than 10 percent of the population resided in them. The general pattern was for a large region to have one dominant city which was connected by markets, political authority, and religion to smaller cities which, in turn, were tied to smaller villages (Lenski, Lenski, and Nolan, 1991). With industrialization, however, the scale and nature of cities, and the relations among them, were dramatically transformed.

In the agrarian era, cities were trade/market, political, and religious centers, with some productive units revolving around crafts, arts, public administration, and financial services. With industrialization, cities became entrepreneurial structures, helping to pull labor, capital, and technology together into factories near raw resources and transportation routes. Cities have always attracted migrants, but industrialization accelerated the pull factors, although the push factors associated with the lack of opportunities and misery of rural peasants were certainly a powerful force (indeed, since early industrial cities were such unpleasant places, people who migrated to them must have been desperate).

Early Urban Ecology

It was during this early phase of industrialization that sociologists became interested in the dynamics of cities (Park, 1916; Hurd, 1903). These analysts first tried to understand the patterns of city growth and to explain the way in which urban areas become differentiated into distinctive areas and zones (McKenzie, 1933). One early model saw cities as manifesting a **concentric zone** pattern, with rings of distinct areas fanning out from the central business district (Park and Burgess, 1925; Park, 1936). Another theory, the **sector model,** saw cities as revealing distinctive sectors like slices of a pie from the central business district (Hoyt, 1939). And a third early approach, the **multiple nuclei model,** saw cities as having not just one center, but alongside, distinct sectors which did not reveal any clear pattern like concentric zones in a circle, or pie sections (Harris and Ullman, 1945).

Each of these early approaches sought to understand why cities grew in certain patterns. They all had a vision of land use as competition for resources—the land itself, transportation routes, housing, retail clients, and other resources. The areas of a city were the result of this competition of people and business for these resources, as fueled by the real estate market. Thus, slums were areas where those with few resources were forced to secure housing; the central business district was the high-rent area where those businesses and professions with money could afford rents; and so on for affluent housing, warehousing, and other zones, sectors, and nuclei of cities. Despite its limitations, this kind of

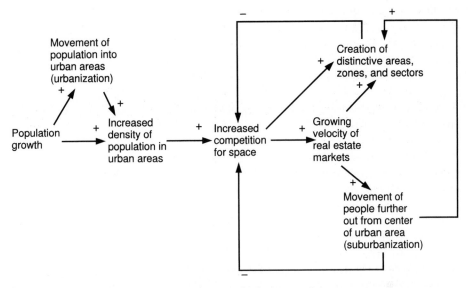

FIGURE 10-3. Early urban ecologists' view of urban growth processes

ecological analysis had an important point to make: Cities are the organization of people in space; this organization will, to some degree, reflect competition for this space; and the present and future distribution of people, housing, businesses, parks, transportation routes, cultural centers, government offices, and the like will be the outcome of this competition (Hawley, 1950, 1981). But other forces were also at work, changing the nature of the urban playing field on which competition for resources occurs.

Other Influences on Urbanization

One set of changes was the development of transportation and communication technologies. New modes of transportation—trolleys, trucks, cars, and airplanes—dramatically changed where people *had* to live. They could move further out, and with cars they did not have to stay near a rail line. As a result, the population of urban areas, especially in the United States, began to move outward, away from the crowding, noise, and pollution of a city's center. And with these people went business to serve them. Radio, and later television, facilitated this process, enabling people to maintain cultural and psychological contact with core urban areas. And the development of electric power, along with refrigerators and other household conveniences, made movement outward physically more comfortable (J. Turner, 1976).

Another set of changes revolved around productive technologies. Old factories could be stacked up on top of one another, but new factories began to use the assembly line and hence required space to line up productive tasks. Space was, at this early stage, cheaper in the outlying regions, and so, workers and service businesses to help them began to move where the jobs were.

Still another force was political. People in outlying suburbs wanted to govern themselves, free of the corruption of "big city" politics, and so they created separate governments for the communities surrounding the city. And once they could control their own destiny over such matters as zoning, housing, parks and recreation, schools, and the like, they became ever more attractive to residents and business.

These changes created **suburbanization,** or the process of creating self-governing communities around a larger core city. As suburbs began to grow, pulling people, business, industry, and government services with them, they often depleted the core city of its more affluent residents and most importantly of its tax base. Such was clearly the case with suburbanization in America. The result was a central city core, with the remnants of an old business district (which, at times, has been revitalized) along with corporate, cultural, and government centers in the midst of large pools of poor, and in the case of the United States, the ethnic poor (who because of open discrimination in housing could not leave for the suburbs until the last three decades). Thus, the suburbs often became more prosperous than the city, and in so doing, they too attracted their own core of corporate headquarters, government offices, and cultural centers.

Another thing also happened as the suburbs spread: they began to bump into one another, creating large **urban corridors** and **metropolitan regions** of several and, in some cases, many cities having economic, demographic, governmental, transportation, and environmental effects on one another (Dogan and Kasarda, 1988). This trend has gone furthest in the United States—Los Angeles to San Diego and Los Angeles to Riverside, San Bernardino, and Ventura; San Francisco Bay Area; Washington-Baltimore; New York-New Jersey, and so on for all populous states in America. Similar trends can be seen in Japan, and in some parts of Europe.

Those recent patterns of urbanization have involved some movement away from urban corridors, but often these movements are simply the vanguard of urban growth that will help connect the suburbs of an emerging corridor. At other times, a new center of urban activity is created, setting into motion, once again, the process of urbanization followed by suburbanization.

In the United States, this pattern of urban development has created many problems, a few of which I should mention (Turner and Musick, 1985). First, there are the financial problems of the older core cities which must provide services for commuters and urban poor at a time when the tax base to pay for these services has fled to the suburbs and beyond. Second, there are the governmental problems with respect to such matters as zoning, police, fire, education, transportation, environment, water, and sewage in large urban areas. For, these matters are divided into so many separate municipalities that they duplicate one another's services and make regionwide planning over sewage, transportation, environment, and basic services difficult. And third, there is the aggravation of inequalities that comes from the more affluent and white living in suburban communities with better schools, cleaner air, and more public services, while the poor and especially the ethnic poor must live in the decaying cores of large cities with poor schools, high crime, dirty air, and few public services. It is from these problems of urbanization in America that you may seek to run (further into the suburbs or exurbia), but none of us can truly escape them.

THE ENVIRONMENT AND ECOSYSTEM

It is, at times, hard to remember that humans are only one species among millions. Our complex patterns of organization sometimes insulate us to such a degree from immediate interaction with the natural environment that we forget a very fundamental fact: Like any animal, we are dependent upon complex chains, cycles, and flows among species as well as between species and the physical-chemical environment. The science of *ecology* studies these interrelations among species and the physical-chemical conditions of all life. And since we are the most disruptive species on earth, the analysis of **ecosystems,** or the particular patterns of relations among species and their physical-chemical environments, must include the study of human culture and social organization (J. Turner, 1976, 1977, 1985c; Turner and Musick, 1985).

Ecosystem Processes

For our purposes, we might visualize the ecosystem as a web of chains, flows, and cycles among those forces sustaining life. A **chain** is a form of interdependence among species; and the most important example is a **food chain** in which one species becomes food for another. At one end of this chain are microorganisms which take energy directly from the sun, whereas at the other end are animals like you and me who eat a wide variety of other animals and plants. A **cycle** is a form of interdependence which feeds back on itself, creating a loop; and a good example is the photosynthesis of the sun's energy by plants which then become food for herbivores (plant eaters), some of whom become food for carnivores (meat eaters), and all of whom become food for microorganisms that decompose dead plants and animals into nutrients for plants engaged in photosynthesis of the sun's energy. A **flow** is the broader movement of forces, energy, and various forms of organic and inorganic matter through an ecosystem. In the cycle above, the sun's energy flows through the ecosystem, with much of it lost as heat; or the forces of wind, rain, and tidal energy flow through ecosystems, taking with them other organic and inorganic materials.

Of particular importance are those chains, cycles, and flows which renew the soil, air, and water. For without these **renewable resources,** as they are often called, plant and animal life would not be possible—and this, of course, includes you and me. *Stock resources,* such as fossil fuels, metals, and chemicals, are stored in the ecosystem and are not renewable; indeed, they are taken out of the ecosystem and hence depleted, although many are recyclable as well. While depletion of stock resources is a problem for humans today, it is not nearly so fundamental as the disruption of the chains, cycles, and flows that renew the water, soil, and air on which life on earth depends. Thus, patterns of human organization have depleted many of the earth's stock resources, but more significantly, human culture and organization are disrupting the processes of regeneration of renewable resources.

Ecological Disruption

Industrial production and mechanized agriculture generate an enormous tonnage of waste residues—sewage, carbon dioxide, heat, chemicals, organic wastes, pesticides, freon, industrial slag, radioactivity, nitrogen oxides, carbon monoxide, ash, sulfur, heavy metals, and so the list goes. As these residues are dumped into the ecosystem, they begin to disrupt those processes that renew the soil, water, and air as well as basic chemical balances such as the ozone layer; and as a result, they begin to kill off species in those chains, cycles, and flows on which we as a species depend.

Air pollution is affected directly by chemicals spewed into the air, as are chemical balances in the upper atmosphere (for example, the clear depletion of the ozone layer that protects us from the sun's ultraviolet rays). These conditions pose health problems, but the more fundamental problem stems from the runoffs from toxic chemicals dumped into lakes, rivers, and streams which flow to the oceans and begin to kill off many microorganisms and, potentially, the ocean's phytoplankton , that produces 80 percent of the air in our atmosphere. Soil pollution comes from the dumping of wastes, particularly harmful residues of pesticides and chemical fertilizers, which accumulate and percolate through the soil, killing off the microorganisms that aerate and refertilize the soil. Moreover, these wastes disrupt the food chains of larger animals or directly kill insects and animals. The end result is that many of the organisms responsible for the renewal of the soil are being destroyed, reducing the capacity of the soil to produce crops for food. Water pollution is a particularly difficult problem because water flows to all parts of the ecosystem. And if waste residues enter at one point in the ecosystem, they are moved to other points, becoming more concentrated and killing both micro and more macro organisms.

Water and soil pollution are given much less attention than air pollution; and yet they are far more serious for maintaining balances in the ecosystem. They are less visible and immediate, but they are more significant for the long-run survival of humans and other species. Air pollution may take a few years off your life, but damage to water and soil could kill off the species.

Pollution and Sociocultural Organization

The basic problem in both local and world ecosystems is you and I, along with all our fellow human beings. As populations have grown, as industrial production has expanded, as high-yield mechanized agriculture has become necessary to feed us all, and as consumption and needs for the "good life" have escalated, humans produce more, consume more, and dump more. And the more we dump, the more disrupted are those processes which renew the air, soil, and water.

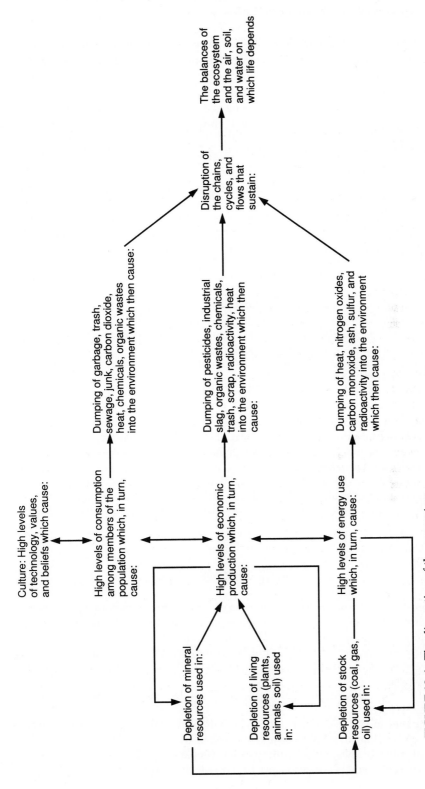

FIGURE 10-4. The disruption of the ecosystem

At the cultural level, values and beliefs emphasize achievement, consumption, and materialism, which in turn create demand for production and consumption of goods. These cultural tenets encourage the development of mass-produced goods requiring high levels of energy and widespread use of chemicals, most of which find their way into the ecosystem. And to consume many goods also means that many of them are dumped when no longer needed, again finding their way into the ecosystem.

These cultural and economic patterns are reinforced by political systems where increased production and consumption are necessary for the legitimacy and careers of politicians. Stratification aggravates these political pressures because those who enjoy the good life usually want more, while those who do not have the good life want at least a piece of affluence. The end result is more pressure for mass industrial and agricultural production, with its inevitable concomitant: pollution and disruption to the ecosystem

SUMMARY

1. The number of people, their distribution and patterns of organization, and their effects on the environment are all interrelated and important topics.
2. The science of demography is the study of population, its size and growth, its characteristics, and its movements (see Key Terms for definitions of key ideas). Of particular importance are growth patterns and the operation of the demographic transition.
3. Community is the organization of people in space, and the most important community process is urbanization or the movement of people to concentrated living space. Suburbanization and the creation of metropolitan regions are the most recent manifestations of the urbanization processes.
4. Ecosystems are constructed from the relations among life forms and inorganic matter through a series of chains, cycles, and flows. Patterns of human organization now disrupt these processes as they sustain the renewable resources on which all life on earth depends.

KEY TERMS

age composition   The percentage/proportion of a population in various age brackets.

age-specific death rate   The number of deaths per 1000 people in a particular age range or bracket, such as 65- to 75-year-olds, or any bracket chosen for analysis.

age-specific fertility rate   The number of live births per 1000 people in a particular age range or bracket, such as 15- to 25-year-olds, 26- to 40-year-olds, or any range chosen for analysis.

community   A social structure that organizes the residence and activities of people in physical space.

concentric zone model   A model of urban growth that sees urbanization as a sequence of rings, moving out from the central business district.

crude birth rate   Number of live births per 1000 people in a given year.

crude death rate   Number of deaths per 1000 people in a given year.

demographic transition The pattern of population growth in the transition to modernity, during which death rates decline first in the face of continued high birth rates followed, eventually, by a decline in birth rates.

demography The science of population processes, especially the characteristics, distribution, movement, and growth/decline of populations.

ecosystem The system of relations among life forms, as well as between life forms and the physical environment.

ecosystem chain/food chain The linking of life forms as food for one another.

ecosystem cycle A form of interdependence in which processes fold back on themselves, creating cycles of events and interdependencies.

ecosystem flow The movement of energy, organic matter, and inorganic matter through an ecosystem.

emigration Movement of people *out of* a society.

ethnic composition The proportions of various ethnic subpopulations in a society and the birth, death, and growth rate associated with each.

general fertility rate The total number of live births in a given year for each 1000 women in their child-bearing years (usually defined as 15 to 44 years of age).

immigration Migration of people *into* a society.

infant mortality rate The number of 1-year-olds and below per 1000 live births who die in a given year.

internal migration Movement of people *within* a society.

metropolitan region An area where the suburbs developing around older large cities become contiguous.

migration The movement of people into, out of, and about a society.

multiple nuclei model A view of the city emphasizing that there are several centers in addition to the central business district.

rate of population growth The increase (decrease) in the size of a population in a given year calculated by dividing the size of a population at the beginning of a year into the net increase (or decrease) of people during the year.

renewable resources Those resources which can be renewed by virtue of ecosystem chains, flows, and cycles. Air, water, and soil are the three most basic renewable resources.

sector model A model of urbanization viewing the city in terms of distinct sectors, like slices of a pie, that emanate from the central business district.

sex ratio The proportion of men to women in a population.

size of population The absolute number of people in a society.

suburbanization The migration process of generating self-governing communities around a large, older city.

urban corridors See metropolitan region.

urbanization The increasing concentration of ever-larger populations in space.

CHAPTER 11

Disorder, Deviance, and Dissent

The organization of humans is not a well-ordered bee-hive. Overpopulation, crowding, inequality, injustice, discrimination, and other disruptive forces generate disorder, foster deviance, and drive people to revolt. It is difficult to open a newspaper today without seeing someone who was killed, some group that is angry and protesting, someone who is openly deviating from conventions, or some groups that stand in open conflict or defiance of the law. While we may decry these events, or even be scared of them, we must recognize that they are inevitable in a large and urban society that reveals inequalities, clear patterns of discrimination, and open injustices. Under these conditions, people get angry, they strike out as is illustrated in the picture above, they retreat into deviance, they organize to protest, they attack and flout conventions, and in so many ways make life more chaotic and disorderly. We cannot expect less, although by understanding the forces of disorder we can perhaps mitigate their eruption and lessen their danger.

THE PROBLEM OF ORDER

Social life involves a perpetual standoff between those forces which operate to maintain the social order and those forces which produce disorder and change. In a real sense, we live in the midst of a constant struggle between mechanisms of social control and social tendencies for deviance, conflict, and dissent. This societal battlefield has no right and wrong sides; for the forces of control are not always benign nor are those of deviance and dissent always malevolent. Thus, the imputed rightness or wrongness of these dynamics is less relevant than their inevitability. The battle never ends, for it addresses the most fundamental sociological question: How is some degree of order to be maintained in a society? Indeed, the very first sociologists —Comte, Spencer, Marx, Durkheim, Weber—wanted to know the answer to this question. For them, as for us today, the social world is rife with tension and conflict and with change and transformation. One does not need to advocate the status quo to realize that societies which cannot provide some provisional answers to this question are marked by constant turmoil and change and that although conflict and change can often improve unpleasant conditions, there must also be some way to create cooperation and consensus among people in society. Without these, society collapses or, as is often the case in human affairs, it becomes an arena of constant upheaval.

Thus the problem of order revolves around questions of social control. As a functional theorist might ask: How are people to play roles in ways that allow them to interact and cooperate? How are people to come to agree about what is right and wrong, proper and improper? How are disputes and disagreements to be resolved and mitigated? In some societies, answers to these questions come effortlessly, without great thought or reflection. In other societies, control is a constant headache. People are alienated, they disagree, they fight, they refuse to get along. Here is the stuff of conflict theory. These problems of social control are most likely to occur in societies that are large, complex, and stratified. Let me elaborate on this point.

Forces of Disorder

One force that determines whether order is threatened in society is the *size* of a population. Large populations are always more difficult to organize than smaller ones, because as the number of people increases, face-to-face contact among everyone is ever more problematic. There is not enough time to see, talk to, and know others. Moreover, the quality—the intensity of emotion, affection, and mutual trust—of the interaction decreases. And so, when people cannot interact directly and cannot feel a sense of solidarity with one another, a very powerful force of social control is weakened. In addition, those who do interact frequently come to form subpopulations, and they often develop their own subculture and lifestyle. This gives them a sense of solidarity. But it also does something else: It makes them *different* from others. It isolates subpopulations from one another and makes them strangers, and in so doing, it increases their chances of conflict or at least of disagreement, resulting in problems of control among diverging subpopulations.

Larger populations also present real difficulties for distributing resources and coordinating activities. When people cannot talk things over and agree informally, how do virtual strangers come to decide who does what and who gets what? The market economy, where people buy and sell goods and services, is one answer but an incomplete one. Another answer is the consolidation of power so that there is a "political force" that can coordinate actions, distribute resources, and regulate potential conflicts in markets.

A second force that escalates problems of order is social differentiation. *Differentiation* is simply the process of creating differences—in culture, in occupational roles, in income, in family structure, in types of economic arrangements, and in all the things that people, groups, and organizations do. The greater the number of such differences, the more differentiated the population. Differentiation results from increases in population size, since people get isolated from one another and develop their own distinctive subcultures and ways of doing things. In addition, supporting a large population requires new, more complex economic arrangements, with people playing specialized roles and working in organizations that produce the volume and varieties of goods and services necessary to support a larger number of people. The degree of differentiation can vary, depending on particular circumstances, but in the end, differentiation will increase with population growth. Such differences always create problems of social control: How are people in different subcultures, economic roles, communities, regions, and work organizations to be coordinated? Who is to keep them from fighting? Who is to regularize market exchanges among them? The answer to these questions is that government's regulatory activities must expand, creating yet another source of social differentiation.

Population growth and social differentiation are linked in turn to a third force that escalates the problem of maintaining order in societies: *inequality*. As populations grow and people do different things, it is inevitable that some people get more money, power, and prestige than others. Complete social equality is really possible only in very small populations where the differences between people's activities and lifestyles are not great. But as populations grow and differentiate, so does inequality—a truly volatile force behind conflict and tension in human societies. Inequalities sometimes create societywide revolutions. More often they generate limited skirmishes between those who have and those who do not have particular resources. As conflict theories emphasize, many of the most interesting events around us are triggered by inequalities—labor strikes, demands for equal rights for women, and racial and ethnic tensions. Change-producing social movements—the labor movement, the abolitionist movement, the women's suffrage movement, the current women's movement, and the civil rights movement—all emerged and spread in response to inequalities. Confrontation and violence are often a part of these movements as forces for change and forces for social control clash. The reconciliation of these forces eventually comes from governmental responses—for example, new laws, new enforcement agencies, and new procedures for redressing grievances. Without government, inequality would be a perpetual conflict-producing machine. With it, someone is at the controls—at least some of the time.

Macro Forces of Social Control

Thus, social life in large, differentiated societies characterized by inequality is filled with potential for disagreement, dissent, and disorder. In his *Leviathan*, the seventeenth-century British social philosopher Thomas Hobbes (1651) proposed that the only solution to such problems is for everyone to agree to subordinate themselves completely to political authority—that is, to accept government and rule by "Big Brother." In contrast to Hobbes, the eighteenth-century economic philosopher Adam Smith (1776) took a utilitarian view, seeing an "Invisible Hand of Order" as emerging out of unregulated, free competition in markets where the laws of supply and demand would rule and govern society.

While the debate of these old social philosophers may not seem relevant today, curiously our urban society reflects a kind of compromise between their conflicting ideas. We live in a society where cultural values extol freedom and individualism; our dominant system of economic beliefs stresses laissez-faire and economic competition among individuals; our social beliefs emphasize "doing your own thing," "being your own person," "sticking to your convictions," and "not knuckling under." Many of our political beliefs involve a distrust of "big government" and a conviction by many that all government is inefficient. Our heroes are rugged individualists who do what they want rather than what they are told. Thus, our cultural beliefs clearly favor Adam Smith's position over Thomas Hobbes'. But as I have already mentioned, big government is inevitable, as size, differentiation, and inequality increase (see also Chapter 9 on polity). And so, many of our most cherished cultural beliefs do not correspond to the realities of social life in large, complex societies. Imagine a society like ours governed solely by the laws of supply and demand. How would greed be controlled? What would keep people from cheating? Inevitably, whether we like it or not, political authority—laws, police, courts, jails—must emerge to answer these questions. Adam Smith's Invisible Hand of Order becomes very visible in the real world.

Without extensive government control, what would society be like? Who would build roads? Who would control pollution? Who would check consumer fraud? Who would keep banks from collapsing with your and my money? Who would take care of the poor, the indigent, and handicapped, the helpless old? Who would keep corporations from getting so large that they could wipe out their competition and charge us at will for basic services? Who would deal with criminals? Who would stop conflicts? Who would run the schools? Who would build universities and colleges? Who would finance disease control? Who would preserve natural resources for recreational use? These and thousands of other tasks cannot be performed by private corporations operating under the profit motive in a free market. If private control were actually attempted, society would collapse. The problems of social control would simply overwhelm us and leave us isolated in a rather cold world. True, we have much to grumble about, but without government, we would not even have the luxury of grumbling.

But Hobbes probably went too far in his advocacy of governmental power, as power alone cannot maintain order. The use of power generates resentments on the part of those subject to power. Indeed, it becomes a source of inequality and hence potential conflict, as conflict theories always emphasize. A society that must be perpetually conquered cannot be ruled, as the Soviet Union recently discovered.

Thus, the social order cannot be sustained for long, either by Smith's Invisible Hand or by Hobbes's Leviathan. True, markets and government are essential to social control in complex societies, but either alone produces social disorder. Moreover, macro-level forces of control never work effectively unless reinforced by people's daily interactions and routines at the micro interpersonal level.

Micro-Level Forces of Social Control

Much social order comes, as interactionist theory would emphasize, from informal interpersonal processes. While the macro dilemma of power versus markets plays itself out, people manage to get along, conform, and remain satisfied. Such is not always the case, but ultimately the problem of order is lodged in the processes of interaction.

One crucial interaction process is, as we saw in Chapter 5, socialization. By learning in interaction with others a common culture or repertoire of symbols, we go a long way toward resolving the problem of order. If you and I did not share some level of consensus over values, beliefs, and norms, we would enter situations with no clear expectations, no standards by which to evaluate each other's and our own conduct, and no instructions about how to behave. We would have to create these standards, and as a result our interaction would be awkward, stressful, and perhaps conflictual until we negotiated a common understanding. Thus, one of the essential processes of social control is our socialization into a shared repertoire of symbols and symbol systems, a force of social control that is also emphasized by functionalists (Parsons, 1951). And once we implicitly recognize the importance of such shared symbols, we socialize ourselves. We actively look for and learn about the operative norms, beliefs, and values, because we know how important they are in getting along with others. When you enter into a new situation where you are a bit uncertain of the relevant cultural beliefs and norms, you become highly sensitized and aware. You want to know the cultural codes. And the desire and willingness to be guided by such codes are integral parts of a powerful mechanism of social control.

This need to know the cultural codes, like the acquisition of the codes themselves, is largely the result of socialization. This is another way, then, that early socialization acts as a mechanism of social control (Parsons, 1951). In addition, we acquire those motives which energize us to occupy social positions and to play roles. If we were apathetic and alienated, we would not want to play roles and we could not depend on others. Society could not control us because we would not care. Without socialized motivations, therefore, the commitment to the social order and the willingness to subject oneself to cultural guidance would not exist. And no matter how motivated we are to abide by cultural codes, we must have the interpersonal skills—role taking, role making, dramaturgical, and ethnomethodological—to function in society. Socialization gives us these; and without them, we could not adjust, readjust, and fine-tune our responses to each other. Finally, our acquisition of a self-conception gives us a steady compass by which to assess our conduct and the reactions of others to us. If we did not have a self to sustain in interaction and if we did not constantly evaluate ourselves, it would be hard for others to respond to us or to control us. The confirmation of self gives us a stake in interaction; and this is what gives others the power to control us—within limits, of course.

The process of mutual sanctioning is also an intrinsic part of all interactions, and it is crucial to social control. As you and I role-take with others, reading their gestures and thinking of appropriate responses, we are also being sanctioned. Those gestures are telling us how well we are doing in the situation; if we are doing something wrong, the gestures of others—their frown, hurt look, or their words—tell us and we change our behaviors. If we could not assign gestures some symbolic meaning and if we could not role-take and imagine ourselves in one another's place, social control would lose its subtlety and grace. We would have to club people into submission. We still do this occasionally, but far more important and effective are the subtle and sometimes unconscious orchestration of gestures which tell people when they are doing things right or wrong.

Recall from Chapter 5 that rituals are a form of interaction, requiring certain stereotyped behaviors on specific occasions or in particular contexts. They are, in essence, yet another way of controlling our responses to each other and of maintaining the social order because they help us typify one another, frame the situation, and take cognizance of relevant cultural systems. Rituals ensure that certain predictable responses will occur. When we buy goods at a store, we engage in rituals—"hello, how are you," "just fine," "nice day," "yes it is," "have a good day," "thanks," etc.—and the interaction moves smoothly. In other words, it is controlled and regulated. And we are grateful because it keeps us from having to do too much interpersonal work with a stranger. All rituals thus control interaction. We are being told what to do and we know how to respond to one another.

The separation of potentially incompatible activities—activities where different cultural symbols, interpersonal styles, and rituals apply—is yet another process of social control. Much of this separation is done for us by the larger social structure, and so this process of control comes from the outside. But we implicitly recognize its importance as we shift from one stage to another. For example, family activities are segregated from work activities in complex societies, since the expectations placed on family members are different from those placed on workers. People thus leave the home for work, thereby separating in time and place conflicting norms and role enactments. If family members "bring their work home with them," there are usually tensions in the household; or if people work in their home or have a "family business," there are extraordinary burdens on everyone. In complex societies, then, it is essential to segregate incompatible activities, thereby avoiding the tensions of having to reconcile different cultural expectations and dramaturgical requirements.

Thus, much of the essence of social control resides in the interpersonal realm—that is, in the sharing of cultural symbols, in socialization, in interactive sanctioning, in rituals, and in segregation of incompatible interactive requirements. In small-scale groupings and populations, these informal processes are all that is necessary for people to get along and cooperate. But when populations get large, when social differentiation increases, and when inequalities become more prominent, interpersonal control can break down, and in fact it can even work to create new problems of control, deviance, and dissent.

DEVIANCE

Deviance is behavior which violates widely held norms; and as societies get larger, more complex, and more diverse, the rates of deviance increase because both formal and informal forces of social control become inadequate. In fact, the forces of social control can actually help produce deviance. By examining diverse theories of deviance, we can get some understanding as to why deviance is inevitable as the forces of disorder and social control increase.

The Functional Theory of Structural Strain

The functional theorist, Robert K. Merton (1968), long ago proposed a theory of **structural strain**—often termed *anomie theory*—to explain deviance. In any society, Merton argued, there are culturally defined success goals and various legitimate means to achieve these goals. High rates of deviance emerge when the legitimate avenues to these success goals are limited, creating a structural strain between means and goals for those who do not have access to legitimate means. A society like ours, for example, stresses monetary and occupational success, but limits the available means to achieve this success, thereby generating structural strain. You are pursuing a legitimate means to the success goals of the United States; and in Merton's terms, you are already a "conformist" because you accept goals as legitimate (indeed, you may lust after material success) and you use legitimate means to achieve them (unless, of course, you cheat on your exams).

Other people, however, experience strain and deviate in several ways. One is what Merton called *innovation*, where success goals are accepted, but the legitimate means are rejected in favor of illegal and illegitimate means—that is, crime. Criminals want what you want—material success—but they use illegitimate means to pursue this goal. Another kind of adaptation to structural strain is *ritualism*, where the success goals are rejected or forgotten in favor of slavish conformity to legitimate means. The slavishly conformist bureaucrat who "goes by the book" is such a ritualist—as we observed in Chapter 7 on groups and organizations. Yet another adaptation to means-ends stress is *retreatism*, where both the success goals *and* means are rejected. Dropouts, drug addicts, members of deviant sects, and the like fall into this category. And a final adaptation is *rebellion*—a topic to be examined in more detail later in this chapter. Here, new goals and new means are used as people rebel against the existing "system," demanding new ways of doing things.

In Merton's theory, then, a wide range of behaviors is to be understood in terms of the disjuncture between the availability of legitimate means and the intensity of success goals. A society like the United States, revealing considerable inequality (see Chapter 8) and extolling the virtues of material success, should have high rates of deviance in terms of Merton's theory. And not surprisingly, we do. Crime is high, and retreatist subgroups exist, and although a societywide rebellion is not likely, there are some rebellious subgroups.

Conflict Perspectives on Deviance

Merton's structural strain theory emphasizes that legitimate means are not equally available to all; conflict theory focuses on this point. Lower-class persons, women, and many ethnic minorities simply do not have the same degree of access to the means of success as more affluent, white males. Access to legitimate means is, therefore, a valued resource over which there is conflict. Conflict theory also stresses that those who hold power are also able to define success goals, as well as legitimate and illegitimate means, in ways that favor them.

While the conflict argument is often stated in the extreme (Quinney, 1970, 1979, 1980), the general argument is worth reviewing. The norms which define deviance are, conflict theorists argue, those of the powerful. Laws and their enforcement emphasize the illegality of activities which are offensive to the morality of the privileged classes and which threaten their property and affluence (Turk, 1969). Stated less stridently, the laws and their enforcement are greatly influenced by the distribution of power and privilege. Poor people who are more likely to steal, use drugs, and carry weapons must confront strict laws against them and harsh enforcement of these laws compared to affluent people who commit white-collar and corporate crimes like embezzlement, industrial pollution, health and safety violations, consumer fraud, election fraud, political dirty tricks, stock manipulation, and the like. And the more powerful can enlist the support of the broad middle classes to support them. Indeed, by focusing enforcement energies on the crimes of the poor, there is less enforcement of those crimes committed by the nonpoor (Chambliss, 1978), thereby enabling the rich to "get away" with their forms of crime.

Interactionist Approaches to Deviance

For interactionists, the behaviors of individuals are shaped by the responses of others. And when others *label* a person's acts as deviant, the individual can often be forced into the role of deviant. How is this possible?

Labeling theory emphasizes that the labels attached to people's behaviors are crucial in the genesis and maintenance of deviance (Lemert, 1951, 1967; Scheff, 1966). When people are labeled deviant—as criminals, delinquents, crazy persons, drug users, alcoholics—they can often respond to these labels by fulfilling the expectations contained in the label. We all know, to some extent, the roles of deviants; and if we were consistently labeled, how would we respond? We might well be driven to act as we were labeled.

But the process of labeling is more complex (Liska, 1981). When we are labeled deviant—say, as an alcoholic, criminal, a delinquent, prostitute, or mental patient—we often carry a record of this label, such as a police file, a blank period of biography, a hospital record, etc. The label thus becomes formalized and institutionalized with the result that employers, landlords, potential friends, welfare agencies, and others respond *as if* we were still deviant. Such labels deny people the chance to escape from deviance and force them back into deviant roles. These pressures are compounded by the inability to acquire new, nondeviant interpersonal ties, for who wants to interact with a prostitute, delinquent, mental patient, or alcoholic? And over time, as the label is applied and enforced, people acquire a self-conception of themselves as deviant in terms of the label, and they come to act in ways that reflect this deviant self-conception, thereby ensuring that the label sticks.

These labeling processes are, no doubt, part of the biography of any deviant. Sometimes the labels have been informal; at other times an "official" record is accumulated. But for each, the label often has generated interpersonal and institutional responses which kept people from escaping their label and which have communicated the evaluation, assessment, and expectation of others about their deviance. Thus, whatever the initial causes of deviance, powerful forces are in operation that sustain deviance once labeling occurs.

Another type of interactionist theory about deviance emphasizes the transmission of deviance through interaction and socialization. Perhaps the most famous of these is the **differential association theory** (Sutherland, 1939; Sutherland and Cressey, 1986). In this theory, individuals who interact in situations where deviance is approved will acquire a high ratio of deviant to nondeviant images and definitions. The result is that these individuals will be disposed to commit deviant acts, especially when they encounter deviant orientations early in life and in long-term interactions with those they admire and care about. Thus, if people must live in environments where there are many images, definitions, and role models of deviance, they are more likely to have early, close long-term interactions with others who impart these deviant orientations. As a result, their patterns of differential association will distort their definitions of proper behavior, their self-definitions, and their perceptions of opportunity in ways that encourage deviance. And once labeled as a deviant, it will become difficult for these individuals to alter this preponderance of deviant definitions about how to view themselves, assess opportunities, and act in the world.

Utilitarian Theories of Deviance

Control theory blends many aspects of these other theories into a rational choice perspective (Hirschi, 1969). The basic question is what keeps people from being deviant in light of the fact that there are many rewards or utilities for being deviant? Ultimately, the answer to this question is that it would cost too much to deviate because of social attachments to nondeviant others and groups, because of investments in nondeviant activities, because of the time spent in nondeviant activities, and because of acquired beliefs in conformity to norms. Conversely, for those who are deviant, these costs are not so great.

For deviants, there are no strong *attachments* and bonds to others who would disapprove of deviants. Indeed, from a control theory perspective, the career of any deviant is punctuated by a lack of attachments, or very weak attachments (Hirschi, 1969; Liska, 1981; Kornhauser, 1978) to others, even those engaged in deviance. Without attachments, there is less to lose from being deviant; and since much deviance is rewarding, it will increase among those whose attachments are weak. There is also the question of "investments" in nondeviant careers. The more we have invested in education, years on the job, house, car, and other possessions, the more we risk in being deviant. We can lose these investments, and so, we perceive deviance as potentially costly. But for those who do not have investments, the costs of deviance are much less. There is also the matter of "involvements," or time and energy spent in conformity to norms. Time and energy are limited, and if our attachments and investments have created pressures to conform, there is less time and energy available for deviance. The extra energy is costly to mobilize, and the time is difficult to find; and so, when people are involved in nondeviance and are spending much time and energy on conformity, they have less to expend on deviance. And finally, there are "beliefs" and other cultural symbols about how people should behave; and if we have internalized those stressing conformity, it becomes psychologically and emotionally costly to violate them. Having a conscience is another way of saying that it is too costly to violate norms and values about what should be and what should occur.

Thus, from a control theoretical viewpoint, those who deviate have weak attachments to others, few investments in nondeviance, less time and energy committed to conformity, and fewer beliefs about conformity to mainstream norms. As a consequence, the costs of deviance are less to these individuals; and since deviance can be rewarding, they become more likely to perceive "rationally" the rewards of deviants as exceeding the costs of deviance. For you and me (well, me for sure), the reverse is true: attachments, investments, involvements, and beliefs make it too costly to deviate.

In sum, these various theoretical approaches can provide much insight into deviance today in America. There is enormous structural strain stemming from inequality; we are all bombarded with the notion of material success in a society that limits the opportunities for many to achieve this success (see Chapter 8 for more details). There is also considerable inequality in how deviant acts are defined by laws and enforced by agencies; and this inequality favors the rich over the poor in how deviance is treated. When deviant acts are committed, labels are easily applied by police, courts, hospitals, and other agencies which stigmatize deviants and help sustain deviant careers, especially for the poor who have no other resources to fight against labels. There are clear areas and regions in America where definitions supporting deviance exceed those against it, forcing those who must live in these regions to differentially associate with definitions, techniques, beliefs, and norms favoring a deviant career. And there are rewards for deviance—instant money for selling drugs, local fame for acts of violence, "easy" income for robbery, quick gratifications for murder and assault, etc.—which are not counterbalanced by high costs from attachments, investments, involvements, and beliefs.

We should expect, therefore, high rates of deviance in the United States; and perhaps it is wise to be less shocked and morally outraged and more attuned to what needs to be done in light of these theories. More punishment and enforcement will not work to stop crime and other acts of deviance; rather, policies must be directed at reducing the disjuncture between success goals and available means, at redressing the imbalance in how poor and rich criminals are treated, at mitigating the effects of labels, and at increasing the human costs of deviance by increasing attachments, investments, involvements, and beliefs in "the system" for those who would deviate.

DISSENT

Unruly crowds, riots, revolts, and collective violence are very much a part of human societies. We cannot read a newspaper or watch television on a given day without hearing about internal dissent and conflict within some society in the world, including our own. Why, then, is dissent such a pervasive phenomenon?

To answer this question, we must enter the subfield in sociology called **collective behavior** which examines sudden transformations of culture and social structure. At times dissent is largely symbolic, involving fads and fashions that violate the public's sense of decorum; at other times, dissent involves noisy crowds and protests; at certain moments crowds turn ugly, creating more violent riots; at still more intense moments, protesting crowds become larger and more focused and form a revolutionary force that can potentially topple those in power; at another moment, such crowds are implicated in a longer-term social movement for change; and at those moments when all else fails, protest can become organized into warring factions in a societywide civil war. Thus, the form of dissent and collective behavior can vary in its scale and scope, its level of violence, and its effects on the organization of a society.

Preconditions of Dissent: Inequality

Dissent is protest against existing social arrangements, and so, ultimately, collective behavior begins with people's perception that something is wrong and must be changed. These perceptions do not have to be explicitly formulated, at least at beginning stages; rather, individuals more often feel and sense a grievance or sense of dissatisfaction. The functional theorist, Neil Smelser (1963), has termed this initial condition **structural strain**.

What contributes to such strain? The most consistent force behind strain is inequality and stratification. As all conflict theories would emphasize, inequality in the distribution of resources is the underlying source of protest; and when people begin to feel that this inequality is unfair and unjust, the level of structural strain increases. If power is too concentrated and arbitrary, if markets generate great material differences, and if honor and prestige are horded by a few and denied to most, then the level of structural strain is high. Moreover, if inequality is associated with economic, political, and social domination of those without resources by those with them, then the level of structural strain is even higher (Stark, 1992, p. 614). People resent being told what to do and having their lives controlled by others; and they begin to get angry and perceive that something must be done.

The Intensification of Dissent

When people begin to "share their grievances," the potential for dissent is increased (Smelser, 1963; R. Turner and Killian, 1987). The sharing of grievances is facilitated by several conditions, initially articulated by Karl Marx and Friedrich Engels (1848) and later incorporated into modern theories. First, if dominated segments of a society have social ties and networks, these can be used to communicate their grievances; and the mutual give-and-take of such communication often begins to arouse people's frustration and anger, while bringing into focus the sources of their grievances (Zald and McCarthy, 1979). Second, leadership is essential, for people do not spontaneously focus their anger and mobilize; they must be led by others with the ability to articulate grievances and convince them that something must be done. Third, beliefs must be articulated so that people have symbols with which to unite and justify their grievances and potential actions (Smelser, 1963). Fourth, the sense of deprivation and grievance experienced by people must escalate, creating a gap between what they receive and what they expected; and the more rapidly this sense of relative deprivation develops, the greater the effect on intensifying grievances (Davies, 1962, 1969).

These forces have mutual effects on one another: Networks of communication reinforce beliefs about deprivations, often escalating them; leaders articulate and expand beliefs, thereby feeding the channels of communication; as grievances are shared, leaders are given credence, while beliefs are reinforced; and as beliefs, leaders, and communication channels reciprocally reinforce one another, grievances escalate.

Collective Outbursts and Crowd Behavior

When the preconditions for dissent have been intensified by the forces discussed above, collective outbursts become more likely. Much of the subfield of collective behavior examines the dynamics of such crowd behavior. Early **contagion theory** stressed that as people interact, they begin to bounce grievances and angry moods off one another, heightening their mobilization. This process is circular and escalating, because as people read one another's gestures and, in turn, gesture back their anger, the intensity of the situation is ratcheted up; and when this occurs, the mutual gesturing becomes ever more intense. As this process unfolds, people become highly suggestible to the responses of others, and as a consequence, a "mob" can suddenly move in a particular way, and people can do things that they would ordinarily never consider doing. While a certain amount of emotional contagion is, no doubt, involved in crowd behavior, more recent theories stress additional factors.

Convergence theory emphasizes that people are not so much transformed and swept away by emotional contagion, as they are self-selected to engage in certain lines of behavior. When people gather in a crowd, they do so because they have certain grievances in common and are *already* prepared by beliefs, leaders, and previous communications to act in certain ways (Cantril, 1941). When students protested in the 1960s and early 1970s, they were ready to do certain things; they were not overrun by a "mob mood," although some emotional contagion was, no doubt, involved. Similarly, in the lynching of blacks in the south during the early decades of this century, those who gathered were of similarly low economic background and were already prepared to vent their fears in this most heinous act (Cantril, 1941).

In contrast, **emergent norm theory** questions the assumptions of both contagion and convergence theories. For there is often a lack of initial convergence among crowd members' orientations and dispositions, and individuals are not just overwhelmed by contagious moods and emotions. Rather, as all interactionist theories emphasize, individuals are seen to look for and find meanings by reading one another's gestures, like any other interaction situation (Turner and Killian, 1987); and out of such role taking, they develop new norms and standards about how to behave. And, they interpersonally reward one another for conformity to these emergent norms. These norms can, of course, encourage violent behavior, from looting to lynching, but such behaviors involve the same basic interaction processes as in noncrowd activities: copresence, role taking, emergent norms, and conformity to norms.

These theoretical approaches to crowd behavior need not be seen as contradictory. There usually is some self-selection of individuals into the crowd situation, usually in terms of shared grievances. There is also a certain amount of emotional charge and contagion, but this is controlled and channeled by emergent norms. The basic types of **crowds** reflect the interplay of these forces (Blumer, 1978). A "casual crowd" is a collection of people who have little else in common besides their copresence and stimulation by a common event, such as observing some highly visible stimulus like an automobile accident. A "conventional crowd" involves people self-selected and assembled for a specific purpose, such as observing a game. An "expressive crowd" is a self-selected gathering of people who intend to be influenced by normatively circumscribed emotional contagion, as is the case at a religious revival, rock concert, or political rally. And, an "acting crowd" is a collection of people who are self-selected, emotionally aroused, and normatively engaged in aggressive acts, such as looting and rioting. As one goes from a casual to an acting crowd, self-selection, emotional contagion, and emergent norms specifying violation of conventional norms all increase. This is what gives them such volatility, as well as the potential to change social structures.

But whether this potential is realized depends upon other social conditions.

Rioters can be crushed, or they can topple a government; and mass rallies can fizzle, or they can mobilize sentiments and prompt further action. Much depends upon the broader social and cultural context of a crowd's formation.

The Context of Crowd Behavior

If crowd activities are part of a larger *social movement* or part of an organized and systematic effort to change particular conditions, they tend to become expressive crowds which mobilize people's sentiments and emphasize grievances. Crowds thus become part of the strategy for exerting pressure for change. The mass demonstrations for Civil Rights in the early 1960s, for example, were the basic element of an organized movement; and they were used not only to call attention to the plight of black Americans, but also to force patterns of white domination in politics, schools, economy, and public facilities to change.

Yet, crowds can still spark violence even when part of a well-organized social movement. Often the violence is initiated by those charged with social control—the police and the army, for example—or from those in a casual crowd, or self-selected expressive crowd, watching a demonstration. Suddenly, these crowds become an acting crowd, attacking members of an organized demonstration. Indeed, the strategy of protests is to incite reactions in order to dramatize the plight of those for whom the demonstrators protest.

Social movements can also cause crowds to become violent indirectly, by arousing emotions and shared grievances of people who then engage in crowd behavior independently of the movement's organization and leader. For example, most of the riots in America's black slums in the 1960s were caused by a casual crowd—people sitting and standing outdoors on a hot summer night watching a routine arrest by the police. Because the Civil Rights movement had activated people's grievances and aroused emotions about the domination and abuse of black Americans, the casual crowd on a hot summer night quickly turned into an acting crowd, setting off a chain of events leading to emergent norms that condoned the looting and destruction of property. These crowd members shared what Smelser (1963) has termed a "generalized belief" about their plight; they responded with disproportionate emotion to a "precipitating incident," or an event such as a routine arrest, that sets into motion an acting crowd. Such motion is particularly likely when people's sense of deprivation escalates as a result of rising expectations that cannot be met or sudden downturns which increase the gap between what people have had in the past and what they now get. Such was the case in the Los Angeles riots of 1992, where the sense of deprivation of blacks suddenly escalated after the verdict in the Rodney King case. In either case, relative deprivation increases, and people are mobilized to act with only the slightest provocation.

Historically, crowds have erupted with such force that they have deposed political regimes. Such crowds usually emerge in the context of high inequality, emergent leaders, generalized beliefs, communication networks, and weakened political authority. The acting crowd in one area becomes the stimulus for crowd formation in other areas, soon creating such a strong wave of dissent that a

revolution, a rapid and violent overthrow of a political regime, occurs. The French Revolution, the revolution in Iran overthrowing the secular shah and creating the current religious polity in that society, and the street demonstrations that brought down the Soviet Union demonstrate how rapidly crowds can destroy a regime *if* it is politically weak and vulnerable (Goldstone, 1990; Skocpol, 1979). But events in China during the late 1980s, and elsewhere throughout the history of large societies, indicate that revolutionary crowds can be crushed when the regime is still in control of the means of coercion and when the crowds have few organizational resources of their own.

For crowds to be successful in changing a society, they must be able to mobilize resources—organizational structures, leaders, networks of communication, beliefs, people, money, and at times coercive capacities (McCarthy and Zald, 1977; Zald and McCarthy, 1979). Most successful revolutions, or social movements, had organizations, leaders, generalized beliefs, some money, and coercive capacity; and when the crowds erupted, they could be sustained or channeled toward goals.

From a rational choice perspective, **resource mobilization theory** stresses this point, arguing that social movements and other change-producing patterns of collective behavior emerge only when there are resources (Tilly, 1978; Zald and McCarthy, 1979). There are always grievances in a society, but most never generate collective movements for lack of a resource base. As a result, individuals calculate that the costs of failure far outweigh their current deprivation, and they therefore do not participate in a collective action. But when the costs of deprivations and grievances are high and the rewards associated with success in dissent are high, then people will join and participate. What tips the balance of people's calculations? Resources: leaders, ideologies and generalized beliefs, organizational structures (unions, churches, secret societies, etc.), finances, communication networks, large numbers of potential recruits, and if needed, coercive capacities. When resources can be mobilized, it is rational to incur the costs and risks of joining; when resources cannot be mobilized, it is rational to pass and continue to endure the costs of deprivations.

Again, context is important. If resource mobilization must face equally well organized opposition, it is less likely to occur or to be effective when it does occur. But if opposition is weak or divided, then the mobilization of resources for dissent can proceed, and people will think it rational to join in.

The Aftermath of Dissent

When dissent becomes widespread in a society, the forces of social control have broken down and the forces of disorder have increased. As a result, a society will never be the same—whether for the better or worse. If episodes of dissent have been successful, patterns of inequality will change, as will the institutional structures sustaining the old patterns. Cultural beliefs will change in ways legitimating new structures. But there is often an ironical twist to these changes: Power must often become more concentrated in order to implement changes and to stave off counter–social movements or counterrevolutions in which advocates of the old order try to restore things to where they were. As a basic rule, the more violent the change-producing dissent and the greater the changes ushered in, the more power must be concentrated to hold things together. And ironically, such power can become yet-another source of inequality, domination, and rising grievances—a fact emphasized by most conflict theories. Indeed, the seventy-year history of the Soviet Union displays all the elements of this sad story—a supposedly liberating revolution, followed by ever-more-concentrated power to hold the new order together, eventually causing grievances to rise to the point of forcing its collapse. If dissent is unsuccessful, much the same situation prevails: Power is concentrated to keep a lid on dissent, thereby escalating the grievances of individuals. Such is currently the case in China—where power is the lid on a powder keg.

If dissent occurs in a democratic context, however, it can at times work to release tensions and increase the viability of a society—a fact emphasized by more functional theories (Coser, 1956). Conflict need not force reactive repression, but instead may foster accommodation. The Civil Rights movement in the 1960s was one such movement. And the collective actions of blacks in what used to be called Rhodesia (now Zimbabwe), while punctuated with violence and reactive concentrations in power, changed the system without excessive violence and without creating a new form of coercive domination. The fate of South Africa is now in the balance, although once again the change may come more rapidly and peaceably than once feared.

Thus, power and dissent always stand in a delicate balance. Too much coercion and domination create, in the long run, dissent; too much dissent, even when successful, causes new concentrations of power fostering further dissent down the road. Political democracy institutionalizes dissent, but never completely; and as a result, social movements often bordering on rebellion and even civil war emerge in even the most democratic society. The capacity of a society to absorb and accommodate rather than to repress dissent is a key to its stability and viability. These are not abstract issues, for you confront them each time a crowd forms, a subgroup protests some condition, or a broad spectrum of people mobilize to address a grievance. I have lived through, and participated in, two such movements—the Civil Rights movement and the antiwar movement. You will, no doubt, be involved in one such movement, or at least watch from the sidelines. At stake will be the capacity to maintain order, accommodate grievances, and stabilize reactive concentrations of power.

SUMMARY

1. Society is always an uneasy standoff between the forces promoting order and those causing deviance, dissent, conflict, and disorder.
2. A number of interrelated forces will inevitably generate pressures for disorder: (a) increases in population size, (b) escalated differentiation, and (c) increased inequality.
3. At the macro level of society, social control is promoted by (a) governmental regulation and (b) market exchanges.

4. At the micro level of social organization, social control is promoted by (a) socialization of personality, (b) mutual sanctioning, (c) rituals, (d) role segregation.
5. Each of the major theoretical perspectives offers a theory on the causes of deviance. Functional theories stress the structural strain between cultural goals and the distribution of means. Conflict theories argue that laws and enforcement procedures help the affluent and work against the poor. Interactionist theories stress the labels given to people and the socialization process. And utilitarian theories emphasize the calculations of costs, investments, involvements, and beliefs in the genesis of deviance or conformity.
6. Dissent is the process of mobilizing to protest against aspects of a society. Such dissent is generated by inequalities, which serve as a basic precondition; and then, dissent is intensified when people share grievances, form networks, communicate, develop leaders, articulate beliefs, and experience relative deprivation. With these preconditions and their intensification, a number of theories have been offered to explain collective outbursts and crowd behavior: (a) contagion theory stressing the face-to-face interaction of individuals, (b) convergence theory emphasizing self-selection of predisposed individuals into crowd situations, (c) emergent norm theory stressing that through interaction, people develop norms in crowd situations which then guide their behavior. Crowd behavior is then initiated with precipitating incidents that galvanize generalized beliefs expressing grievances. To become an effective social movement, those in crowds must have resources to sustain their protest activities.

KEY TERMS

collective behavior   A field of study focusing on the sudden transformations of culture and social structures through such processes as dissent, riots, revolutions, fads, and social movements.

contagion theory   An early theory of collective behavior emphasizing the effects of interaction in intensifying people's emotions and, hence, the potential for collective behavior.

control theory   A utilitarian theory of deviance stressing that calculations of cost and investments determine whether or not people will deviate.

convergence theory   An approach emphasizing that people self-select themselves into crowd situations rather than getting swept away by a "mob mood."

crowd   Gatherings of people acting together with reference to some stimulus, situation, or goal.

deviance   Behavior that violates accepted norms.

differential association theory   A theory arguing that deviance is created when there is an excess of criminal to noncriminal definitions of appropriate behavior in a person's biography.

emergent norm theory   A symbolic interactionist theory stressing that collective behavior in a crowd is like all interaction and involves mutual role taking and the development of norms about how to behave.

labeling theory   A theory arguing that the deviant labels given to people are a major cause of their deviance.

resource mobilization theory   An approach to the study of social movements emphasizing that crowd mobilization and persistence of a social movement are related to the resource base of those involved.

revolution   A rapid and violent mobilization of people who seek to overthrow a political regime.

structural strain   Robert Merton's "anomie theory" emphasizing that rates of deviance increase when there is a disjuncture between goals and the means to achieve these goals. Also, Neil Smelser's basic precondition, rooted in inequality, for collective behavior.

CHAPTER 12

Social Change

For most of human history—some 40,000 years—change was very slow. Our remote ancestors were for 30,000 years simple hunters and gatherers, hardly changing over the millennia. Then with the development of agriculture, change became more common, but it was still slow. Now, over the last three hundred years, change is constant and incessant. It cannot be avoided; there are few places to go hide or to find "the simpler life." Each generation must now live in a very different world than the previous one, and increasingly, each person must change their jobs and skills during their lifetime. We can no longer muddle through with what we learned earlier. Such rapid change forces us all to be different than our ancestors who could enjoy a particular way of living throughout their lifetime. We must now learn to adapt to the juggernaut that has been unleashed by our culture and ways of organizing ourselves. As the discontinuity pictured above illustrates, the old, traditional church with its spires oriented to the heavens must now exist alongside, and increasingly utilize, newer ways of communicating with the heavens and each other.

For 30,000 years of our existence as a species, the basic nature of human organization did not change. Small bands of nuclear families wandered a territory, collecting what they needed to survive. Then, anywhere from 12,000 to 18,000 years ago, people began to settle down and practice horticulture, and the nature of human organization was never to be the same. Compare present-day American society—big, complex, volatile, and dynamic—with a small band of hunters and gatherers; and we can immediately see *how much* change has occurred over the last 10,000 to 12,000 years. And much of this change has occurred in just a few hundred years.

Change is not, however, always cumulative, continually adding new elements to the past. Societies have often collapsed and disappeared. Indeed, for most of the agrarian era—from four to five thousand years ago up to just a few hundred years ago—change has been somewhat cyclical. Empires arose, reached a zenith in terms of size, complexity, and culture—only to fall apart and regress back to simpler forms. Yet, over the long haul, these cyclical movements have been accompanied by slow and incremental increases in technologies which, in turn, subtly changed economic and other institutional forms (Lenski, Lenski, and Nolan, 1991). These incremental increases were just that, incremental and hardly observable to the people living through them. But then came a great breakthrough, building on the slow changes of the past and adding new dynamic elements. This breakthrough is called the **industrial revolution** because it revolutionized human social organization; and perhaps we are now living through yet-another dynamic period of change—the information revolution—which will significantly alter how we and our descendants live. Change and transformation, then, are part of our lives; and it is wise to understand more about this basic contingency of the modern era.

FORCES OF CHANGE

Culture and Social Change

Since cultural symbols guide human interaction and social organization, change in these symbols will, in turn, have profound effects on social relations and structure. Of course, cultural symbols typically change with alterations in the structures that they regulate, but for the moment, let us analyze the power of cultural change by itself.

Probably the most potent source of social change in human affairs has been **technology,** or knowledge about how to manipulate the environment (Lenski, Lenski, and Nolan, 1991). For, as humans have developed new knowledge about how to gather resources, how to produce goods and services, and how to distribute these, all other social relations have changed. Indeed, the basic types of societies that have existed—hunting and gathering (and more specialized variants like fishing and herding), horticulture, agricultural, and industrial—are defined by their technologies, as these symbols shaped the structure of the economy. **Innovation,** or the development of new technologies, has thus been a powerful change-producing force in human societies.

Another source of cultural change in human societies stems from **evaluative beliefs,** or those cognitions that people hold about what should occur and exist in basic social contexts. By far the most powerful beliefs are those associated with religion. As new conceptions of the supernatural and of people's obligations to this realm have emerged, basic social structures have correspondingly changed. For example, Max Weber (1904) developed the controversial thesis that emergence of Protestantism caused people to become oriented to hard work, saving, investment, and accumulation—the impetus for the emergence of capitalism and industrialization. Similarly today, we can observe the spread of Islam throughout the middle east and northern Africa and the transforming effects of its beliefs on, for example, government, education, and sex roles.

Cultural symbols change through two basic processes. One is **diffusion,** or the spread of symbol systems from one population to another. Languages, values, beliefs, institutional norms, and technologies have all been subject to diffusion, and today, it is easy to observe this process. For example, at one time beliefs and institutional norms, as well as technologies, about how to organize industrial economic activity spread from England to continental Europe and then to the east, especially Japan; today, beliefs and norms about the organization of work are coming back to us from Japan, as American corporations attempt to become more competitive in the world system. In fact, the existence of a world market economy, as well as highly developed communications media and systems of transportation, ensure that diffusion will be rapid and widespread. At one time in human history, diffusion was necessarily slow; today, it is inevitably rapid.

The other source of symbolic change is structural. As people cope with new problems and concerns, they reorganize activities; and as they do so, they alter cultural symbols. At first they change norms, because these are what most directly and immediately guide their actions. Over time, beliefs about what occurs and should occur begin to change in order to correspond to altered patterns of social relations, and if these changes in social structures, norms, and beliefs are sufficiently large and widespread, values or standards of right and wrong may also change. For example, industrialization in the undeveloped world has this effect: Certain economic relations are changed which, in turn, successively alter norms, beliefs, and values.

This relationship between cultural and structural change is, of course, reciprocal. If new symbols diffuse into a society or are created as social relations are altered, they often feed back and accelerate the very changes which created them. For example, if ideas about how to organize a workplace filter into a society, these changes in work make people more receptive to further diffusion of these ideas; or if work norms change by internal processes of reorganization, once these norms exist, they accelerate change and reorganization of work. Thus, change-producing ideas are not like the Goodyear blimp, floating above the action; they are implicated in that action, being produced by it and, reciprocally, feeding back and affecting the flow of interaction and the patterning of social structures.

Social Structure and Change

Social structures can, by themselves, be sources of change. For, built into most patterns of social relations are the seeds of change. Let me explore a few of the key sources of such changes.

Inequality and Change

One principal source of structural change is inequality and the creation of class, sexual, and ethnic categories. As all conflict theories would stress, inequality in the distribution of money, power, prestige, health, education, and other valued resources generates a basic tension between those who have and those who want these resources. Such tension need not erupt into violent conflict, but it creates pressures on social relations. Those who have resources work to keep them by consolidating power, by draping themselves in legitimating beliefs, and by resorting to naked coercion. Often, those without resources can do little but grumble and perhaps periodically riot; yet, when deprivations escalate and people can begin to organize, more far-reaching changes can result. Thus, inequality is like a sociocultural pressure cooker; the lid can be kept tight, at least for a time, but the pressure builds and causes change, sometimes gradually but often violently.

This source of structural change is dramatically escalated by ethnicity. When the disadvantaged are a distinctive ethnic subculture and are subject to discrimination, the normal tensions associated with inequality are magnified. For, the ethnic subculture—its values, beliefs, norms, and organizations—becomes a vehicle for communication of grievances, emergence of leaders, and codification of beliefs. These forces will increase the likelihood of protest and change, especially if an ethnic subpopulation already has some resources—money, pockets of local power, symbols, and organizational structures—which it can spend in addressing its grievances. Those without such minimal resources—such as black slaves in the pre-Civil War south in America—are less able to protest, but the existence of an oppressed ethnic population will, over the long run, produce pressures for change.

In fact, we can generalize from the case of ethnicity and inequality: As a general rule, inequalities create political pressures for change when they produce distinctive subcultures which have unifying cultural symbols, viable social structures, and some financial resources. The subculture serves as a kind of launching pad for a social movement and, at times, for the crowd behavior that goes along with a social movement (see last chapter for more details). Thus, if a social class, sexual category, age group, or any category produced by inequalities can become a subculture, it can more readily mobilize and cause change.

Subcultures and Change

Let me extend this general rule further: The existence of distinct subcultures, per se, produces pressures for change, even if there is little inequality associated with their situation. People in different ethnic subpopulations are likely to have diverging beliefs and lifestyles; and when they come into contact, conflict and change can occur. Similarly, other subcultural clashes can force change. For example, tensions between youth and older generations have often produced change. The 1950s, for example, created semirebellious groupings of youth, personified by James Dean, or a young Marlon Brando, and even Elvis Presley, who forced a loosening of norms about proper behavior; the youth of the 1960s broke these norms open even more, creating more tolerance for distinctive and different ways of living. Even deviant subcultures have generated change, as is best illustrated in how Americans now respond to homosexuality. Thus, as divergent subcultures come into contact, change is inevitable as accommodations and compromises are made. And big, complex societies like the United States, which have so many diverse subcultures, will inevitably undergo change from this source.

Institutions and Change

Basic institutions often change of their own accord, in response to their own internal dynamics. A capitalist economy, for example, is self-transforming; it constantly expands markets, creates new businesses, changes consumer preferences, and reorders the nature of the workforce. Similarly, a political democracy is self-transforming: Its very nature is to allow the "will" of people and interest groups to determine what goals will be pursued, what activities will be considered important, and what resources will be used; and as various interests exert pressures, change is inevitable. The converse of a capitalist economy and democratic political system also generates change, as we have seen with the collapse of the Soviet empire in 1991. For, totalitarian political regimes and regulated economies circumscribe people's activities and dictate their preferences to the point of apathy and stagnation, often bringing the system down.

Other institutional structures, such as education, science, medicine, law, religion, and even family are also self-transforming. In each, the very nature of their operation can generate change. For example, science seeks new knowledge which can be used to develop new, change-producing technologies; medicine attempts to improve health and, in so doing, changes the nature of medical care systems; law often attempts to reinterpret its statutes or to extend them to new arenas; religion frequently becomes more secular as it becomes established and, in so doing, invites more evangelical and fundamentalistic competitors; and family relations can change as members reassess their relations.

Because institutions are interrelated, each influencing the others, change in one causes changes in the others. Thus, institutions change not only because of their internal dynamics, but also in response to one another. This domino effect, when coupled with internal self-transforming processes within institutions, can create an endless impetus for change. For example, your family has changed dramatically from the one I grew up in: Your mother is much more likely to have worked (as will you if you are, or plan to be, a mother); your family is, on average, smaller than its counterpart in the 1940s (and may become even smaller as the burdens of children weigh on the lifestyles and energy of working parents); and your family is probably more egalitarian than the one of the 1940s and 1950s, and the one you create in the future will certainly be more egalitarian (indeed, you and your spouse will have to renegotiate constantly your relationship). These and other changes came primarily from changes in the economy, as well as from the internal tension associated with inequalities between men and women in the household. These changes will, in turn, produce further changes in sex roles in general, politics (women will become more prominent in the halls of power, despite a lot of male foot dragging), and schools (in order to accommodate working mothers). And as these changes in other institutions occur, they will redouble back and cause additional changes in your or your children's family.

In the past, this chain of change was much slower. Institutions were more stable; and while kings and empires came and went, most people did what they had always had been doing. Now change in institutions is more rapid, and we feel the effects more dramatically in all spheres of institutional life—work, family, school, politics, law, and religion. Thus, once institutions reveal a rapid self-transforming capacity, their interconnectedness makes our lives seem, at times, like a dizzy blur of transformation. Such is modern life; we must all get used to it, or find a place to run and hide.

Demography and Change

Population processes can exert great pressures for change. When a population increases in size, new forms of economic productivity become necessary to feed, house, and clothe the larger citizenry; new patterns of political and legal organization often become necessary to regulate and control the restive masses; new schools and patterns of education become essential to socialize the increasing numbers of young; and so it goes. Population growth is thus a powerful dynamo in a society; it demands institutional responses and change. Conversely, a declining population can also exert pressures for change, but with less urgency. As numbers decline, as was the case for much of eastern Europe under communist rule for the four decades after World War II, there are fewer workers for the economy and fewer children for schools.

The patterns of movement of a population also cause change. If a population becomes urban, with massive influxes of rural peasants and farmers to cities, as is now the case in much of the Third World, enormous pressure is put on the urban infrastructure, creating vast slums and shantytowns of desperate and restive people. This situation, in turn, forces adjustments of government, schools, and economy. Conversely, as has been evident in the United States, some urban areas are losing population, leaving behind the less mobile poor and elderly who require government services on a declining tax base. This situation has forced changes in local governance, welfare, schools, and other urban institutional structures.

Migration into and out of a society, or its key areas, also has great effects on social structure. For example, the influx of Mexicans into the southwest is dramatically changing not only the culture of this region, but its economy, patterns of governance, social services, and schools. Similarly, the influx of many of your relatives in the last century and early decades of this century into urban areas also forced changes in the basic institutions of these areas. Out-migration, or emigration, also affects a society, especially if a particular class of citizens leaves. If the educated, professional, or entrepreneurial workforce leaves—the "brain drain," as it is called—the economy, government, and schools will be adversely affected; or if low-wage workers leave and create a labor shortage, then other problems will ensue, although when the poor leave, their migration often helps reduce the pressures on government, schools, and other institutions.

The age structure of a population also creates pressures for change. A population whose proportion of young relative to old is declining, as is the case in the United States and much of Europe, will experience problems finding enough tax revenues (from the young who work) to support the elderly (who do not work). Conversely, a society which has a very young population, as is the case in most of the societies of Latin America, Asia, and Africa, will face the problem of creating jobs, schools, and social services for the young as they grow older—a situation that often undermines the legitimacy of political leaders and, as a consequence, causes changes in political institutions.

Thus, as I emphasized in Chapter 10, population size, composition, and movement are not passive forces. On the contrary, they force change. A casual look at the Third World will tell you this, but we can look closer to home and see the pressures on social structure and culture that come with immigration, internal migrations, and graying of the citizenry. Members of younger age cohorts in America are likely to have to make the most significant adjustments to these demographic forces, as they must pay for the medical and other government benefits given to the elderly.

INTERPRETATIONS OF CHANGE

From its very beginnings, sociology as a discipline sought to understand change (Nisbet, 1966, 1969). Indeed, the founders of sociology all attempted to explain the great transformation of their time: industrialization and its effects on the reorganization of societies, social relations, and personal life. More recent sociologists have continued in this tradition, seeking to understand the transformations associated with postindustrialism and the emerging information age. Let me review, in broad strokes, some of the models used to interpret social change.

Cyclical Models of Change

Herbert Spencer (1874–1896) was the first sociologist to develop a cyclical model. For Spencer, any type of society on an evolutionary scale tends to cycle between what he termed a "militant" and an "industrial" profile. A *militant society* is one where power is concentrated and centralized, whereas an *industrial society* is one where power is decentralized. Each of these poles, Spencer argued, generates pressures for movement to the opposite pole. A centralized system overregulates, creating economic stagnation and resentments which eventually are articulated in beliefs and political pressures for deregulation and decentralization of power. In contrast, a decentralized system underregulates, generating problems of coordination and control which lead to the emergence of beliefs and political movements for tighter regulation through the centralization of power. Thus, one crucial dynamic in a society revolves around the oscillation between centralized and decentralized power—a process made dramatically evident by the fall of the highly centralized Soviet empire to a more decentralized cluster of independent states.

Another early cyclical theory was developed by the economist turned sociologist, Vilfredo Pareto (1916). Much like Spencer, Pareto argued that political centralization leads to economic contraction which, in turn, causes dissatisfaction in the population and stagnation in the development and flow of capital. This situation created pressures for decentralization, but this decentralization of power causes so much economic expansion and speculation that capital is expended (or frittered away as in the United States during the 1980s) to the point of chaos, thus forcing increased concentration of power to regulate economic activity. These processes are, however, greatly constrained by cultural beliefs, for there is a lag between when change is needed and people's beliefs that change is appropriate. People hold onto their beliefs, and this cultural force works against change. But once beliefs begin to change as the situation worsens, they then accelerate changes in political regulation, causing the emergence of new kinds of leaders.

Dialectical-Conflict Models of Change

Cyclical models are, in a sense, **dialectical** because they argue that inherent in one state of social organization—whether centralization or decentralization of power—are the seeds of transformation to an opposite state of organization. Thus, inherent in political centralization is the stagnation and resentment that cause change to decentralization; and built into decentralization are the seeds of chaos and speculation that cause change to a more centralized political system.

Karl Marx, and modern-day Marxists, have also developed dialectical models of change which likewise emphasize that the seeds of transformation are built into social forms, but unlike cycle models, they stress an evolutionary movement of societies toward a communist utopia. Obviously, this utopian state of communism is downplayed in contemporary models; indeed, most Marxists would deny naive notions of "end states," but if we scratch the surface of their models, the notion that "something better" than capitalism is in our future can almost always be found. We need not accept these implicit assumptions to see the strong points of Marxist models, however.

One type of dialectical conflict theory emphasizes the internal contradictions of a given system of social organization. As Marx emphasized, a given pattern of economic organization creates the impetus for its own transformation by enabling the disadvantaged to become organized in the pursuit of their interests in changing the system (Marx and Engels, 1848). Thus, in early capitalist industrial systems, workers are placed in situations (degrading factories and urban areas) where they can communicate, develop leaders and ideologies, and politically mobilize to force change. The great revolution by the proletariat never occurred in the way visualized by Marx, but the forces emphasized by Marx (worker mobilization to realize their interests) did cause some redistribution of income and power in capitalist societies so that workers could enjoy a better life.

This line of argument emphasizes an important source of change: inequality. A complex system of social organization creates inequality and, for a time, operates to aggravate the plight of those at the bottom. But as their resentments build and they become organized to pursue their interests in redistribution, they force change in politics, in economic activity, and in the distribution of valued resources (Dahrendorf, 1959). This kind of argument—first given forceful expression by Marx and carried forward by Marxists—represents an important insight into how the world operates.

An extension of these ideas has occurred with the development of **world systems analysis**. The argument here is that the dynamics of inequality extend to the world economic system. That is, the unit of analysis is not *a* society but *a system* of societies. For just as a given society reveals inequality, so the world system of societies evidences change-producing patterns of inequality. Immanuel Wallerstein (1974) has been the most consistent advocate of this position. For Wallerstein, a pattern of inequality is evident in world capitalism: The "core" geographical area contains those nations which are most economically developed and which, by virtue of their economic power (via their multinational corporations in alliance with their governments), exploit other poorer regions, taking their resources and giving little back; the "periphery" consists of those societies which supply the raw materials that ensure the profits and prosperity of the core; and the societies of the "semiperiphery" fall in between the core and periphery, often serving as conduits of resources flowing from the periphery to the core. Even when the core invests capital in the periphery, the investment is narrow and does not encourage broadly based economic development that can help a society; and this situation is aggravated by the fact that the wealth of a nation—its raw materials—is being taken out at low prices, thereby robbing a society of the wealth that could finance its future development. Thus, a small "class" of core nations is seen to exploit the mass of peripheral nations, and in so doing, this core aggravates world-level inequality. In many of these Marxist-inspired world systems theories, there is a hidden presumption, or hope, that as capitalism spreads and as this exploitation aggravates inequalities at a world level, the "contradictions of capitalism" will reach a point where conflicts will force some redistribution from the core to periphery. This presumption aside, world systems models emphasize an important dynamic of social change: The flow of resources across societies and the existence of tension-producing patterns of world inequality can erupt into conflict and, hence, social change.

Functional-Evolutionary Models of Change

Evolutionary models emphasize the cumulative nature of social change. Over the long run of history, societies have become bigger and more complex—moving from simple hunting and gathering to horticulture, and then to agrarian, and from there to industrial and postindustrial profiles. Most early sociologists posited evolutionary stages of development from simple to complex, but the most sophisticated of these theories were functional. These functional theories emphasized that evolution involved a process of increasing growth of the population, the necessity for differentiation of social structures to support the larger population, and the emergence of new mechanisms for integrating and coordinating this larger and more differentiated population.

Herbert Spencer (1874–1896) probably developed the most detailed of these early evolutionary theories. For Spencer, the evolution of societies had historically moved through several distinct stages: simple without a leader (hunting and gathering), simple with a leader (horticulture), compound (advanced horticulture), doubly compound (agrarian), and finally treble compound (modern, industrial). During this evolution, societies had become more differentiated (or "compounded" in his terms) along three functional axes: (1) the productive-reproductive (those positions and social units involved with economic production and with socialization of new members into the society), (2) the regulatory (those positions and social units involved in political control), and (3) the distributive (those positions and units facilitating the movements of goods, services, information, and other resources). As differentiation along these axes occurred, problems of coordination and control escalated, forcing the elaboration of those structures that facilitate (1) the interdependence of units on each other (markets and exchange, roads and other means of communication and transportation), and (2) the political regulation and coordination of units (laws and regulatory agencies).

Émile Durkheim (1893) borrowed much from Spencer, but he shifted the emphasis to the functional importance of cultural systems. For Durkheim the progressive differentiation of society into ever-more-specialized positions created a problem of how people could share common cultural symbols when they performed such diverse activities and, thereby, had such divergent experiences. His answer was that evolution involved the "generalization" of values in order that they would be sufficiently broad so as to apply to everyone's different life situation. At the same time, institutional norms for all major spheres of activity— family, work, religion, politics, and the like—would have to become clear and specific so that people would know how to behave and respond. Thus, values would say something like "work hard," but beliefs and norms in the workplace, family, school, and other institutional spheres would indicate how this value would be realized. Thus, as social structure differentiates, so must culture; but it does so, Durkheim believed, in ways that give people a common set of unifying symbols, while at the same time providing normative guidance in their various specialized activities.

More recent functional theories of societal evolution (Parsons, 1966, 1971) pursue these early themes. Evolution revolves around growth in the size and complexity of society, creating problems of integration. These problems are resolved at the structural level by the concentration of regulatory power (that is, government regulation), by the elaboration of market systems for carrying out exchanges and thereby fostering interdependencies among social units (you and me in labor markets; producers and buyers of goods, services, and virtually anything in other markets), by the expansion of bodies of law and courts to guide exchanges and to constrain the powers of government, by the extension of citizenship and voting rights to the population, and by the creation of a generalized sense of community through highly general values and beliefs.

Conflict-Evolutionary Models

Marxist models have evolutionary elements, but there are other, non-Marxist conflict theories that incorporate both the Marxian emphasis on inequality as a driving force in evolution and the functional stress on differentiation and integration. In these theories (Lenski, 1966; J. Turner, 1984a), evolution is seen as ultimately fueled by advances in technology which, in turn, have increased productivity. Such increases in production result in a larger economic surplus which is usurped by some and used to concentrate power and increase their privilege. Once power exists it can be used to extract more surplus, thereby escalating inequality. As long as technological advance and increased productivity ensue, this system of surplus extraction, concentration of power, and increased inequality continues—reaching its peak in agrarian societies with absolute monarchs and a hereditary nobility who control a vast pool of poor peasants. But inequality creates pressures for change, as those without power and privilege mobilize to do something about their plight. At times, these mobilizations lead to the collapse of a society, but they also cause some redistribution of power and wealth. Especially with industrialization, and the differentiation of economic positions and elaboration of markets, power becomes more democratic and, with democracy, government is forced to give to the less privileged new services—education, job security, health care, pensions, welfare benefits, and all the social service and welfare programs of a modern industrial society. Such redistribution generates a sense of national identity and commitments to general values and beliefs of the society as a whole, thereby providing a basis for integration of the population.

Postindustrial and Postmodern Models

A large body of literature has emerged on *postindustrial* and *postmodern* societies, the current state of culmination from past evolution. These terms do not mean the same thing, but they denote a kind of philosophical comment on modern society. They are not theory, but they try to indicate the state and direction of contemporary societies—thereby making them good candidates for closing a chapter on social change.

Postindustrial commentaries emphasize the transformations associated with further technological advances in production and communication. As machines can perform many of the routine productive tasks, the nature of work and society is transformed. Work roles will require greater skill and training, thereby making education an ever more important institutional system. Jobs will involve processing information as opposed to "things"; and the media of communication will enable people to work and live in less concentrated ways than the traditional city and urban corridor. A different kind of person will emerge—mobile, flexible, educated, professional, and secular (Bell, 1973; Hage and Powers, 1992).

Postmodernist commentaries emphasize that modern societies are becoming so fluid that a "decentering" is occurring: Regulation and control by government and organizations are lost as hyperdifferentiation of positions occurs, as cultural values and beliefs become too abstracted and remote, as markets become complex and able to buy and sell almost anything, as neighborhood and community are lost in constantly mobile suburbanites, as democratic government becomes a media circus without meaningful programs and platforms, and as com- munications media and information networks detach people from the workplace. People thus become disconnected from one another in work, home, neighborhood, politics, and culture. Thus, the rationality of modernism—as manifested in factory and bureaucracies—has given way to nonrational fluidity and chaos.

These portrayals have a clear moral bias, but they force us to think about the nature of modern society, as it has evolved and developed. As a participant in this society, you can evaluate the validity of the claims made by postindustrial and postmodern thinkers. Are these portrayals accurate? My sense is that they are dramatically overdrawn, but these kinds of commentaries make us think about the effects of evolutionary change in our lives.

SUMMARY

1. The rate of social change has dramatically accelerated in the last few hundred years. Change can be cumulative, but the history of human societies reveals sudden reversals. Such was particularly the case for the agrarian era.
2. Change can come from cultural forces, particularly (a) innovations in technology, (b) evaluative beliefs, and (c) diffusion of symbol systems. Such cultural changes are intimately connected to changes in structures, serving to initiate changes in structure or, at the very least, accelerating already initiated structural changes.
3. Social structures reveal several major sources of change, including (a) inequality and the resulting conflict over resources, (b) subcultures seeking to overcome disadvantages, (c) institutions that reveal processes generating their own transformations.
4. Demographic processes are also an impetus to change, especially changes in a population's size, its movement patterns, and its age structure.
5. The study of change is at the center of all sociological analysis, from the beginnings of the discipline up to the present. A number of basic models has been developed to explain change, including: (a) cycle models emphasizing movement of societies back and forth between two basic states, (b) dialectical-conflict models stressing the change-producing dynamics inherent in inequalities, (c) functional-evolutionary models stressing the movement from simple to complex societal forms and the corresponding effort to meet new needs and requisites, (d) conflict-evolutionary models that see the driving force behind movement from simple to complex societies as inequalities emerging from the reorganization of societies in terms of new technologies, and (e) loose commentaries, whether "postindustrial" or "postmodern," on the transforming effects of societies with advanced information technologies and media systems.

KEY TERMS

dialectic/dialectical   The line of argument asserting that inherent in one social form are the processes for its transformation.

diffusion   The spread of cultural symbol systems from one population to another.

evaluative beliefs   Cognitions that people hold about *what should* occur in basic social contexts.

industrial revolution   The harnessing of inanimate sources of power to machines and human labor, and the consequent reorganization of the economy, society, and culture in the 1800s and up to the present.

innovation, technological   The development of new knowledge about how to manipulate the environment.

postindustrial   Commentaries revolving around the cultural and structural transformations associated with further advances in technologies for production, communication, and transportation.

postmodern   A loose set of social commentaries on the decentering of societies through hyperdifferentiation, loss of core values and beliefs, overextension of markets, loss of neighborhood and community, media domination of politics, culture, and social ties.

technology   Systems of symbols organized into knowledge about how to manipulate the environment.

world systems analysis   The analysis of the patterns of inequality in power and economic resources of nations and the resulting patterns of political and economic domination among nations.

EPILOG: A Long Note to Students on the Uses of Sociology

To look at the present-day world, many problematic issues dominate social life: How are we to reorganize American corporations in the face of world economic competition? How can we create work settings that are more meaningful for workers? How can we transport people to work in a less congested way? How do we deliver welfare? How do we organize medical services in a less costly way? How do we educate students better in the age of global economic competition? How can we house everyone? How are we to reduce poverty? How can we mitigate racial and ethnic tensions? How are we to plan more efficiently the growth of cities? How is government to be made more efficient and less unwieldy? How do we sustain delicate ecological balances?

These and other questions are real, immediate, and relevant to all of us. They are sociological because an answer to each will require *understanding of the ways in which people are organized*. Organizational problems and dilemmas are thus the lifeblood of sociology. Today, we need new and expanded knowledge and understanding of human behavior and organization; and as a result there will be jobs and careers for sociologists who can collect, analyze, and interpret data on human populations and who can provide advice on how to resolve the innumerable organizational problems and dilemmas that confront American society.

There will be, therefore, a long-term invasion of sociologists into nonacademic jobs. This is an invasion not just of M.A.s and Ph.D.s, but also of B.A. majors in sociology and of students with degrees in other fields who take a number of sociology courses to broaden their perspective. Some may consider this an invasion of the Visigoths, but I prefer to think of us as a liberating army. In any case, the invasion will be a quiet one, occurring as many different kinds of sociologically trained people assume an equally wide range of jobs. Not all of these will be glamour jobs, involving sociological pronouncements that gain the ear of movers and shakers in the corporate and governmental bureaucracies.

To give just a few examples, we will probably be seeing sociologists as data analysts, office heads, sales directors, labor-management facilitators, eligibility workers in the welfare system, heads of adoption agencies, city planning directors, patrol officers on the police force, parks and recreation directors, liaison personnel in the various agencies of city government, redevelopment directors, community organizers, census bureau statisticians, social workers, management consultants, advertising executives, insurance agents, and housing developers. Thus, as this very short listing of job options underscores, the provision of many different kinds of human and organizational services will be the avenue of sociological invasion. In all these jobs, knowledge of organizational dynamics, human behavior, and cultural diversity is essential. For some jobs, this knowledge will need to be extensive and supplemented by skills in theory, methods, and statistics. In others, the knowledge can be rudimentary but will provide an orientating perspective with which to approach a job and a means for interpreting and dealing with on-the-job experiences.

The increasing range of jobs for which sociological training is relevant is the result of the transformation of the economy and government. A postindustrial economy increasingly employs people in service, nonmanual jobs. As machines take on more tasks, the need for personnel to service the productive process grows dramatically. In the private sector, productive activity involves dealing with people, clients, governmental agencies, and other corporate units; and as a result, work has a clear sociological bias. In government, regulatory and service functions increase; and virtually all these functions are sociological in character because they involve providing human services and coordinating activity.

You may not want to read any further, but if you are still curious, let me now go back over each chapter of this book and indicate why the topics covered have important implications and career application. Let me start with Chapter 2.

If you want to become a professional sociologist, you must learn theory and research methods. The ability to gather, analyze, and interpret data is in great demand by government and business. Most students do not, of course, plan to be professional sociologists. But almost all professional jobs will require you to deal with information presented in statistical form and to bring the analytical skills of a theorist to its interpretation. You will therefore need to understand how data are collected, what the methodologies involved are, and how data are analyzed; at the same time, you will need analytical skills, which training in theory can give you, to interpret data and to make informed decisions based upon this interpretation. Most government agencies and private corporations collect hordes of data, pass it around on their computer networks, and use it in making decisions. Those who know how to collect, analyze, and interpret such data will have the advantage in these agencies and corporations. To enter the world without the basic tools of social science is to place yourself at a great disadvantage.

Finally, you confront statistics and other types of analyzed data every day in your nonprofessional life—on television, in the newspaper, on the radio, and in conversations with friends. You have often heard people spout data and facts. You and I live in a world where facts are often statistical facts. Without knowledge of proper methods for collecting, analyzing, and interpreting such facts, you can be manipulated. Many of the "facts" on the media are, as I have discovered, just plain wrong, and anyone with just a little training can see the problems with these "facts." For example, the divorce rate in America, the crime rate, the rate of employment/unemployment, the "leading economic indicators," the consumer price index, and the rate of increase or decline in almost anything have been misrepresented on television. Most of this misrepresentation has come from the ignorance of the TV producers and commentators, although some of it may have been deliberate. Moreover, I have read many stories in the newspaper and magazines that are so flawed methodologically (that is, in how the data have been collected) as to be worthless. Yet most people will believe them. You should not, but unless you have further training you will be manipulated.

Thus, since so much of the information to which each of us is exposed is, in reality, packaged data, we can all be easily misinformed if we do not understand methodological procedures. If only for your own enlightenment in a world filled with information, you must know something about the procedures of social science.

Turning to the implications of Chapter 3, we can see clearly that if we wish to understand how we as individuals behave, knowledge about cultural coding is essential. What language systems do we have? What is the nature and level of our technologies for manipulating the environment? What profile of basic values do we hold? What kinds of beliefs—both factual and evaluational—do we use in key situations? How aware of crucial institutional norms are we? What is the content of our stocks of knowledge? And what subculture(s) are we members of? A simple answer to these questions can tell us a great deal about ourselves—how we see the world, what we are likely to do, what will make us happy or angry, and how we are prepared to deal with other people.

What is true for ourselves is also true for others. If we want to understand other people, or maybe help them, we need to know about their cultural coding. People's personal miseries and their maladjustments to social conditions are always to some extent a cultural problem. People often hold contradictory beliefs. They can also have trouble reconciling their beliefs to the requirements of a situation. Or, they can simply be unaware of the beliefs and norms of a situation. I am not saying that individual problems are always strictly cultural, but I am saying that there are always cultural elements. Many personal problems revolve around the conflicts, passions, emotions, and contradictions that values, beliefs, stocks of knowledge, and institutional norms can mobilize.

Thus, if you want a job that involves helping people—whether as a teacher, social worker, psychologist, or probation officer—you need to understand the dynamics of culture. You need to know the elementary things that I imparted in Chapter 3 and much, much more. But for our purposes, the essential point is this: We must be aware of the cultural legacy that each individual carries. Much of what a person is, can be, and hopes to be is a reflection of the profile of culture that he or she carries. Skilled practitioners need to know how to get at, and get inside, this cultural content in people's heads. Further training in sociology can help.

At a more macro level, when you desire to help whole groups and populations of people, knowledge of cultural processes is also essential. If we want to help a group, we have to understand the common culture of its members. If we want to slow the birth rate of people, we need to know their values, the relevant beliefs, and the crucial norms that lead them to have numerous children even when birth-control pills have been made available. If we want to help an ethnic population adjust to life in a society, we need to know the points of variation or conflict between its culture and that of the mainstream. If we want to initiate a political movement—say equal rights, civil rights, workers' rights—a large part of our task involves changing people's beliefs and altering institutional norms.

And even if you are not interested in helping people or saving the world, a knowledge of cultural dynamics can help you. In fact, even if you are only interested in helping yourself make more money, knowledge of the cultural values, beliefs, and norms of those with whom you deal is essential. For, we all live in a world of subcultures, both subtle and obvious. Within an organization, beliefs and norms vary from the top to the bottom levels. Within a community and between communities, there are cultural variations. In the broader society, some differences have their roots in ethnic, class, and regional cultural systems. If you must deal with people from different walks of life, you need to be aware of cultural variations and the processes that produce and sustain these variations. Sociology can help on this score; thus, as purely a matter of career training, it behooves you to delve further in a sociology curriculum.

Finally, simply recognizing the facts of cultural variation and the processes by which these are sustained will make you a better, more enlightened, and tolerant person. Few sociologically trained individuals carry a "red neck" and intolerant mentality. If only for your own enlightenment, further study into the world of symbols and culture can be useful.

Turning to the message of Chapter 4, I emphasized that social structures, from the smallest group to whole societies, have great power over us. What makes social structures doubly powerful is that they overlap and are laced together in a web of interdependencies. It is hard to find cracks in between them, to isolate yourself and to break loose. This interconnectedness makes life in modern societies complex and bewildering. It also presents the society as a whole with real organizational problems and dilemmas to go along with the personal frustrations that each of us feels in a social fabric that is often tightly woven around us. Retreatism and despair are frequent responses to our sense that we are cogs in a vast social machine beyond our full comprehension.

I propose an alternative: Strive to understand this machine, learn how it works, and if necessary, take it apart and build a new one. There are too many people in this world and too few mountaintops and other places for us to retreat. We must develop expertise in how groups, organizations, communities, social categories, and basic institutions work and operate. Here is where the career opportunities will be.

You and I live in a complex world, in which the organization of people and the delivery of services have become major industries—much like steel, mining, and railroads in the last century. And yet in some ways, current thinking about these new industries lags on the level of that of the last century. On the one hand, this lag means that there are some prejudices against sociology, but on the other hand, the previous failure to use sociology and sociologists means that there will be a burst of opportunities in the future. You may believe that I am overly optimistic, but even if you are correct, there will at least be some beginning attempts to use sociology. That is, even if we view the future less optimistically, industry and government will begin to look for people who understand social structures and who can help organize activity and deliver services. Indeed, they have already done so, but quietly. They have been tiptoeing around the cost accountant, the bottom-line hard-liners, and the laissez-faire captains of industry. There are, then, opportunities for those who wish to enter quietly and be on the ground floor.

Career and vocational interests aside, there is another sound reason for you to learn about the subfields of sociology dealing with social structure: to increase your awareness of the forces impinging on you. Knowing something about the complex structure of modern societies will make each of us a better individual and will allow us to cope and to maintain sanity in what is often an insane world.

Equally important, your more humanitarian desire to help people can be seen in a new light. Simple solutions in a complex world will usually fail. Whether our goal is eliminating poverty as well as racial and sexual injustice, cleaning up the environment, reducing worker alienation, increasing economic productivity, or any of a host of other goals, we all must approach cautiously. In working toward such goals, you will have to confront and overcome the power of social structure and culture. These forces represent a dragon that cannot be easily tamed to our purposes. In dealing with problems rooted in social structures, you will confront well-entrenched cultural beliefs and institutional norms; you must deal with powerful vested interests that have a stake in what you want to change; you must cope with ignorance and stupidity among people; you must contend with the interconnectedness of structures which are embedded in one another and therefore are much more difficult to change; and you must accept the current state of sociological ignorance as to how the social world operates and what the consequences of your efforts might be. Thus, you must approach the task of amelioration as a knight in very tarnished armor who is going against a very powerful dragon.

Yet, if the task seems hopeless, the solution is not abdication to the ignorant, to ideologies, to those "who have had revealed unto them the simplistic solution." My sense is that the difficulties that confront humane "social engineering" should be seen as not only a challenge but also a great opportunity. To be a highway engineer is, to my taste, a bit boring and predictable. The parameters and formulas are in most cases known. But to try to build a better society is to confront an unknown where we are just beginning to learn the parameters and formulas. For those of you who wish to understand human organization in order to change it for the better, really exciting challenges await us.

For those who acquire facility in gathering and analyzing information on social structure and for those who develop conceptual and theoretical acumen on basic social processes, there are real but as yet unrealized opportunities to do something constructive. You may not get rich, at least for the present, but you can get a sense of satisfaction from doing something important—helping to create new forms of human organization.

In Chapter 5, I stressed that anything that you do involves interaction—with others in a specific context, with remote others, and with various reference groups. Success in a career is largely dependent on how effective we are in interpersonal relations. True, motivation and intelligence are critical, but equally essential are our interpersonal skills. How well can you role-take? Can you effectively present yourself and manage emotions? Can you make a role so that others feel comfortable with you? Can you frame? Can you use rituals effectively? Can you recognize the reference groups of others? Can you reconcile the expectations of immediate others with reference groups? If you can answer yes to these questions, you will go far. Some people do this naturally and implicitly, without great agonizing about their relations with others. Others are less adept and can profit from further sociological analysis on how interaction operates. You can view such further study as career training; and I suspect that it is as important as the "pre" (medicine, law, business, etc.) courses that many students are taking these days. Courses in social psychology, interpersonal relations, roles and interaction, micro social processes, and the like can greatly facilitate your career—whatever its specific nature.

The reason for this is simple: Most jobs involve delivering services and working with people in organizations. Few of you will be tilling the soil, operating the blast furnace, or putting windshields on Fords. Most of you aspire to own a business or to be a manager in some kind of corporation or a successful employee in a governmental bureaucracy—whether the public schools, police, welfare system, or foreign service. All these kinds of jobs involve dealing with people—clients, peers, bosses, subordinates. Understanding the dynamics of interaction can give you an enormous advantage in such "people work."

Furthermore, there are professional careers for people trained in interpersonal relations. While psychologists have traditionally held sway in the certification of counselors of various types, sociologists are now also involved in the counseling revolution, and in increasing numbers. In particular, sociological degrees are useful for those who provide counseling for interpersonal problems; they are useful in marital counseling; probation and corrections, executive workshops on employee relations, mediation services for adversarial conditions in industry, and a host of other problem areas where *relations* among people, groups, and organizations are at issue. Sociology is far better training than psychology for these kinds of professional careers. Such training begins with an understanding of human interaction.

Finally, knowledge of interpersonal dynamics can, to put it simply, make you a better person. Such knowledge can enhance your understanding of yourself, your appreciation of others, and your abilities to cope with friends, lovers, and strangers. So much human happiness depends on the quality of our relations with others that it is well worth our while to know something about how interpersonal processes work.

Looking at the implications of the material in Chapter 6, one thing is evident: socialization is big business, as well as a substantial part of big government. Probably the most visible socialization careers are to be found in the school system. Teachers socialize their students not just through the content of the curriculum but also in more subtle ways. What schools and their professionals do is "teach bureaucracy" to children. Playing roles in bureaucratic organizations requires a host of interpersonal skills, a set of motivational dispositions, and a willingness to control emotions and to define oneself in terms of organizational criteria. Learning how to play bureaucracy is the hidden curriculum of the schools; and as you read these words, you are still learning (in this case, how to work without direct teacher supervision, how to manage your time, how to conform to performance standards, etc.). All of us who are involved in education, then, are also in the socialization business. And it is a big, big business and always will be. Even with any future declines in birth rates, there will still be a substantial invasion of newborns across the borders of society.

True, teaching is no longer a glamorous occupation. Times are tough in this field because school budgets are low and because so much of a teacher's time is devoted to maintaining order and control in large and diverse classes. But there are jobs, and potentially, these can be gratifying jobs. Not everyone can be or wants to be a high-pressure, high-income dynamo. Moreover, the number of high-income niches is small, and most jobs are deadly dull and bureaucratic. Many of you have high hopes, and most of you will be disappointed—not for lack of ability, but for lack of luck or available opportunities. Teaching can be a very gratifying job, if one views it in the proper perspective. You are in essence engaged in one of the functionally most important tasks in the society: helping to mold new generations. Granted, schools can be unpleasant places, but so can most bureaucracies. At least schools are not dull, in contrast to most bureaucracies.

When you seek occupations with higher pay and prestige —lawyering, doctoring, entrepreneuring, accounting, and the like—you *may* make more money, but competition is severe, and these are now very glutted fields. Moreover, I doubt that you will ever get in these fields the same gratifying sense that you are helping society and helping people. If you view educational careers in this perspective, I hope they appear more attractive.

While education is the General Motors of the socialization business (or maybe the Toyota these days), professionals specifically trained in socialization have many other career options. A few of the more obvious possibilities include social work, child guidance, clinical counseling, probation, and juvenile corrections. There are also new, emerging careers for those trained in adult resocialization. The field of gerontology (the study of aging), which is rapidly expanding in a time when our population is growing older, involves among other things helping people to adjust to being old, being alone, and being ill, and to survive in other new situations. The field of "sensitivity training" for workers of all sorts—executives, bureaucrats, production-line employees—is also expanding, as it is becoming evident that mutual understanding among workers and satisfaction on the job are related to productivity in both industry and government. Thus, the personnel offices of both industry and government have new kinds of professionals. Moreover, companies and government often bring in consultants from the outside to help them deal with resocialization of workers and with structural changes in the organization.

In almost any occupation you can think about in our rapidly changing society, there is a need to change with the times. As people get older, this is more difficult; and as a consequence, new professionals are employed to facilitate readjustments (that is, resocialization) to new and altered conditions. Even if you are not one of these professionals, you yourself will have to change and readjust. Indeed, you may have to resocialize yourself if no one is there to help. Knowing something about the dynamics of socialization can assist you in making these readjustments and hence in becoming a more satisfied and successful worker.

Finally, as with all sociological inquiry, you can be a better person with knowledge about socialization. By knowing how socialization operates and by examining your own personal experiences in light of this knowledge, you can gain perspective on the past and better deal with the future. For all these reasons, then, it is worth your while to look into more sociology courses on this most fundamental form of human interaction—socialization.

As I stressed in Chapter 7, the basic structures organizing modern life are groups and organizations. And these are at the center of contemporary problems, and they will be part of the solutions to these problems. The problems of American corporations in the world system, the high cost of medicine, and the red tape of governmental bureaucracies all highlight long-standing problems in bureaucratic organizations. This set of facts signals that there are career opportunities for those who know about organizations. It is, for example, no coincidence that sociologists with expertise in complex organizations are on the faculties of schools of business and public administration; for, making a profit or delivering a public service effectively is a matter of organization. People who have knowledge of how organizations operate will, I think, be in increasing demand. To take advantage of these opportunities, one will have to become credentialed with higher degrees, but the extra years in the organizational behavior tract of a business school or in a similar tract in a sociology department will prove worth the effort.

Aside from these opportunities, it is useful to understand organizations because your job and career advancement will depend upon it. In all likelihood you will work in a complex organization; and your effectiveness in your job will depend upon seeing the bigger picture of where you stand in relation to organizational processes in general.

As you work in an organization, membership in group structures is inevitable. Thus, much of your immediate routine will involve group activities, and hence, it is important to know about group processes as well. Not only can this knowledge help in career success, it is useful in all social relations as well. For most activity within and outside work is performed inside a group structure. Knowledge of the basic dynamics of groups will enable—indeed, empower— you to become a more effective participant and, equally significant, to enjoy your relations in groups even more.

More practically, there are real job opportunities for those who understand group processes. Within corporate America, for example, there has been a dramatic increase in interest about "group dynamics." Since most work activity within corporate organizations occurs in groups, profits made by these organizations will be directly affected by the productivity of groups. And there is increased concern not only with productivity issues but also with worker contentment. In addition, groups and organizations are becoming more heterogeneous—that is, there are more women and minorities in them. This change has been slow, but at least there is now an awareness that the consequences of integration by sex, race, and ethnicity need to be better understood. Even executives are being trained—usually in nice places near the ocean—on group dynamics and sensitivity. As corporate decisions must consider "the human element," executives must trade in their Adam Smith for Joyce Brothers and, increasingly, for some sociological references. In all of this activity, sociology has much to offer. We are *the* discipline that studies groups and group processes, and as a result, there are careers for those who understand these processes. Even if you do not want to be an expert but only a successful participant, knowledge of group processes can give you a decided advantage in work activities.

As I indicated in Chapter 8, it is not difficult to locate yourself and others in a class position, an ethnic subpopulation, and hopefully, in a sexual category. Once you have done this, you have a rough idea of how much, and what kinds, of valued resources you can command and will be able to garner in the years ahead. This is useful knowledge personally, if only to make you more sure about where you stand within the stratification system. If you are poor, if you are a woman, and or if you are part of a dark-skinned minority, it will not be easy, and perhaps you do not need sociology to tell you this. But the study of stratification in its class, ethnic, and gender dimensions can provide great insight into the broader sociocultural constraints on, and obstacles to, your well-being in American society. These topics are worthy of additional courses of study.

Speaking practically, inequality creates career opportunities. Many of the ultimate outcomes of inequality—crime, drugs, slums, welfare, public health problems, unplanned babies, and the like—generate social service careers. Even when the political climate is not favorable to "helping people," there are opportunities because the consequences of inequality cannot be completely swept under the rug. And, despite all the problems in these careers—comparatively low pay, bureaucratic red tape, political apathy, low prestige in the public's eye— they do something very important: They help people. Such careers have an intrinsic capacity to reward, and you should not be too quick to reject them for the more glamorous professions, most of which are glutted and require additional credentials.

Inequality is inevitable in large, complex societies, and it creates many problems for people and society as a whole. Most sociologists want, in some way, to help solve these problems. And thus, most sociology courses can provide you with training that can help you become a better-prepared professional to deal with them in whatever line of work you choose. Even if you opt for the glamorous fast track, you will as a citizen need to be informed about the problems generated by inequality; your taxes, your sense of safety, your domestic tranquility, and hopefully, your sense of justice require that you be better informed about the dynamics of inequality and stratification. Inequality and stratification will not go away; and the problems that ensue will not be solved by simplistic political and ideological slogans. They will be mitigated by sociologically informed citizens, practitioners, and politicians.

As I emphasized in Chapter 9, most of the positions that you occupy and the roles that you play all occur within an institutional context. And these contexts are interrelated, one institution interfaces with another, forming a web of interconnections. Your life is thus circumscribed by this web, and at times you may feel like a fly who is caught in this web. At other times institutions seem remote, but your daily life is affected by the norms, cultural beliefs, and networks of positions that make up major social institutions. Think about your daily routines—involving class, studying, shopping, health centers, library, work, workshop, and family. All of these occur within institutions—educational, economic, familial, religious, medicine, and science. Thus, if only to understand for yourself the forces impinging on your lives, specific courses on each institution are useful. In all sociology departments, courses on each basic institution are offered; they are usually called the "sociology of" (family, education, law, religion, science) or some other title like "political sociology," "economic sociology," or "medical sociology." They are worth taking because they will, if nothing else, tell you about the constraints on your life and, in so doing, make it easier for you to cope.

There is also a practical reason to think about institutions. Since they exist to deal with basic human problems, there is money to be made for those who understand them. The tensions and problems in families require trained personnel to understand them and help those in trouble; sociology is one of the career paths to acquiring this training. The problems of the American education system are well known, and there is a need for practitioners who can do research on these problems or who can help administer the solutions; again, sociological training in education and in complex organizations is essential. The analysis of politics is, to put it crudely, "big business"; and it is often done by those who are not very well trained to look at the broader dynamics of power; sociological training can, I think, be a good place to begin a career in the halls of power or as an analyst/journalist/consultant to political processes. Sociologists have tended to cede the analysis of the economy over to economists, with what I see as disastrous results; and so, increasingly, noneconomists who see the broader picture beyond immediate market processes are being consulted. This trend has created new opportunities for sociologists who can analyze the economy in its institutional and cultural context. Medical sociology is the biggest section in the American Sociological Association; and many of its members are practitioners, either doing medical research (because sociological methods are so essential to this research) or on the front lines of delivering and organizing medical programs for clients. As American medicine undergoes profound reorganization in the next decade, the opportunities for sociologically trained professionals will increase dramatically. The remaining institutions—science and religion—remain primarily academic; and if you wish to study these, your best career choice is to stay in school and become a member of academia.

But careers aside, let me emphasize again that for your personal understanding of the Big Forces controlling your life, the study of institutions is essential. If only to be a more informed citizen, who must vote for politicians who set policies on basic institutions, you should know if they are being unrealistic or if they are proposing sensible policies. Sociology can help in making such assessments.

Turning to the topics of Chapter 10—demography, ecology, and community—many technical careers are available in these areas. In demography, you will need to be good at statistics, but there are many kinds of jobs for people who can use statistics in counting people as well as in analyzing their characteristics and movements. Government is certainly one of the sources for jobs in demographic work—from the Bureau of the Census through the other executive departments of the federal government down to state and local governmental agencies. But the private sectors is also interested in this expertise—from market research firms or divisions in companies to long-term forecasting of demographic trends by banks, insurance companies, and brokerages.

Careers in urban and ecological issues are less clear, but plentiful. Urban planning is a feature of all levels of government and requires trained personnel. Assessment of environmental impacts is another basic feature of economic activity these days, and environmental engineering is becoming a track in engineering schools as well as a market for private companies. Thus, those trained in urban and environmental issues will be able to find jobs—jobs which can make a difference in the society.

Careers aside, the immediate relevance of demography, urban communities, and ecological processes to your lives should be obvious. The size and composition of your community, your living space now and in the future, and the quality of your environment are all issues which sociological training can help you understand, for these issues are related to the cultural and structural forces of the American society and of other societies in the world. Since they are such basic features of your life now, and far into the future, it is worth taking more sociology courses to put into perspective these important questions.

As the topics of Chapter 11 implied, you and I live in a violent society where many people hold intense grievances. You know this because you avoid certain areas of the society and certain people. For, as a society with considerable inequality, and a large poverty sector, it is inevitable that there will be both high rates of deviance and dissent. People will commit crimes to get what you seek—material success—and they will carry great resentments over their domination which can, at any moment, erupt into individual acts of violence or, if preconditions and intensification processes exist, into crowd behavior and dissent. Thus, simply as a member of American society, it is important to understand the forces producing deviance and dissent. In any sociology department, there are usually several courses on criminology, perhaps one or two on deviance, and at least one on collective behavior and social movements; these can be very useful as survival training in American society.

Many of the job opportunities for sociologically trained people can be found in the problems of social control in a society. The vast agencies and bureaus at all levels of government dealing with crime and other forms of deviance represent a large number of job opportunities for sociologically trained workers. These jobs require those who understand the sociocultural context of deviance; and sociology is where training in these contexts is most complete. Police work, probation, prisons, juvenile halls, and special schools for the delinquent are all jobs in social control; mental health hospitals and clinics, social work agencies, alcoholism and its treatment, and drug addiction centers are also jobs in social control, both inside and outside of government. These are important jobs, and since the problems of social control in American society will not go away, there will be an expanding number of career opportunities in these and related areas.

Finally, as Chapter 12 made clear, the pace of social change is accelerating. You will perhaps experience even greater changes in your lives now and into the next century than I did growing up in the post-World War II era. And so, if nothing else, you will have to adjust constantly to change. Many of you will have to work in complex, flexible organizations where your status set will be constantly changing, and your roles and role sets will be periodically reshuffled. You will have to be more attuned to others emotionally as you coordinate activities with them, for much of the work that you do will require flexible coordination and mutual adjustments rather than conformity to established protocols. You will experience less hierarchy, authority, and emphasis on normative conformity in less bureaucratic organizations, and while these were constraining, the security and routine that they provided in older bureaucratic organizations will be gone. You will have to cope with uncertainty, anxiety, and stress; you will have to hustle and produce—or else. This can seem exciting, but it is a bit scary in a society with a loose safety net. All of this will be true for only some of you, however; for many others, there will still be many routine bureaucratic jobs, but these will not be cutting-edge jobs.

As the nature of work and organizations changes, your nonwork life will require adjustments. You may not be able to settle and lay down roots in a community; your home and work may be less separated with the ability to plug electronically into work from home, and vice versa. These changes will alter family life, leisure, politics, voting, shopping, and virtually all activities.

These changes will, for many, be easy. As I watch students today, they have already become attached to their computers; and they have little trouble adjusting to the rapid flow of information and to the necessity of being near their machines. Yet, change always produces personal and societal problems, and it is here that new kinds of careers are to be made. For, as the personal problems of individuals in a change-oriented world escalate, as organizations seek to adjust to ever new technologies, and as people try to adapt to these organizations and technologies, hosts of new and unimagined problems will emerge. These problems will generate jobs and careers for those trained in sociology—personal counseling, management consultants, job retraining, impact assessment, the interface of people and information machines, and many other activities that will emerge in the information age. Change is thus more than something to which you must adjust and accept; it is also an opportunity for building a career for which sociological training will be essential.

In sum, then, there are real job opportunities for those with sociological training. Equally important there are opportunities to learn about yourself and the world around you in sociology courses. Thus, whether for a career or personal enlightenment, I invite you to pursue sociology further.

Glossary

age composition   The percentage/proportion of a population in various age brackets.

age-specific death rate   The number of deaths per 1000 people in a particular age range or bracket, such as 65- to 75-year-olds, or any bracket chosen for analysis.

age-specific fertility rate   The number of live births per 1000 people in a particular age range or bracket, such as 15- to 25-year-olds, 26- to 40-year-olds, or any range chosen for analysis.

analysis   A stage in the scientific method in which the data collected are systematically assessed in order to determine what has been discovered.

applied sociology   The effort to use sociological knowledge in dealing with problems and events.

autonomy versus doubt   The second stage in Erik Erikson's development scheme, running to the third year of a child's life, during which a child's degree of success in learning gives it either a sense of autonomy or doubt and shame.

avunculocal rule   A residence rule specifying that a married couple and their children are to live with the male's mother's brother.

backstage   Erving Goffman's term denoting areas of privacy where the self-conscious manipulation of gestures can be relaxed.

beliefs   Systems of symbols organized into cognitions about what should exist or occur, as well as what does exist and occur, in specific types of social situations.

bilateral descent   A rule of descent specifying that the male's and female's side of the family and kin network will be given equal importance.

bourgeoisie, the   In Karl Marx's analysis, those who own and control the means of production in capitalist societies.

capital   The implements of economic production, and the money used to purchase these implements.

caste system   A stratification system with clearly marked class divisions, in which people are born into a particular class and have little chance for mobility to a different class.

categorical structures   Structures created when cohorts and types of individuals are defined and treated differently on the basis of their perceived attributes and characteristics.

charismatic leader   Max Weber's term for those who, by virtue of their personal qualities, can mobilize subordinates in a system of inequality to engage in conflict with
superordinates.

chiefdom   A form of polity in which one man comes to dominate decisions among
populations organized on the basis of kinship rules.

clan   A kinship structure created when lineages are linked together by a descent rule.

classes   For Max Weber, those who share a common set of life chances and opportunities
in markets; for Karl Marx, the divisions in a society reflecting ownership of the means
of production; for more general analysis, the differences among subpopulations by
virtue of their respective shares of valued resources.

clinical sociology   A term used to describe the activities of sociologists who use sociological knowledge to assess a situation for a client and to develop solutions for this
client.

coercion   The use of physical force in social relations.

coercive organizations   Those bureaucratic structures in which members are forced to
remain isolated from the society.

collective behavior   A field of study focusing on the sudden transformations of culture
and social structures through such processes as dissent, riots, revolutions, fads, and
social movements.

collective conscience   Émile Durkheim's term for systems of cultural symbols that
people in a society share and use to regulate their affairs.

community   A social structure that organizes the residence and activities of people in
physical space.

concentric zone model   A model of urban growth that sees urbanization as a sequence
of rings, moving out from the central business district.

concrete operational stage   The third stage of cognitive development in Jean Piaget's
scheme, lasting from seven to eleven years of age, during which children learn to use
logic and reasoning, although abilities to employ abstract reasoning remain limited.

conflict of interest   Karl Marx's term for the basic tension and incompatibility of goals
between those who control resources and those who do not.

conflict sociology/conflict theory   The view that the main dynamic of human social
relations and patterns of social organization is tension and conflict over the unequal
distribution of resources.

conflict theories   Explanations that seek to understand phenomena in terms of the
tensions inherent in the unequal distribution of resources.

contagion theory   An early theory of collective behavior emphasizing the effects of
interaction in intensifying people's emotions and, hence, the potential for collective
behavior.

control group   Those subjects in an experimental design who are not exposed to a
stimulus of interest and who are used as a basis of comparison with those exposed
to the stimulus.

control theory   A utilitarian theory of deviance stressing that calculations of cost and
investments determine whether or not people will deviate.

convergence theory   An approach emphasizing that people self-select themselves into
crowd situations rather than get swept away by a "mob mood."

credentialism The reliance, indeed overreliance, on educational credentials for placement in the economy—a practice that stimulates credential inflation.

crowd Gatherings of people acting together with reference to some stimulus, situation, or goal.

crude birth rate Number of live births per 1000 people in a given year.

crude death rate Number of deaths per 1000 people in a given year.

cultural conflict Differences in cultural values and beliefs that place people at odds with one another, and hence, in potential conflict.

cultural contradiction Inconsistencies in the various systems of symbols making up the culture of a society.

cultural directives The profile of values, beliefs, norms, and other symbol systems that individuals use in guiding their behaviors and interactions.

culture Those systems of symbols that humans create and use to guide behavior, interaction, and patterns of social organization.

culture, material The term used by some analysts to denote the artifacts and objects created by humans.

data Information about the empirical world.

demographic transition The pattern of population growth in the transition to modernity, during which death rates decline first in the face of continued high birth rates followed, eventually, by a decline in birth rates.

demography The science of population processes, especially the characteristics, distribution, movement, and growth/decline of populations.

descent rules Norms specifying whether the male's or female's side of the family and kin network are more important in terms of property and authority.

deviance Behavior that violates accepted norms.

dialectic/dialectical The line of argument asserting that inherent in one social form are the inherent processes for its transformation.

differential association theory A theory arguing that deviance is created when there is an excess of criminal to noncriminal definitions of appropriate behavior in a person's biography.

diffuse status characteristics Those features reflecting an array, or a set, of status positions occupied by an individual which an individual carries into a group and which serve as a basis for members' responses.

diffusion The spread of cultural symbol systems from one population to another.

discrimination The differential treatment of others, especially those of an ethnic group or a gender category, so that they receive less valued resources.

economy, institution of The organization of technology, capital, and labor into structures for the purpose of gathering natural resources, producing goods and services, and distributing these goods and services to members of a society.

ecosystem The system of relations among life forms, as well as between life forms and the physical environment.

ecosystem chain/food chain The linking of life forms as food for one another.

ecosystem cycle A form of interdependence in which processes fold back on themselves, creating cycles of events and interdependencies.

ecosystem flow   The movement of energy, organic matter, and inorganic matter through an ecosystem.

education, institution of   Formal bureaucratic structures designed to (1) socialize and facilitate the placement of people into positions in society, (2) store knowledge, and (3) generate new systems of culture.

ego   Sigmund Freud's term to denote the process of reconciling id impulses with superego constraints, often forcing the use of repression and defense mechanisms.

emergent norm theory   A symbolic interactionist theory stressing that collective behavior in a crowd is like all interaction and involves material role taking and the development of norms about how to behave.

emigration   Movement of people *out of* a society.

emotions   The moods or states of individuals revolving around, and involving elaborations of, such primary states as anger, fear, sadness, happiness, and surprise.

endogamy   A rule specifying that individuals must marry within another kin group or community.

enlightenment, the   A broad intellectual movement in the eighteenth century in which nonreligious thinking about the universe was encouraged.

entrepreneurship   The organizational forms and capacities that coordinate technology, capital, and labor.

ethnic composition   The proportions of various ethnic subpopulations in a society and the birth, death, and growth rate associated with each.

ethnicity   Those behavioral, cultural, and organizational characteristics that distinguish subpopulations in a society.

ethnocentricism   The tendency to view one's own culture or subculture as superior to the culture of other people or societies.

ethnomethods   A concept introduced by Harold Garfinkel to denote the implicit interpersonal signals emitted to create the presumption that people in interaction share a common view of reality.

evaluative beliefs   Cognitions that people hold about *what should* occur in basic social contexts.

exogamy   A rule specifying that individuals must marry outside a kin group or community.

experimental group   Those subjects in an experimental research design who are exposed to a stimulus of interest to the investigator.

experiments/experimental designs   A research design in which extraneous influences are controlled in an effort to isolate the effect of some specific stimulus.

extended family unit   A kinship unit created when several nuclear units are joined in one household.

formal operational stage   The fourth and last stage of a child's cognitive development in Jean Piaget's scheme, lasting from twelve years of age to adolescence, during which the ability to use abstract representations of the world develops.

frames/framing   The term employed by Erving Goffman to denote the process of using gestures to include (or exclude) certain matters as in (or outside) the interaction.

front   Erving Goffman's term to denote the use of gestures to present oneself in a particular way and in a particular mode of action.

frontstage   Erving Goffman's term denoting situations where individuals consciously manipulate gestures in ways designed to elicit desired responses from others, especially with respect to one's sense of self.

functionalism   An approach to the analysis of phenomena in terms of their consequences for the needs or requisite of the larger social whole in which they are located. This approach was first used in sociology by Herbert Spencer.

functional theory   Explanations that seek to understand phenomena in terms of their consequences for a larger social whole.

game stage   George Herbert Mead's second stage in the socialization of children, during which they develop the capacity to role-take with several others simultaneously, to read their perspective, to evaluate oneself from this perspective, and to cooperate in groups of others.

gender/gender differentiation   The process of culturally defining the appropriate positions, roles, and demeanor for men and women.

gender processes   Those cultural and social forces that affect the positions occupied and roles played by men and women in a society.

gender stratification   The situation where the positions typically occupied by men and women habitually receive different levels of valued resources.

general fertility rate   The total number of live births in a given year for each 1000 women in their child-bearing years (usually defined as 15 to 44 years of age).

generalized other   George Herbert Mead's term denoting the community of attitudes or perspective of social groupings. The capacity to role-take with varieties of generalized others marks the third and final stage of childhood development because it is now possible to assume broader cultural perspectives and use these for self-evaluation and regulation of behavior.

generativity versus self-absorption   The seventh stage in Erik Erikson's developmental scheme, lasting through mature adulthood, during which success in family, work, and community lead to a feeling of being able to give to others, or if not, to self-absorption and stagnation in life.

government, structure of   The organization of leaders, power, and decision making in a society.

groups   Small social structures composed of only a few different status positions, small numbers of incumbents, relatively dense ties among positions, and clear cultural expectations about role behaviors.

groupthink   The process in group decision making in which members reinforce one another to the point that the decision does not bear a close relationship to the realities of the situation.

hierarchy of the sciences   Auguste Comte's view that the sciences could be arranged in a hierarchy in terms of when they emerged and the complexity of their subject matter. Sociology, not surprisingly, was at the top of the hierarchy, just above biology.

histories/historical research   A type of research design in which information about the past is gathered systematically.

hypothesis   A statement of what one expects to be found in a research project. Hypotheses are often derived from theories and represent the predictions that a general theory makes for a specific empirical case(s).

id   Sigmund Freud's term for impulses and needs, many of which cannot be expressed in society because they violate taboos and conventions.

identity formation versus confusion   The fifth stage in Erik Erikson's developmental scheme, lasting for the duration of adolescence, during which the ability to establish relations and enjoy success leads to a sense of identity or confusion about who and what one is.

immigration   Migration of people *into* a society.

impression management   Erving Goffman's term to denote the deliberate manipulation of gestures and physical props in order to project a particular image of oneself to others.

incest rules   Norms prohibiting sex and marriage among parents and offspring, and at times other closely related kin.

income distribution   The percentage of total income held by different percentages of the population, usually calculated in terms of income fifths.

industrialization   The process of harnessing inanimate sources of power and machines attended by labor to the gathering of resources, the production of goods and commodities, and the distribution of goods and commodities.

industrial revolution   The harnessing of inanimate sources of power to machines and human labor, and the consequent reorganization of the economy, society, and culture in the 1800s and up to the present.

industriousness versus inferiority   The fourth stage in Erik Erikson's developmental scheme, running from six to thirteen years, during which the degree of success in groups and projects provides a sense of industriousness or failure.

infant mortality rate   The number of 1-year-olds and below per 1000 live births who die in a given year.

informal system   The system of ties that people develop within the formal structure of an organization; such ties often supplant, but always supplement, formal lines of authority.

initiative versus guilt   The third stage in Erik Erikson's developmental scheme, lasting from four to six years of age, during which success in exploring the environment and in forming positive relations provides a sense of initiative or failure, shame, and guilt.

innovation, technological   The development of new knowledge about how to manipulate the environment.

institutionalized discrimination   Patterns of systematic discrimination against an ethnic subpopulation, a gender category, or some other cohort of people that are legitimated by cultural symbols, carried out informally and formally, and built into the structures of a society.

institutional norms   Systems of symbols organized into very general expectations about behavior in basic types and classes of situations in a society.

institution/social institution   Societywide structures that organize groups, organizations, and the community with respect to basic human and organizational needs.

integrity versus despair   The final stage in Erik Erikson's developmental scheme, corresponding to old age, during which individuals see meaning and continuity in their lives, or experience despair.

interaction   The process of individuals mutually emitting gestures, interpreting these gestures, and adjusting their respective courses of action.

interactionism An approach to the analysis of social phenomena, inspired by early American philosophers and sociologists, that stresses the importance of understanding the dynamics of face-to-face contact and interaction among individuals.

interactionist theories Explanations that seek to understand phenomena in terms of the mutual, face-to-face gesturing activities of individuals who attempt to confirm self and to construct joint lines of conduct.

internal migration Movement of people *within* a society.

intersocietal systems Processes that create relations among societies, including trade, war, migrations, and political or economic coalitions.

intimacy versus isolation The sixth stage in Erik Erikson's developmental scheme, lasting through young adulthood, during which stable and positive relations produce a capacity for intimacy.

kinship, institution of The organization of marriage and blood ties among members of a society into structures that have consequences for regularizing sex and mating, providing for biological and social support, socializing the young, and placing the young into adult positions.

labeling theory A theory arguing that the deviant labels given to people are a major cause of their deviance.

labor The persons performing economic activities.

language Systems of symbols used in communication.

law of the three stages Auguste Comte's view that ideas, and society as a whole, pass through three stages: (1) the theological, where religious ideas dominate; (2) the metaphysical, where systematic thought is stressed, and (3) the positivistic, where science comes to dominate.

leadership, governmental The ability of some in a society to make decisions for mobilizing resources and coordinating activities.

legitimacy The acceptance by those subject to power of the right of those using power to do so.

lineage A kinship structure created when several extended family units are linked together by descent and residence rules.

marriage rules Norms specifying who can marry whom in a society, and when.

matrilineal descent A rule of descent specifying that the woman's side of the family and kin network (especially her male kindred) are to be the most important in terms of property and authority.

matrilocal rule A kinship norm specifying that a married couple and their children are to live with the female's family and kin.

means of production Karl Marx's term for the nature and organization of the economy in a society.

medicine, institution of Those structures in a society designed to develop and use secular knowledge to diagnose, prevent, and treat illness and disease.

metropolitan region An area where the suburbs developing around older large cities become contiguous.

migration The movement of people into, out of, and about a society.

mind George Herbert Mead's term to designate the process by which individuals covertly rehearse alternative lines of conduct, anticipate or imagine the consequences of each of these potential lines of behavior, and select that line of behavior most likely to facilitate cooperation.

moiety   A kinship unit created when clans are linked together.

motives/motivation   An individual's level of energy, and nature of energy, devoted to occupying positions and playing roles in society.

multiple nuclei model   A view of the city emphasizing that there are several centers in addition to the central business district.

neolocal rule   A residence rule indicating that a married couple and their children have autonomy in deciding for themselves where to live.

networks (of status positions)   The ties and connections that link status positions together, thereby forming a social structure.

niche density   In organizational ecology, the total number of organizations of a given type seeking the same or similar resources.

norms   Systems of symbols informing individuals about how they are expected to behave and interact in a situation.

nuclear family unit   The family unit created by the married couple and their offspring.

observations   A type of research design in which the activities of individuals in their natural setting are recorded.

open-class system   A stratification system with less clearly demarcated classes and with opportunities for mobility from class to class.

organizations   Goal-directed social structures revealing hierarchies of positions, linked together by authority and clear norms, with increasing numbers of incumbents at the lower levels of the hierarchy.

pantheon   A set of religious beliefs specifying the inhabitants, as well as their relations and life histories, of the supernatural realm.

participant observation   A type of observational research design in which the researcher becomes actively involved with those being studied.

parties   For Max Weber, the organization of power as a distinct basis for inequality and stratification of individuals who bear varying affiliations and access to organizations holding or seeking power.

patrilineal descent   A rule of descent specifying that the male's side of the family and kin network are to be the most important in terms of property and authority.

patrilocal rule   A kinship norm specifying that a married couple and their children are to live with the male's family and kin.

philosophes, the   A lineage of eighteenth-century social thinkers in France who championed the idea of individual freedom from arbitrary political authority. It was from this lineage that Auguste Comte, the founder of sociology, was to draw many of his ideas.

physical props   The use of objects, including the body and its spacing relative to other bodies in the environment, in order to signal a line of conduct.

play stage   George Herbert Mead's first critical stage in the socialization of children, during which they acquire the ability to use, and interpret, gestures with at least one other person.

polity   The generic term for patterns of governance in a society.

postindustrial Commentaries revolving around the cultural and structural transformations associated with further advances in technologies for production, communication, and transportation.

postmodern A loose set of social commentaries on the decentering of societies through hyperdifferentiation, loss of core values and beliefs, overextension of markets, loss of neighborhood and community, media domination of politics, culture, and social ties.

power The capacity to enforce decisions and have one's way.

practice A term often used to describe sociological work that is used for practical purposes and for changing a situation.

prejudices Beliefs about the undesirable qualities of others, especially those in an ethnic group.

preoperational stage The second stage of a child's cognitive development in Jean Piaget's scheme, lasting from two to seven years of age, during which children learn to use symbols to denote objects, although the capacity for use of abstract symbols remains limited.

primary groups Small face-to-face groups in which people feel more involved, more intimate, and more cohesive.

profane Denoting processes in the empirical world, in comparison with the sacred, which is of the supernatural world.

proletariat, the Karl Marx's term for those who do not own the means of production in capitalist society and who must, therefore, work for those who do.

race Perceived biological distinctiveness for categories of individuals.

rate of population growth The increase (decrease) in the size of a population in a given year calculated by dividing the size of a population at the beginning of a year into the net increase (or decrease) of people during the year.

reference group Perspectives of groups, both those in which one is participating and those which are remote, that are used as a frame of reference for self-evaluation and for guiding conduct.

religious beliefs Conceptions about the nature of the sacred and supernatural as well as the entities and forces in the supernatural realm.

religious rituals Stereotyped sequences of behavior designed to make appeals to the forces of the supernatural realm.

religious structure The unit organizing rituals and sustaining religious beliefs and values.

religious values Conceptions of what is right and wrong, as well as what should exist and occur, that are viewed as emanating from supernatural forces.

renewable resources Those resources which can be renewed by virtue of ecosystem chains, flows, and cycles. Air, water, and soil are the three most basic renewable resources.

repressed/repression Sigmund Freud's term denoting the process by which unacceptable impulses (id) are pushed below consciousness by ego processes seeking to conform to superego demands.

research design The explicit procedures that are used in collecting empirical data.

research problem   The first step in the scientific method devoted to establishing what kind of information is to be gathered in a research project.

residence rules   Norms specifying where married couples are to live and reside.

resource mobilization theory   An approach to the study of social movements emphasizing that crowd mobilization and persistence of a social movement are related to the resource base of those involved.

revolution   A rapid and violent mobilization of people who seek to overthrow a political regime.

rituals/interpersonal rituals   The process of using highly stereotyped sequences of behavior to mark the opening, closing, and course of interaction.

role   The behavior of individuals in status positions, as they take account of one another and size up norms and other cultural symbols relevant to a situation.

role conflict   A situation where the roles associated with different status positions are incompatible, placing the individual trying to play the roles of these different positions in a situation of conflict.

role-make   A concept introduced by Ralph Turner to denote the process of emitting gestures in order to create a particular role for oneself in a situation.

role playing skills   An individual's ability and capacity for role taking and role making in interaction with others.

role set   The expected array of behaviors for a given status position.

role strain   A situation where there are either too many or contradictory expectations in the role set of a status position, thereby creating tension and strain for individuals trying to meet all expectations.

role-take   A concept introduced by George Herbert Mead to denote the capacity to read the gestures of others and, thereby, to sense what they are likely to do in terms of their dispositions to act and the cultural symbols relevant to a situation.

romantic love complex   A set of beliefs emphasizing mutual attraction and compatibility as the basis for selecting marriage partners.

sacred   Objects and forces having a special quality because they are connected to perceived supernatural powers.

science   The process in which theoretical explanations about the operation of phenomena in the universe are systematically tested with empirical data.

science, institution of   Those social structures designed to produce secular knowledge (in terms of theory and research) about how the universe operates.

scientific method   The procedures employed in the collection of data. These procedures are designed to test theories or, at the very least, to collect data in ways that are objective and replicable by other researchers.

secondary groups   Large groups where face-to-face interaction among all members is not possible, resulting in a corresponding decrease in intimacy, cohesiveness, and duration.

sector model   A model of urbanization viewing the city in terms of distinct sectors, like slices of a pie, that emanate from the central business district.

self-conception   An individual's view of himself or herself as a certain type of person with particular attributes and, hence, deserving of certain kinds of responses from others.

self/self-concept The capacity to see oneself as an object in a situation and to carry cognitions, feelings, and evaluations of oneself as a certain type of person who is deserving of particular responses.

sensorimotor stage The first stage of a child's cognitive development in Jean Piaget's scheme, lasting to about two years of age, during which children learn to retain images of objects in their environment.

sex ratio The proportion of men to women in a population.

sex/sexual differentiation The biological differences between males and females.

size of population The absolute number of people in a society.

socialization Those interactions instilling in individuals the basic components of personality that are necessary for their participation in society.

society A structure which encompasses all other structures (groups, organizations, institutions, categories, and stratification) and which organizes a population and provides political regulation for these structures in geographical space and in relation to other societies.

socioemotional leader An individual who seeks to smooth out tensions that arise as the members of the group seek to realize the group's goals.

sociology The systematic study of human social behavior, interaction, and organization.

state, the The bureaucratic organization of the center of coercive power, legitimate authority, and civil administration in a society.

status groups Max Weber's term for subsets of individuals who share similar lifestyles, who form ties because of shared culture, tastes, and outlooks, and who, by virtue of these, can command a certain honor and prestige.

status position The location of an individual within a network of positions. A basic unit of social structure.

status set The complex or array of positions that an individual occupies.

stocks of knowledge Implicit stores of information that individuals use to guide their behavior and interaction.

stratification systems Structures revolving around (1) the unequal distribution of valued resources to the members of a society and (2) the distinctive categories thereby created by virtue of the shares of resources held by different subpopulations in a society.

structural strain Robert Merton's "anomie theory" emphasizing that rates of deviance increase when there is a disjuncture between goals and the means to achieve these goals. Also, Neil Smelser's basic precondition, rooted in inequality, for collective behavior.

subculture A subpopulation of individuals in a society that possesses at least some symbols that are unique to this subpopulation and, at times, at odds with the broader culture of a society.

substructure Karl Marx's label for the material, economic base which influences other aspects of a society.

suburbanization The migration process of generating self-governing communities around a large, older city.

superego Sigmund Freud's term denoting the morality of society as it has been absorbed by an individual.

supernatural   A realm where gods and unworldly forces operate.

superorganic   Herbert Spencer's view of sociology's subject matter: the organization of living organisms.

superstructure   Karl Marx's term for those structures and cultural systems determined by the economic base of a society.

surveys   A type of research design in which a sample of respondents is asked an established set or schedule of questions.

task leader   An individual in a group who directs and coordinates other members' activities in order to accomplish the group's goals.

technology   Systems of symbols organized into knowledge about how to manipulate the environment.

tests   The careful gathering of empirical data in order to assess the plausibility of a theory, or hypothesis derived from a theory.

theory   Abstract statements that explain how and why phenomena in the universe operate. Theory is the vehicle in science for understanding.

trust versus mistrust   The first stage in Erik Erikson's developmental scheme, lasting to two years of age, during which a child's experiences with love and nurturance provide it with a sense of trust or mistrust of others.

typifications   A concept introduced by Alfred Schutz to denote the process of categorizing others as an instance of a general class or type which, in turn, enables individuals to respond in stereotypical ways and, thereby, to reduce the interpersonal work in interaction.

unobtrusive observation   A type of observational research design in which the investigator seeks to remain uninvolved with those being studied.

urban corridors   See metropolitan region.

urbanization   The increasing concentration of ever-larger populations in space.

utilitarian organizations   Those bureaucratic structures which people enter on the basis of calculations of costs and benefits.

utilitarian theories   Explanations that seek to understand phenomena in terms of the rational calculations by actors of their costs and benefits.

value-free   Max Weber's term emphasizing that sociology should seek to eliminate bias and moral considerations in an effort to produce objective analyses of social phenomena.

values   Systems of symbols organized into abstract moral ideas about good-bad, appropriate-inappropriate, and right-wrong. Values cut across diverse situations because they are general and abstract.

voluntary organizations   Those bureaucratic structures which people freely may enter and leave.

wealth distribution   The percentage of total wealth held by different percentages of the population, usually calculated in terms of wealth fifths.

world systems analysis   The analysis of the patterns of inequality in power and economic resources of nations and the resulting patterns of political and economic domination among nations.

References

Aitchison, Jean. 1978. *The Articulate Mammal*. New York: McGraw-Hill.

Alexander, Jeffrey C., ed. 1985. *Neofunctionalism*. Beverly Hills, CA: Sage.

Alexander, Jeffrey C., et al. 1986. *The Micro-Macro Link*. Berkeley, CA: University of California Press.

Alford, Robert R., and Roger Friedland. 1985. *Powers of Theory: Capitalism, the State and Democracy*. Cambridge: Cambridge University Press.

Allport, Gordon. 1954. *The Nature of Prejudice*. Cambridge, MA: Addison-Wesley.

———. 1979. *The Nature of Prejudice* (25th Anniversary edition). Reading, MA: Addison-Wesley.

Almgren, Gunnar. 1992. "Demographic Transition." In *Encyclopedia of Sociology*, edited by E. Borgatta and M. Borgatta. New York: Macmillan.

Appelbaum, R. P. 1978. "Marx's Theory of the Falling Rate of Profit." *American Sociological Review* 43 (February):67–80.

Apple, Michael W. 1982. *Education and Power*. Boston: Routledge and Kegan Paul.

Apple, Michael W., and Lois Weis. 1983. *Ideology and Practice in Schooling*. Philadelphia: Temple University Press.

Babbie, Earl. 1992. *The Practice of Sociological Research*, 3d edition. Belmont, CA: Wadsworth.

Bales, Robert F. 1950. *Interaction Process Analysis*. Cambridge, MA: Addison-Wesley.

Bandura, Albert. 1977. "Self-efficacy: Toward a Unifying Theory of Behavioral Change." *Psychological Review* 84:191–215.

Beeghley, Leonard. 1983. *Living Poorly in America*. New York: Praeger.

Bell, Daniel. 1973. *The Coming of Post-industrial Society*. New York: Basic Books.

Bellah, Robert. 1964. "Religious Evolution." *American Sociological Review* 29:358–374.

Bendix, Reinhard. 1968. *Max Weber: An Intellectual Portrait*. Garden City, NY: Doubleday.

Bennett, Neil G., A. K. Blanc, and D. E. Bloom. 1988. "Commitment and the Modern Union." *American Sociological Review* 53:127–138.

Berger, Joseph, T. L. Conner, and M. H. Fisek, eds. 1974. *Expectation States Theory: A Theoretical Research Program*. Cambridge, MA: Winthrop.

Berger, Joseph, M. H. Fisek, R. Z. Norman, and M. Zelditch, Jr. 1977. *Status Characteristics and Social Interaction: An Expectation States Approach*. New York: Elsevier.

Berger, Joseph, S. J. Rosenholtz, and M. Zelditch, Jr. 1980. "Status Organizing Processes." *Annual Review of Sociology* 6:479–508.

Berger, Joseph, David G. Wagner, and Morris Zelditch. 1989. "Theory Growth, Social Processes, and Meta Theory." In *Theory Building*, edited by J. H. Turner. Newbury Park: Sage.

Berger, Joseph, and Morris Zelditch, Jr. 1985. *Status, Rewards and Influence*. San Francisco: Jossey-Bass.

Biddle, Bruce J. 1992. "Role Theory." In *Encyclopedia of Sociology*, edited by E. F. Borgatta and M. L. Borgatta. New York: Macmillan.

Blake, Judith, and Kingsley Davis. 1964. "On Norms and Values." In *Handbook of Modern Sociology*, edited by R. L. Faris. Chicago: Rand McNally.

Blumer, Herbert. 1969. *Symbolic Interaction: Perspective and Method*. Englewood Cliffs, NJ: Prentice-Hall.

———. 1978. "Collective Groupings." In *Collective Behavior and Social Movements*, edited by L. E. Genedie. Itasca, IL: Peacock.

Bourdieu, Pierre. 1984. *Distinction: A Social Critique of The Judgement of Taste*. Cambridge, MA: Harvard University Press.

Bowles, Samuel, and H. Gintis. 1976. *Schooling in Capitalist America*. New York: Basic Books.

Brown, Roger W. 1972. "Feral and Isolated Man." In *Language*, edited by V. P. Clark et al. New York: St. Martin's Press.

Burt, Ronald S. 1980. "Models of Network Structure." *Annual Review of Sociology* 6:79–141.

Camic, Charles. 1979. "The Utilitarians Revisited." *American Journal of Sociology* 85(3):516–550.

Cantril, Hadley. 1941. *The Psychology of Social Movements*. New York: Wiley.

Carneiro, Robert. 1970. "A Theory of the Origin of the State." *Science* 169:733–738.

Carroll, John B., ed. 1956. *Language, Thought and Reality: Selected Writings of Benjamin Lee Whorf*. Cambridge, MA: MIT Press.

Chafetz, Janet Saltzman. 1990. *Gender Equality: An Integrated Theory of Stability and Change*. Newbury Park, CA: Sage.

Chambliss, William. 1978. "Toward a Political Economy of Crime." In *The Sociology of Law*, edited by C. Reasons and R. Rich. Toronto: Butterworth.

Cicourel, A. V. 1964. *Method and Measurement in Sociology*. New York: Free Press.

Coleman, James S. 1991. *Foundations of Social Theory*. Cambridge, MA: Harvard University Press.

Collins, Randall. 1975. *Conflict Sociology*. New York: Academic Press.

———. 1976. "Review of 'Schooling in Capitalist America'." *Harvard Educational Review* 46:246–251.

———. 1979. *The Credential Society*. New York: Academic Press.

———. 1981. "On the Micro-Foundations of Macro-Sociology." *American Journal of Sociology* 86 (March):984–1014.

———. 1984. "Statistics vs. Words." *Sociological Theory* 2:329–364.

———. 1986. "Interaction Ritual Chains, Power and Property." Pp. 177–192 in *The Micro-Macro Link*, edited by J. Alexander et al. Berkeley, CA: University of California Press.

Collins, Randall, and Scott Coltrane. 1991. *Family Sociology*. Chicago: Nelson-Hall.

Comte, Auguste. 1830–1842 [1896]. *Course of Positive Philosophy*. London: G. Bell.

———. 1851-1854. *Systeme De Politique: ou, Traite De Sociologies, Instituant La Religion De L'humanite*. Paris: L. Mathias.

Conrad, Peter, and J. Kern, eds. 1986. *The Sociology of Health and Illness: Critical Perspectives*, 2d edition. New York: St. Martin's Press.

Cooley, Charles Horton. 1902. *Human Nature and the Social Order*. New York: Scribner.

———. 1909. *Social Organization*. New York: Scribner.

Coser, Lewis A. 1956. *The Functions of Social Conflict*. London: Free Press.

Dahl, Robert A. 1961. *Who Governs?* New Haven: Yale University Press.

Dahrendorf, Ralf. 1958. "Out of Utopia: Toward a Reorientation of Sociological Analysis." *American Journal of Sociology* 74 (September):115–127.

———. 1959. *Class and Class Conflict in Industrial Society.* Stanford, CA: Stanford University Press.

Davies, James C. 1962. "Toward a Theory of Revolution." *American Sociological Review* 27:5–19.

———. 1969. "The J-Curve of Rising and Declining Satisfactions as a Cause of Some Great Revolutions and Contained Rebellion." In *Violence in America,* edited by D. Graham and T. Gurr. New York: Bantam.

Davis, Kingsley. 1940. "Extreme Social Isolation of a Child." *American Journal of Sociology* 45:554–564.

———. 1945. "The World Demographic Transition." *Annals of the American Academy of Political and Social Science* 237:1-11.

———. 1947. "A Final Note on a Case of Extreme Isolation." *American Journal of Sociology* 52:432–437.

Davis, Kingsley, and Wilbert Moore. 1945. "Some Principles of Stratification." *American Sociological Review* 4:431–442.

Dogan, Mattei, and John D. Kasarda. 1988. *The Metropolitan Era,* 2 volumes. Newbury Park, CA: Sage.

Domhoff, William G. 1967. *Who Rules America?* Englewood Cliffs, NJ: Prentice-Hall.

———. 1970. *The Higher Circles: The Governing Class in America.* New York: Random House.

———. 1978. *Who Really Rules?* Santa Monica, CA: Goodyear.

———. 1983. *Who Rules America Now?: A View for the '80s.* Englewood Cliffs, NJ: Prentice-Hall.

———. 1990. *The Power Elite and the State.* New York: Aldine de Gruyer.

Durkheim, Émile. 1891 [1975]. *Montesquieu and Rousseau.* Ann Arbor: University of Michigan Press.

———. 1893 [1947]. *The Division of Labor in Society.* New York: Free Press.

———. 1895 [1938]. *The Rules of the Sociological Method.* New York: Free Press.

———. 1897 [1951]. *Suicide.* New York: Free Press.

———. 1912 [1965]. *The Elementary Forms of Religious Life.* New York: Free Press.

Earle, Timothy, ed. 1984. *On the Evolution of Complex Societies.* Malibu, CA: Undena.

Ehrlich, Paul, and Anne H. Ehrlich. 1990. *The Population Explosion.* New York: Simon & Schuster.

Eisenstadt, S. N., and A. Shachar. 1987. *Society, Culture and Urbanization.* Newbury Park, CA: Sage.

Ekman, Paul. 1982. *Emotions in the Human Face.* Cambridge: Cambridge University Press.

Ellis, Albert. 1945. "The Sexual Psychology of Human Hermaphrodites." *Psychosomatic Medicine* 18:108–125.

Epstein, S. 1980. "The Self-concept: A Review and the Proposal for an Integrated Theory of Personality." Pp. 27-39 in *Personality: Basic Issues and Current Research.* Englewood Cliffs, NJ: Prentice-Hall.

Erikson, Erik H. 1950. *Childhood and Society.* New York: Norton.

Etzioni, Amitai. 1961. *A Comparative Analysis of Complex Organizations.* New York: Free Press.

———. 1964. *Modern Organizations.* Englewood Cliffs, NJ: Prentice-Hall.

Feagin, Joe R. 1991. *Racial and Ethnic Relations,* 3d edition. Englewood Cliffs, NJ: Prentice-Hall.

Federal Reserve System. 1992. "Preliminary Report of a Survey of Wealth." Washington: U.S. Government Printing Office.

Freud, Sigmund. 1900. *The Interpretation of Dreams*. London: Hogarth Press.

———. 1938. *The Basic Writings of Sigmund Freud*. New York: Random House.

Fried, Morton H. 1967. *The Evolution of Political Society*. New York: Random House.

Frisbie, Parker W., and John D. Kasarda. 1988. "Spatial Processes." Pp. 629–666 in *Handbook of Sociology*, edited by N. J. Smelser. Newbury Park, CA: Sage.

Garfinkel, Harold. 1967. *Ethnomethodology*. Englewood Cliffs, NJ: Prentice-Hall.

Gecas, Viktor. 1982. "The Self-concept." *Annual Review of Sociology* 8:1–33.

———. 1985. "Self Concept." Pp. 739–741 in *The Social Science Encyclopedia*. London: Routledge and Kegan Paul.

———. 1986. "The Motivational Significance of Self-Concept for Socialization Theory." *Advances in Group Processes* 3:131–156.

———. 1989. "The Social Psychology of Self-efficacy." *Annual Reviews of Sociology* 15:291–316.

———. 1991. "The Self-Concept as a Basis for a Theory of Motivation." Pp. 171–187 in *The Self-Society Dynamic: Cognition, Emotion and Action*. Cambridge: Cambridge University Press.

Gecas, Viktor, and Michael L. Schwalbe. 1983. "Beyond the Looking Glass Self: Social Structure and Efficacy-Based Self-Esteem." *Social Psychology Quarterly* 46:77–88.

Giddens, Anthony. 1971. *Capitalism and Modern Theory: An Analysis of the Writings of Marx, Durkheim, and Max Weber*. Cambridge: Cambridge University Press.

———. 1976. *New Rules of Sociological Method*. London: Hutchinson Ross.

———. 1984. *The Constitution of Society*. Berkeley, CA: University of California Press.

Gilmore, Samuel. 1992. "Culture." In *Encyclopedia of Sociology*, edited by E. F. Borgatta and M. L. Borgatta. New York: Macmillan.

Goffman, Erving. 1959. *The Presentation of Self in Everyday Life*. Garden City, NY: Anchor Books.

———. 1961. *Encounters*. Indianapolis, IN: Bobbs-Merrill.

———. 1967. *Interaction Ritual: Essays on Face-to-Face Behavior*. Garden City, NY: Anchor Books.

———. 1974. *Frame Analysis: An Essay on the Organization of Experience*. Boston: Harper and Row.

Goldstone, Jack. 1990. *Revolution and Rebellion in the Early Modern World, 1640–1848*. Berkeley, CA: University of California Press.

Goode, William J. 1960. "A Theory of Role Strain." *American Sociological Review* 25:483–496.

Habermas, Jurgen. 1970. *Knowledge and Human Interest*. London: Heinemann.

Hage, Jerald, and Charles Powers. 1992. *Post-industrial Lives: Roles and Relationships in the 21st Century*. Newbury Park, CA: Sage.

Hall, Edward T. 1959. *The Silent Language*. New York: Doubleday.

Handel, Warren. 1982. *Ethnomethodology: How People Make Sense*. Englewood Cliffs, NJ: Prentice-Hall.

Hannan, Michael T., and John Freeman. 1977. "The Population Ecology of Organizations." *American Journal of Sociology* 82 (March):929–964.

———. 1984. "Structural Inertia and Organizational Change." *American Sociological Review* 49:149–164.

———. 1986. "Where Do Organizational Forms Come From?" *Sociological Forum* 1:50–72.

———. 1987. "The Ecology of Organizational Founding: American Labor Unions, 1836–1985." *American Journal of Sociology* 92:910–943.

———. 1988. "The Ecology of Organizational Mortality: American Labor Unions, 1836–1985." *American Journal of Sociology* 94:25-52.

———. 1989. *Organizational Ecology*. Cambridge: Harvard University Press.

Hare, A. Paul. 1992. "Group Size Effects." In *Encyclopedia of Sociology*, edited by E. Borgatta and M. Borgatta. New York: Macmillan.

Harris, Chauncey, and Edward Ullman. 1945. "The Nature of Cities." *The Annals of the American Academy of Political and Social Sciences* 242:7–17.

Hawley, Amos H. 1950. *Human Ecology*. New York: Ronald Press.

———. 1981. *Urban Society: An Ecological Approach*. New York: Ronald Press.

———. 1986. *Human Ecology: A Theoretical Essay*. Chicago: University of Chicago Press.

Hechter, Michael. 1987. *Principles of Group Solidarity*. Berkeley, CA: University of California Press.

Heiss, Jerold. 1981. "Social Roles." Pp. 94–132 in *Social Psychology: Sociological Perspectives*, edited by M. Rosenberg and R. H. Turner. New York: Basic Books.

Hirschi, Travis. 1969. *Causes of Delinquency*. Berkeley, CA: University of California Press.

Hobbes, Thomas. 1651 [1947]. *Leviathan*. New York: Macmillan.

Hoyt, Homer. 1939. *The Structure and Growth of Residential Neighborhoods in American Cities*. Washington: U.S. Government Printing Office.

Hunt, Morton. 1985. *Profiles of Social Research. The Scientific Study of Human Interaction*. New York: Russell Sage.

Hurd, Richard M. 1903. *Principles of City Growth*. New York: The Record and Guide.

James, William. 1890 [1980]. *Principles of Psychology*. New York: Dover.

Janis, Irving L. 1972. *Victims of Group-Think*. Boston: Houghton Mifflin.

———. 1982. *Groupthink: Psychological Studies of Policy Decisions and Fiascos*. Boston: Houghton Mifflin.

Johnson, Allen W., and Timothy Earle. 1987. *The Evolution of Human Societies: From Foraging Group to Agrarian State*. Stanford: Stanford University Press.

Kellerman, Henry. 1981. *Group Cohesion*. New York: Grune & Stratton.

Kelley, Harold H. 1958. "Two Functions of Reference Groups." In *Readings in Social Psychology*, edited by G. E. Swanson. New York: Holt.

Kemper, Theodore D. 1987. "How Many Emotions Are There? Wedding the Social and the Autonomic Components." *American Journal of Sociology* 93:379–399.

Kluckhohn, Clyde. 1951. "Values and Value Orientations in the Theory of Action." In *Toward a General Theory of Action*, edited by T. Parsons and E. Shils. New York: Harper & Row.

Kluegel, James, and Eliot Smith. 1986. *Beliefs about Inequality: Americans' Views of What Is and What Ought to Be*. Hawthorne, NY: Aldine.

Kogan, Neil, and M. A. Wallach. 1964. *Risk Taking*. New York: Holt, Rinehart and Winston.

Kornhauser, Ruth. 1978. *Social Sources of Delinquency: An Appraisal of Analytic Models*. Chicago: University of Chicago Press.

Kroeber, A. L., and Clyde Kluckhohn. 1973. *Culture: A Critical Review of Concepts and Definitions*. New York: Vintage Press.

Kroeber, Alfred, and Talcott Parsons. 1958. "The Concept of Culture and Social System." *American Sociological Review* 23:582–583.

La Piere, Richard T. 1934. "Attitudes vs. Actions." *Social Forces* 13:230-237.

Lemert, Edwin M. 1951. *Social Pathology*. New York: McGraw-Hill.

———. 1967. *Human Deviance, Social Problems and Social Control*. Englewood Cliffs, NJ: Prentice-Hall.

Lenski, Gerhard. 1966. *Power and Privilege*. New York: McGraw-Hill, reprinted by the University of North Carolina Press.

Lenski, Gerhard, Jean Lenski, and Patrick Nolan. 1991. *Human Societies: An Introduction to Macrosociology*. New York: McGraw-Hill.

Lieberson, Stanley. 1985. *Making It Count: The Improvement of Social Research and Theory*. Berkeley: University of California Press.

———. 1992. "Small N's and Big Conclusions." *Social Forces* 70 (2):307–320.

Linton, Ralph. 1936. *The Study of Man*. New York: Appleton-Century-Crofts.

Liska, Allen E. 1981. *Perspectives on Deviance*. Englewood Cliffs, NJ: Prentice-Hall.

Long, Larry. 1988. *Migration and Residential Mobility in the United States*. New York: Russell Sage.

Luhmann, Niklas. 1982. *The Differentiation of Society*, trans. by S. Holmes and C. Larmore. New York: Columbia University Press.

Luker, Kristen. 1984. *Abortion and the Politics of Motherhood*. Berkeley: University of California Press.

Malthus, Thomas R. 1798 [1926]. *First Essay on Population*. New York: Kelley.

Marsden, Peter, and Nan Lin, eds. 1980. *Social Structure and Network Analysis*. Newbury Park, CA: Sage.

Marx, Karl, 1867 [1967]. *Capital: A Critical Analysis of Capitalist Production*. New York: International Publishers.

Marx, Karl, and Friedrich Engels. 1846 [1947]. *The German Ideology*. New York: International Publishers.

———. 1848 [1978]. *The Communist Manifesto*. Pp. 469–500 in *The Marx-Engels Reader*, edited by Robert Tucker. New York: Norton.

Maryanski, Alexandra, and Jonathan H. Turner. 1991. "Network Analysis." In J. H. Turner, *The Structure of Sociological Theory*. Belmont, CA: Wadsworth.

———. 1992. *The Social Cage: Human Nature and the Evolution of Society*. Stanford, CA: Stanford University Press.

McCarthy, John D., and Mayer Zald. 1977. "Resource Mobilization and Social Movements." *American Journal of Sociology* 82(6):1212-1241.

McKenzie, Roderick. 1933. *The Metropolitan Community*. New York: McGraw-Hill.

McPherson, J. Miller. 1981. "A Dynamic Model of Voluntary Affiliation." *Social Forces* 59:705–728.

———. 1983. "An Ecology of Affiliation." *American Sociological Review* 48:519–532.

———. 1988. "A Theory of Voluntary Organization." Pp. 42–76 in *Community Organizations*, edited by C. Milofsky. New York: Oxford.

———. 1990. "Evolution in Communities of Voluntary Organizations." Pp. 224–245 in *Organizational Evolution*, edited by Ji Hendra Singh. Newbury Park, CA: Sage.

Mead, George Herbert. 1934. *Mind, Self, and Society*. Chicago: University of Chicago Press.

———. 1938. *Philosophy of the Act*. Chicago: University of Chicago Press.

Mehan, Hugh, and Houston Wood. 1975. *The Reality of Ethnomethodology*. New York: Wiley.

Menard, Scott W., and Elizabeth W. Moen, eds. 1987. *Perspectives on Population*. New York: Oxford University Press.

Merton, Robert K. 1949. "Discrimination and the American Creed." In *Discrimination and National Welfare*, edited by R. H. MacIver. New York: Harper & Row.

———. 1957. "Role-Set: Problems in Sociological Theory." *British Journal of Sociology* 8:106-120.

———. 1968. *Social Theory and Social Structure*. New York: Free Press.

Merton, Robert K., and Alice S. Rossi. 1957. "Contributions to the Theory of Reference Group Behavior." In R. K. Merton, *Social Theory and Social Structure*. New York: Free Press.

———. 1968. "Continuities in the Theory of Reference Groups and Social Structure." In R. K. Merton, *Social Theory and Social Structure*. New York: Free Press.

Meyer, John W. 1977. "The Effects of Education as an Institution." *American Journal of Sociology* 83(1):55–77.

Mills, C. Wright. 1956. *The Power Elite*. New York: Oxford University Press.

————. 1959. *Sociological Imagination*. New York: Oxford University Press.

Miyamoto, Frank S. 1970. "Self, Motivation, and Symbolic Interaction Theory." Pp. 271–285 in *Human Nature and Collective Behavior*, edited by T. Shibutani. Englewood Cliffs, NJ: Prentice-Hall.

Money, John, and Anke Ehrhardt. 1972. *Man and Woman, Boy and Girl*. Baltimore: Johns Hopkins University Press.

Murdock, George P. 1949. *Social Structure*. New York: Macmillan.

————. 1965. *Culture and Society*. Pittsburgh: University of Pittsburgh Press.

Nadel, S. F. 1957. *The Study of Social Structure*. London: Cohen and West.

Niebuhr, Richard. 1929. *The Social Sources of Denominationalism*. New York: Holt.

Nisbet, Robert A. 1966. *The Sociological Tradition*. New York: Basic Books.

————. 1969. *Social Change and History*. New York: Oxford University Press.

NORC. 1982. *Prestige Rankings*. Chicago: National Opinion Research Center.

Pareto, Vilfredo. 1916 [1935]. *Treatise on General Sociology*. New York: Harcourt, Brace, under the title *The Mind and Society*.

Park, Robert E. 1916. "The City: Suggestions for the Investigation of Human Behavior in an Urban Environment." *American Journal of Sociology* 20:577–612.

————. 1936. "Human Ecology." *American Journal of Sociology* 42:1-15.

Park, Robert E., and Ernest W. Burgess. 1925. *The City*. Chicago: University of Chicago Press.

Parkinson, C. Northcote. 1957. *Parkinson's Law*. Boston: Houghton-Mifflin.

Parsons, Talcott. 1951. *The Social System*. New York: Free Press.

————. 1953. "A Revised Analytical Approach to the Theory of Stratification." In *Class, Status, and Power*, edited by R. Bendix and S. M. Lipset. New York: Free Press.

————. 1966. *Societies: Evolutionary and Comparative Perspectives*. Englewood Cliffs, NJ: Prentice-Hall.

————. 1971. *The System of Modern Societies*. Englewood Cliffs, NJ: Prentice-Hall.

Perrow, Charles. 1967. "A Framework for the Comparative Analysis of Organizations." *American Sociological Review* 32:194-208.

————. 1986. *Complex Organizations*. New York: Random House.

Peter, Laurence F., and Raymond Hull. 1969. *The Peter Principle*. New York: Morrow.

Piaget, Jean. 1948. *The Moral Judgement of the Child*. Glencoe, IL: Free Press.

————. 1952. *The Origins of Intelligence in Children*. New York: International Universities Press.

Plutchik, Robert. 1962. *The Emotions: Facts, Theories and a New Model*. New York: Random House.

Plutchik, Robert, and Henry Kellerman, eds. 1980. *Emotion: Theory and Research Experience*. New York: Academic Press.

Pondy, Louis. 1983. *Organizational Symbolism*. Greenwich, CT: JAI Press.

Popper, Karl R. 1959. *The Logic of Scientific Discovery*. London: Hutchinson.

————. 1969. *Conjectures and Refutations*. London: Routledge and Kegan Paul.

Quinney, Richard. 1970. *The Social Reality of Crime*. Boston: Little, Brown.

————. 1979. *Criminology*, 2d edition. Boston: Little, Brown.

————. 1980. *Class, State, and Crime*, 2d edition. New York: Longmans.

Reynolds, Vernon. 1976. *The Biology of Human Action*. San Francisco: Freeman.

Ritzer, George. 1975. *Sociology: A Multiple Paradigm Science*. Boston: Allyn and Bacon.

————. 1988. *Contemporary Sociological Theory*, 2d edition. New York: Knopf.

Roethlisberger, Fritz, and W. J. Dickson. 1939. *Management and the Worker*. Cambridge, MA: Harvard University Press.

Rokeach, Milton. 1973. *The Nature of Human Values*. New York: Free Press.

———, ed. 1979. *Understanding Human Values: Individual and Societal.* New York: Free Press.

Ropers, Richard H. 1991. *Persistent Poverty: The American Dream Turned Nightmare.* New York: Plenum Press.

Rosenberg, Morris. 1979. *Conceiving Self.* New York: Basic Books.

Rossi, Peter, James Wright, and Andy Anderson, eds. 1985. *Handbook of Survey Research.* Orlando, FL: Academic Press.

Sahlins, Marshall. 1972. *Stone Age Economics.* New York: Aldine.

Scheff, Thomas J. 1966. *Being Mentally Ill: A Sociological Theory.* Chicago: Aldine.

Schutz, Alfred. 1932 [1967]. *The Phenomenology of the Social World.* Evanston, IL: Northwestern University Press.

Seboek, T. A., ed. 1968. *Animal Communication.* Bloomington: Indiana University Press.

Seidman, Steven, and David G. Wagner, eds. 1992. *Postmodernism and Social Theory.* Oxford: Blackwell.

Sherraden, Michael. 1991. *Assets and the Poor: A New American Welfare Policy.* Armock, NY: Sharpe.

Shibutani, Tamotsu. 1955. "Reference Groups as Perspectives." *American Journal of Sociology* 60 (May):562–569.

———. 1986. *Social Processes.* Berkeley, CA: University of California Press.

Shotola, Robert W. 1992. "Small Groups." In *Encyclopedia of Sociology,* edited by E. Borgatta and M. Borgatta. New York: Macmillan.

Simmel, Georg. 1903–1904. "The Sociology of Conflict." *American Journal of Sociology* 9 (several issues):490–525, 672–689, and 798–811.

———. 1956. *Conflict and the Web of Group Affiliations,* trans. by K. Wolf. New York: Free Press.

Singer, Milton. 1968. "Culture: The Concept of Culture." In *International Encyclopedia of the Social Sciences.* New York: Macmillan.

Singleton, Royce, and Jonathan H. Turner. 1975. "Racism: White Oppression of Blacks in America." Pp. 130–160 in *Understanding Social Problems,* edited by D. Zimmerman and L. Weider. New York: Praeger.

Sjoberg, Gideon. 1960. *The Preindustrial City.* New York: Free Press.

Skocpol, Theda. 1979. *States and Social Revolutions.* New York: Cambridge University Press.

Smelser, Neil J. 1963. *Theory of Collective Behavior.* New York: Free Press.

Smircich, Linda. 1983. "Concepts of Culture and Organizational Analysis." *Administrative Science Quarterly* 28:339–358.

Smith, Adam. 1776 [1937]. *An Inquiry into the Nature and Causes of the Wealth of Nations.* New York: Modern Library.

Smith, Kevin B. 1985. "I Made It Because of Me: Beliefs about the Causes of Wealth and Poverty." *Sociological Spectrum* 5:17–29.

Spencer, Baldwin, and F. J. Gillian. 1899. *The Native Tribes of Central Australia,* 2d edition. London: Macmillan.

Spencer, Herbert. 1862. *First Principles.* New York: Appleton.

———. 1864–1867 [1887]. *The Principles of Biology,* 2 volumes. New York: Appleton.

———. 1873. *The Study of Sociology.* London: Kegan Paul.

———. 1874–1896 [1898]. *The Principles of Sociology,* 3 volumes. New York: Appleton.

Stark, Rodney. 1981. "Must All Religions Be Supernatural?" In *The Social Impact of New Religious Movements,* edited by B. Wilson. New York: Rose of Sharon Press.

———. 1992. *Sociology,* 4th edition. Belmont, CA: Wadsworth.

Stark, Rodney, and W. S. Bainbridge. 1980. "Secularizations, Revival and Cult Formation." *Annual Review of Social Sciences of Religion* 4:85-119.

Starr, Paul. 1982. *The Social Transformation of American Medicine*. New York: Basic Books.

Stryker, Sheldon. 1980. *Symbolic Interaction: A Social Structural View*. Menlo Park, CA: Benjamin-Cummings.

Sullivan, Harry Stack. 1953. *The Interpersonal Theory of Psychiatry*. New York: Norton.

Sutherland, Edwin H. 1924. *Criminology*. Philadelphia: Lippincott.

———. 1939. *Principles of Criminology*. Philadelphia: Lippincott.

Sutherland, Edwin D., and Donald R. Cressey. 1986. *Principles of Criminology*. Philadelphia: Lippincott.

Tilly, Charles. 1978. *From Mobilization to Revolution*. Reading, MA: Addison-Wesley.

Tumin, Melvin M. 1953. "Some Principles of Stratification: A Critical Analysis." *American Sociological Review* 18:387–393.

———. 1967. *Social Stratification: The Forms and Functions of Inequality*. Englewood Cliffs, NJ: Prentice-Hall.

Turk, Austin T. 1969. *Criminality and Legal Order*. Chicago: Rand McNally.

Turner, Jonathan H. 1972. *Patterns of Social Organization: A Survey of Social Institutions*. New York: McGraw-Hill.

———. 1976. *American Society: Problems of Structure*. New York: Harper & Row.

———. 1977. *Social Problems in America: The Structural and Cultural Basis*. New York: Harper & Row.

———. 1981. "Émile Durkheim's Theory of Integration in Differentiated Social Systems." *Pacific Sociological Review* 24(4):187-208.

———. 1983. "Theoretical Strategies for Linking Micro and Macro Processes: An Evaluation of Seven Approaches." *Western Sociological Review* 14(1):4-15.

———. 1984a. *Societal Stratification: A Theoretical Analysis*. New York: Columbia University Press.

———. 1984b. "Durkheim's and Spencer's Principles of Social Organization." *Sociological Perspectives* 27:21-32.

———. 1985a. "In Defense of Positivism." *Sociological Theory* 3 (Fall):24–30.

———. 1985b. *Herbert Spencer: A Renewed Appreciation*. Newbury Park, CA: Sage.

———. 1985c. *Sociology: The Science of Human Organization*. Chicago: Nelson-Hall.

———. 1986a. "The Mechanics of Social Interaction." *Sociological Theory* 4:95–105.

———. 1986b. "Toward a Unified Theory of Ethnic Antagonism: A Preliminary Synthesis of Three Macro Models." *Sociological Forum* 1 (Summer):403-427.

———. 1988. *A Theory of Social Interaction*. Stanford, CA: Stanford University Press.

———. 1989. "A Theory of Microdynamics." *Advances in Group Processes* 7:1-18.

———. 1990. "Durkheim's Theory of Social Organization." *Social Forces* 68:1-15.

———. 1991. *The Structure of Sociological Theory*, 5th edition. Belmont, CA: Wadsworth.

———. 1993a. "Inequality and Poverty." In *Social Problems*, edited by George Ritzer and Craig Calhoun. New York: McGraw-Hill.

———. 1993b. *Classical Sociology Theory: A Positivistic Interpretation*. Chicago: Nelson-Hall.

Turner, Jonathan H., and Adalberto Aguirre, Jr. 1994. *American Ethnicity: The Dynamics and Consequences of Discrimination*. New York: McGraw-Hill.

Turner, Jonathan H., and Edna Bonacich. 1980. "Toward a Composite Theory of Middleman Minorities." *Ethnicity* 7:144–158.

Turner, Jonathan H., and Randall Collins. 1989. "Toward a Microtheory of Structuring." Pp. 118–130 in *Theory Building in Sociology*, edited by J. H. Turner. Newbury Park, CA: Sage.

Turner, Jonathan H., and Alexandra Maryanski. 1979. *Functionalism*. Menlo Park, CA: Benjamin-Cummings.

Turner, Jonathan H., and Peter Molnar. 1993. "Selection Processes and the Evolution of Emotions in Humans." *Biology and Culture* (in preparation).

Turner, Jonathan H., and David Musick. 1985. *American Dilemmas*. New York: Columbia University Press.

Turner, Jonathan H., Leonard Beeghley, and Charles Powers. 1989. *The Emergence of Sociological Theory*. Belmont, CA: Wadsworth.

Turner, Jonathan H., Royce Singleton, and David Musick. 1984. *Oppression: A Socio-history of Black-White Relations in America*. Chicago: Nelson-Hall.

Turner, Jonathan H., and Charles E. Starnes. 1976. *Inequality: Privilege and Poverty in America*. Santa Monica, CA: Goodyear.

Turner, Ralph H. 1962. "Role-Taking versus Conformity." In *Human Behavior and Social Processes*, edited by A. Rose. Boston: Houghton Mifflin.

———. 1968. "Social Roles: Sociological Aspects." *International Encyclopedia of the Social Sciences*. New York: Macmillan.

———. 1978. "The Role and the Person." *American Journal of Sociology* 84:1–23.

———. 1980. "Strategy for Developing an Integrated Role Theory." *Humboldt Journal of Social Relations* 7:123–139.

Turner, Ralph H., and Lewis M. Killian. 1987. *Collective Behavior*. Englewood Cliffs, NJ: Prentice-Hall.

Turner, Stephen Park, and Jonathan H. Turner. 1990. *The Impossible Science: An Institutional History of American Sociology*. Newbury Park, CA: Sage.

United Nations. 1991. *World Trends in Population*. New York: United Nations Publishing.

U.S. Bureau of the Census. 1983, 1991. *Current Population Reports*. Washington: U.S. Government Printing Office.

U.S. Department of Labor. 1991.

Useem, Michael. 1980. "Corporations and the Corporate Elite." *Annual Review of Sociology* 6:41-77.

Wallace, Anthony F. C. 1966. *Religion: An Anthropological View*. New York: Random House.

Wallerstein, Immanuel M. 1974. *The Modern World System: Capitalist Agriculture and the Origins of the European World Economy in the Sixteenth Century*. New York: Academic Press.

Weber, Max. 1904 [1949]. *The Methodology of the Social Sciences*. New York: Free Press.

———. 1904–1905 [1958]. *The Protestant Ethic and the Spirit of Capitalism*. New York: Scribner.

———. 1905. *The Protestant Ethic and the Spirit of Capitalism*. New York: Free Press.

———. 1922/1978. *Economy and Society: An Outline of Interpretive Sociology*, edited by G. Roth and C. Wittich. Berkeley: University of California Press.

Webster, Murray, Jr., and Martha Foschi. 1988. *Status Generalization: New Theory and Research*. Stanford, CA: Stanford University Press.

Weeks, John R. 1989. *Population: An Introduction to Concepts and Issues*. Belmont, CA: Wadsworth.

Wellman, Barry S., and S. D. Berkowitz. 1988. *Social Structures: A Network Approach*. Cambridge: Cambridge University Press.

White, Lynn K., and Alan Booth. 1985. "The Quality and Stability of Remarriages." *American Sociological Review* 50:689–698.

White, Lynn K., and John N. Edwards. 1990. "Emptying the Nest and Parental Well-Being." *American Sociological Review* 55:235–242.

Whyte, William Foote. 1984. *Learning from the Field*. Newbury Park, CA: Sage.

————. 1989. "Advancing Scientific Knowledge through Participatory Action Research." *Sociological Forum* 4:367-386.

Whyte, William Foote, and Kathleen King Whyte. 1984. *Learning from the Field: A Guide from Experience*. Beverly Hills, CA: Sage.

Wilford, John Noble. 1981. "Nine Percent of Everyone Who Ever Lived Is Alone Now." *The New York Times*, October 6:13.

Williams, Robin M., Jr. 1970. *American Society: A Sociological Interpretation*. New York: Knopf.

Wilson, William J. 1987. *The Truly Disadvantaged*. Chicago: University of Chicago Press.

Wolff, Edward N. 1987. "Estimates of Household Inequality in the United States." *Review of Income and Wealth* 33:231–242.

Zald, Meyer N., and John D. McCarthy, eds. 1979. *The Dynamics of Social Movements*. Cambridge, MA: Winthrop.

Index